RECRUITMENT, RETENTION, AND UTILIZATION OF FEDERAL SCIENTISTS AND ENGINEERS

A Report to the Carnegie Commission on Science, Technology, and Government

Alan K. Campbell and Linda S. Dix, editors

Committee on Scientists and Engineers in the Federal Government

Office of Scientific and Engineering Personnel
National Research Council

NATIONAL ACADEMY PRESS
Washington, D.C. 1990

NOTICE: The project that is the subject of this report was approved by the Governing Board of the National Research Council, whose members are drawn from the councils of the National Academy of Sciences, the National Academy of Engineering, and the Institute of Medicine.

This report has been reviewed by persons other than the author according to procedures approved by a Report Review Committee consisting of members of the National Academy of Sciences, the National Academy of Engineering, and the Institute of Medicine.

The National Academy of Sciences is a private, nonprofit, self-perpetuating society of distinguished scholars engaged in scientific and engineering research, dedicated to the furtherance of science and technology and to their use for the general welfare. Upon the authority of the charter granted to it by the Congress in 1863, the Academy has a mandate that requires it to advise the federal government on scientific and technical matters. Dr. Frank Press is president of the National Academy of Sciences.

The National Academy of Engineering was established in 1964, under the charter of the National Academy of Sciences, as a parallel organization of outstanding engineers. It is autonomous in its administration and in the selection of its members, sharing with the National Academy of Sciences the responsibility for advising the federal government. The National Academy of Engineering also sponsors engineering programs aimed at meeting national needs, encourages education and research, and recognizes the superior achievements of engineers. Dr. Robert M. White is president of the National Academy of Engineering.

The Institute of Medicine was established in 1970 by the National Academy of Sciences to secure the services of eminent members of appropriate professions in the examination of policy matters pertaining to the health of the public. The Institute acts under the responsibility given to the National Academy of Sciences by its congressional charter to be an adviser to the federal government and, upon its own initiative, to identify issues of medical care, research, and education. Dr. Samuel O. Thier is president of the Institute of Medicine.

The National Research Council was organized by the National Academy of Sciences in 1916 to associate the broad community of science and technology with the Academy's purposes of furthering knowledge and advising the federal government. Functioning in accordance with general policies determined by the Academy, the Council has become the principal operating agency of both the National Academy of Sciences and the National Academy of Engineering in providing services to the federal government, the public, and the scientific and engineering communities. The Council is administered jointly by both Academies and the Institute of Medicine. Dr. Frank Press and Dr. Robert M. White are chairman and vice chairman, respectively, of the National Research Council.

Library of Congress Catalog Card No. 90-62688
International Standard Book No. 0-309-04330-1

Additional copies of this report are available from:
National Academy Press
2101 Constitution Avenue, N.W.
Washington, D.C. 20418

S070
Printed in the United States of America

COMMITTEE ON SCIENTISTS AND ENGINEERS IN THE FEDERAL GOVERNMENT

Alan K. Campbell, chair
Vice Chairman
ARA Services, Inc.
(Chairman, Civil Service Commission, 1977-78; Director, U.S. Office of Personnel Management, 1979-80)

Ernest Ambler
(Director, National Institute of Standards and Technology, 1978-1989)

Stephen J. Lukasik
Vice President for Technology
Northrop Corporation
(Director, Defense Advanced Research Projects Agency, 1971-1974; Chief scientist, Federal Communications Commission, 1979-1982)

Howard Messner
Executive Vice President
American Consulting Engineers Council
(Director of administration, Environmental Protection Agency, 1971-1975; Assistant director, Congressional Budget Office, 1975-1977)

Janet L. Norwood
Commissioner, Bureau of Labor Statistics, 1979—

Alan Schriesheim
Director and Chief Executive Officer, Argonne National Laboratory, 1984—

<u>Liaison from OSEP's Advisory Committee on Studies and Analyses</u>
Eli Ginzberg
Director
Conservation of Human Resources
Columbia University

<u>Staff Officer</u>
Linda S. Dix

PREFACE AND ACKNOWLEDGMENTS

Early in 1989 the Carnegie Commission on Science, Technology, and Government—concerned with the use of science and technology in this country, particularly by government at all levels—asked the National Research Council's Office of Scientific and Engineering Personnel (OSEP) to conduct an exploratory study of the organizational and institutional processes that may affect the ability of federal government to attract and retain scientists and engineers. The committee established to conduct this investigation undertook specific activities to understand what those mechanisms are and their impact on the ability of the federal government to retain, attract, and provide a good working environment for scientists and engineers:

- A literature review was completed to determine previous examinations of this topic;
- Staff contacted the 13 distinguished scientists who have received the Alan T. Waterman Award from the National Science Foundation, asking them to comment on the factors that influenced their decisions not to seek federal employment after graduate school as well as factors that might affect their considerations about federal employment today.
- Directors of 22 federal laboratories—varying in mission, size, and geographical location—were asked to consider organizational and decision-making processes that may affect federal government recruitment, retention, and utilization of scientists and engineers.
- Placement officers in approximately 50 U.S. institutions—liberal arts colleges and research universities, both public and private—were asked for data on the recruitment activities of federal agencies directed toward their students, the interest of their graduates in federal employment, and trends in the numbers of agencies visiting their campuses and graduates actually taking federal employment.
- Four papers dealing with topics that might shed additional light on the federal government's ability to recruit and retain scientists and engineers were commissioned (see Appendix B).
- A workshop was held in Washington on February 23, 1990, at which representatives of approximately 25 federal agencies briefed the committee on the most influential factors relating to recruitment, retention, and utilization of scientists and engineers; organizational and decision-making processes that relate to them; and mechanisms undertaken to maintain a stable work force of scientists and engineer (see Appendix C).

Information gleaned from these several sources led to the Committee's determination that several issues require further examination. It is hoped that readers—particularly the Carnegie Commission on Science, Technology, and Government and those policy-makers in position to redirect the federal initiative for recruiting, retaining, and utilizing the scientific and engineering work force—will find the information useful.

For their many contributions to this exploratory study, the Committee on Scientists and Engineers in the Federal Government is grateful to the following individuals: David Z. Robinson, executive director, and Jesse Ausubel, director of studies, Carnegie Commission on Science, Technology, and the Government; William D. Carey, chairman, and Alan Fechter, executive director, OSEP; and Eli Ginzberg, liaison to this committee from OSEP's Advisory Committee on Studies and Analyses. In addition, providing useful information throughout the study were several staff from the Office of Personnel Management: Constance Berry Newman, director; Dona Wolf; Phillip A.D. Schneider; John Curnow; Andrew Klugh; Paul Thompson; Leonard Klein; Sandra M. Payne; Martin Reck; Barry Shapiro; George Steinbauer; Barbara Fiss; and Ruth O'Donnell. We also appreciate the assistance provided by staff in the U.S. Merit Systems Protection Board—John M. Palguta, deputy director, Office of Policy and Evaluation, and Paul VanRijn. Furthermore, the Committee learned much about the day-to-day experiences of those responsible for recruiting and managing the federal scientific work force from federally employed scientists and engineers throughout the country—both through discussions at the committee-sponsored workshop and through correspondence. We are particularly appreciative of comments received from scientists and engineers who, although not contacted directly by the committee, had learned of this study and sent us pertinent information. Response to this exploratory study has been intense, confirming the belief of the sponsors and committee that the issue under study—the ability of the federal government to recruit, retain, and utilize scientists and engineers effectively—cannot be determined in a simplistic fashion but requires a deeper investigation to verify the perceptions and findings reported here.

CONTENTS

EXECUTIVE SUMMARY		1
I.	INTRODUCTION	5
II.	FINDINGS	7
	Availability and Relevance of Data on the Federal Science and Engineering Work Force	8
	Management Practices Relating to the Career Work Force	11
	Trends Regarding Presidential Appointments	27
III.	ISSUES REQUIRING FURTHER ANALYSIS	29
BIBLIOGRAPHY		33

APPENDIXES

A:	Related Materials	37
B:	Commissioned Papers	75

- *Recruitment, Retention, and Utilization of Scientists and Engineers in the Federal Government: Results of a Literature Review* by Linda S. Dix, **77**
- *Quantitative Inputs to Federal Technical Personnel Management* by Charles E. Falk, **95**
- *Meeting Federal Work Force Needs with Regard to Scientists and Engineers: The Role of the U.S. Office of Personnel Management* by John M. Palguta, **111**
- *Differences in Recruitment, Retention, and Utilization Processes: A Comparison of Traditionally Operated Federal Laboratories, M&O Facilities, and Demonstration Projects* by Sheldon B. Clark, **121**
- *The Political Appointments Process and the Recruitment of Scientists and Engineers* by James P. Pfiffner, **133**

C: Workshop on Recruitment, Retention, and Utilization of Federal Scientists and Engineers   143
- Agenda, **145**
- List of Participants, **147**
- Proceedings, **149**

ABBREVIATIONS

CDC	Centers for Disease Control
CPDF	Central Personnel Data File
CSRA	Civil Service Reform Act
DOL	Department of Labor
ERL	Environmental Research Laboratories
GAO	General Accounting Office
IDA	Institute for Defense Analysis
MSPB	Merit Systems Protection Board
NBS	National Bureau of Standards
NIST	National Institute of Standards and Technology
NOSC	Naval Ocean Systems Center
NRC	National Research Council
NRL	Naval Research Laboratory
NSF	National Science Foundation
NWC	Naval Weapons Center
OMB	Office of Management and Budget
OPM	Office of Personnel Management
OSEP	Office of Scientific and Engineering Personnel
OSTP	Office of Science and Technology Policy
PACE	Professional and Administrative Career Examination
PHS	Public Health Service
PMI	Presidential Management Intern
S&E	Scientific and engineering

EXECUTIVE SUMMARY

While the world is being transformed by science and technology, the Carnegie Commission on Science, Technology, and Government is endeavoring to identify mechanisms by which "the branches of the U.S. government encourage and use the contributions of the nation's scientists and engineers [and] incorporate scientific and technical knowledge into policy and administrative decision-making" (The Commission, 1990). Approximately 200,000 scientists and engineers are directly employed by the federal government (Figure 1), and the President makes about 150 appointments of individuals to leadership positions of importance to science and engineering (see Appendix A, Table 11). Thus, the Commission asked the National Research Council's Committee on Scientists and Engineers in the Federal Government to review what is known about the ability of federal agencies to recruit, retain, and utilize scientists and engineers effectively.

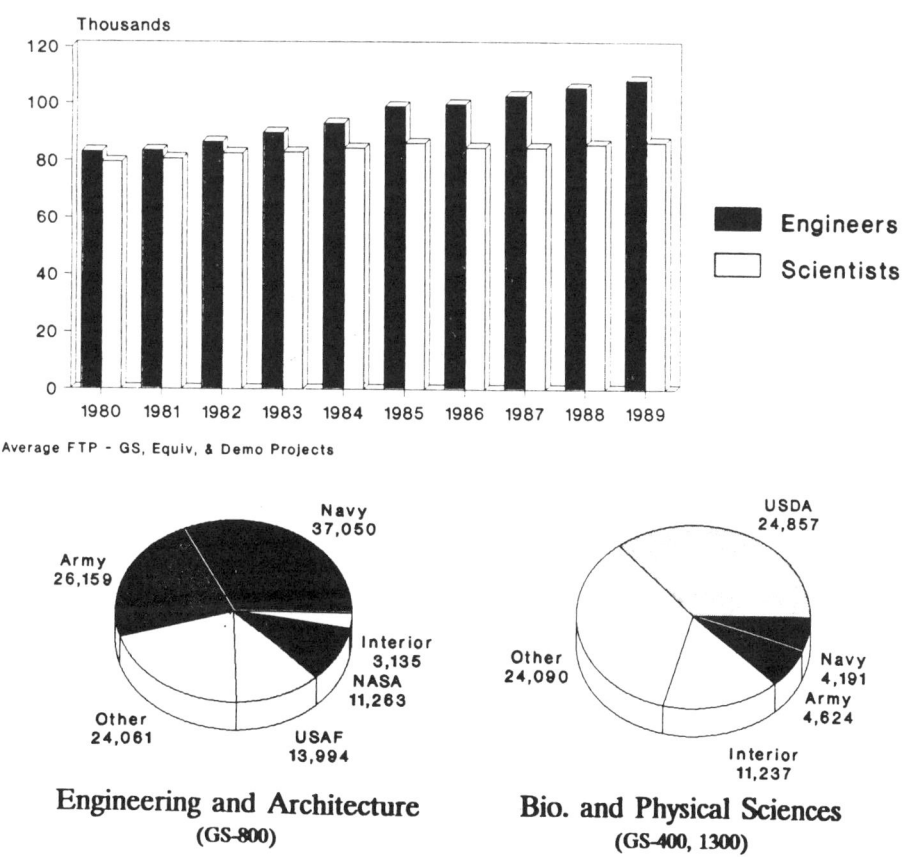

SOURCE: U.S. Office of Personnel Management, *Federal Staffing Digest* **2**(3: Spring 1990):8.

Figure 1. Federal employment of professional scientists and engineers, September 1989.

Relative to the set of questions put to the Committee, this report does not give precise responses but, rather, sheds light on the confusion associated with many of those questions. The Committee accumulated information from various sources: a literature review of previous examinations of this topic and commissioned papers (see Appendix B); discussions with staff at the Office of Personnel Management (OPM) and the National Science Foundation and with eminent scientists, engineers, and managers of federally employed scientists and engineers; and a workshop at which personnel specialists and line managers of the government's scientists and engineers discussed their experiences concerning recruitment, retention, and utilization of scientists and engineers (see Appendix C). At the same time, the Committee met several times to evaluate the information received, to identify additional needs, and to agree upon its findings.

Findings

Based on the activities that it undertook, the study committee focuses this report of its findings on three broad areas: the availability and relevance of data on the federal science and engineering work force, management practices relating to the career work force, and trends regarding presidential appointments.

Availability and Relevance of Data on the Federal Science and Engineering Work Force

1. The Central Personnel Data File (CPDF) maintained by OPM from data supplied by individual federal agencies presents a general picture of the federal work force, including scientists and engineers, based on broad occupational classifications. A primary purpose of the CPDF is to provide federal employment information for government-wide policy development and oversight. However, it is not now a management tool helpful to individual federal agencies. (See pages 8-10.)

2. Managers of the federal science and engineering (S&E) work force have been unable to agree on what constitutes accurate measures of the quality of that work force. Some CPDF data can be used as proxies to input measures of quality—such as the highest academic degree conferred on an employee. In addition, OPM has recently undertaken a study of work force quality, surveying a sample of non-DoD scientists and engineers. (See pages 10-11.)

Management Practices Relating to the Career Work Force

3. Perceptions about factors affecting the federal government's ability to recruit and retain scientists and engineers have remained basically the same for the past 30 years, in spite of specific efforts by OPM and individual federal agencies to enhance such recruitment and retention. (See pages 11-18.) Table 1 lists several barriers to this ability and mechanisms that could improve their effectiveness.

TABLE 1: Barriers to Effective Recruitment and Retention of Scientists and Engineers and Mechanisms to Reduce Them

Barriers	Mechanisms
Inadequate compensation	Pay banding, recruitment bonuses, occupation-specific pay scales.
Lengthy time required to extend an offer of employment	Direct-hire authority, simplified hiring procedures, increased personnel authority for line managers.
Difficulty of promotion after reaching GS-12 level	Pay banding.
Restricted role of line managers in personnel decisions	Flexibility in increasing salary without promoting, increasing personnel authority for line managers, occupation-specific salary schedules.
Excessive paper work	Direct-hire authority, computer-assisted classifications, more generic classifications.
Questionable tie between performance and pay	Performance appraisals and multiple components of pay increase that are not mutually exclusive; bonuses; awards
Personnel ceilings and reductions in force	Using adjunct personnel such as postdocs; flexibility in considering force factors other than seniority; simplified classification systems that enable the labs to retrain RIFed staff.

4. To fulfill the missions of federal agencies, science and engineering activity can be undertaken under a variety of scenarios—including the traditional setting within an agency, demonstration projects, federal laboratories, and managed-and-operated (M&O) facilities. Demonstration projects authorized by OPM and the contracting out of S&E work seem to have provided agencies with the flexibility deemed necessary to overcome some of the difficulties associated with recruitment, retention, and utilization of scientists and engineers. (See pages 18-24.)

5. The extent to which scientists and engineers are utilized effectively varies from agency to agency. (See pages 24-25.)

6. Many within the broader S&E community are concerned about the effects of the changing U.S. demography on the federal government's ability to recruit and retain qualified U.S. citizens. Several managers of federal scientists and engineers revealed difficulties in hiring women and minorities. CPDF data on the race/ethnicity and sex of federal employees, used by agencies such as the Equal Employment Opportunity Commission to monitor a variety of federal affirmative action programs, could also indicate where the federal government might pursue initiatives to respond to projected shortages of scientists and engineers, tapping groups currently underrepresented in the sciences and engineering. (See pages 26-27.)

7. Government policies that limit the hiring of foreign nationals may have adverse effects on agencies' abilities to perform S&E work. (See page 27.)

Trends Regarding Presidential Appointments

8. There is growing concern about the adequacy of the political appointments process and the impact of political appointees on the fulfillment of federal S&E work. (See pages 27-28.)

Issues Requiring Further Analysis

Based on these findings, the Committee identified six candidates for further analysis:

- What mechanisms and scenarios for conducting federal S&E work could be employed on a wider basis to enhance recruitment, retention, and utilization of federal scientists and engineers?

- What can be done to enhance federal recruitment of scientists and engineers, especially women and minorities at the entry level, and retention of all scientists and engineers at the midcareer level? What institutional decision-making processes should be altered and in what way? Should the relationship between OPM and the individual federal agencies be different for scientists and engineers than it is for other federal personnel?

- What steps must be taken to heighten the awareness within agencies of the mechanisms established by OPM to alleviate many of the problems that they encounter in recruiting and retaining scientists and engineers?

- How can the Central Personnel Data File be more useful to agencies facing difficulties in recruiting and retaining scientists and engineers?

- Are there too few scientists and engineers in the federal government? Or are there too few _highly qualified_ federal scientists and engineers?

- What can be done so that the political appointment process enhances the recruitment, retention, and utilization of scientists and engineers in federal government?

I. INTRODUCTION

Scientists and engineers are a vital part of this country's work force—as shown by their participation in all sectors of the economy. The focus of this report is on the approximately 202,300 scientists and engineers employed by the federal government, primarily in the National Aeronautics and Space Administration (NASA) and the departments of Defense, Commerce, Agriculture, Interior, Health and Human Services, and Transportation. Comprising 10.7 percent of the federal work force, scientists and engineers are classified into one of seven broad occupational categories: social scientists; computer specialists; biological scientists; agricultural scientists; engineers; physical scientists; and mathematical and computer scientists (see Appendix A, Table 1). A vital and necessary resource for the government to serve the nation, federal scientists and engineers are employed in:

- research;
- development;
- design;
- data collection, processing, and analysis;
- natural resource operations;
- management;
- installation, operations, and maintenance;
- planning;
- testing and evaluation;
- research contract and grants administration;
- construction;
- production;
- scientific and technical information;
- standards and specifications;
- regulatory enforcement and licensing;
- teaching and training; and
- technical assistance and consulting.

Yet some people feel that federal agencies are not very successful at recruiting and retaining the most capable scientists and engineers. One individual corresponding with the study committee viewed the system as a "ponderous bureaucracy" making

> decisions based on pork-barrel grounds rather than meaningful technical objectives.... Hiring of staff is at best tortuous.... [There are] arbitrary limits on personnel, mountains of paper that confront the hiring

manager—The working scientist has little control of his project in many cases.[1]

As a result of this perceived lack of success in attracting and keeping talented scientists and engineers and the alleged inadequacy in the administration of this work force, the Carnegie Commission on Science, Technology, and Government asked the Office of Scientific and Engineering Personnel to convene a committee to examine this issue more closely. OSEP established the Committee on Scientists and Engineers in the Federal Government to undertake this task. The charge of the Committee was to consider organizational and decision-making processes that may affect the recruitment, retention, and utilization of scientists and engineers by the federal government. This activity is the first stage of a multiphased project, with the second phase expected to go into greater depth and develop action-oriented recommendations. The Commission requested the Committee to examine the general processes that now affect recruitment, retention, and utilization and the data available to enable one to comment on those processes; to conduct a preliminary assessment of current problems, emphasizing federal organizational capability to implement policy; and to identify possible changes that might be made to improve the effectiveness of the federal government.

---

[1] George A. Paulikas, group vice president of the Aerospace Corporation, to Alan Fechter, November 13, 1989.

II. FINDINGS

Among the questions underlying this study were the following:

- What kind of information is needed to know whether the federal government is able to recruit and retain S&E personnel?
- Is there an analytical capability within the federal government to predict changes in the composition of its S&E work force and to ascertain whether it effectively recruits, retains, and utilizes scientists and engineers?
- Where are policy options developed? Who should make policy decisions and recommendations?

Basic to understanding the ability of the federal government to recruit, retain, and utilize scientists and engineers effectively is knowledge of the federal personnel system in general. OPM, established as the successor to the U.S. Civil Service Commission with the passage of the Civil Service Reform Act of 1978, is the central personnel management agency within the federal government. As such, OPM has a broad mandate:

> to exercise leadership in Federal personnel administration . . . to concentrate its efforts on planning and administering an effective Governmentwide program of personnel management . . . to see that agencies are performing properly under civil service laws, regulations, and delegated authorities. . . . OPM will have the opportunity for innovative planning for the future needs of the Federal work force, executive and employee development, and pilot projects to test the efficacy of various administration practices.[2]

According to OPM director Constance Berry Newman,

> The Office of Personnel Management has been charged with devising an overall human resource system for the federal government that specifically addresses our recruitment and retention problems. Scientists and engineers represent one of the most difficult job categories for which to recruit, sometimes allowing essential government functions to suffer from staff shortages and a lack of clear management.[3]

---

[2] "Legislative History of the Civil Service Reform Act of 1978," House Committee on Post Office and Civil Service, Committee Print No. 96-2, 96th Congress, 1st session (1979), p. 1470.

[3] Letter to Frank Press, chairman of the National Research Council, December 3, 1989.

However, OPM may, and has, delegated authorities to individual federal agencies to enhance S&E recruitment, retention, and utilization.

Based on the activities that it undertook in the conduct of this study, the Committee focuses this report on the role of OPM and other federal agencies by examining three broad areas: the availability and relevance of data, management practices, and presidential appointments. In this section, findings within each of these categories are presented, along with elaborative information.

Availability and Relevance of Data on the Federal Science and Engineering Work Force

1. **The Central Personnel Data File (CPDF) maintained by OPM from data supplied by individual federal agencies presents a general picture of the federal work force, including scientists and engineers, based on broad occupational classifications. A primary purpose of the CPDF is to provide federal employment information for government-wide policy development and oversight. However, it is not now a management tool helpful to individual federal agencies.**

One question of concern to the Carnegie Commission on Science, Technology, and Government was whether any agency of the federal government maintains data on federal scientists and engineers that would indicate the degree to which their retention and utilization is effective. The Committee learned that data on each federal employee, not just scientists and engineers, are compiled in OPM's Central Personnel Data File (CPDF), which consists of descriptive and dynamic data (see Appendix A, Table 2, for a listing of some information that can be obtained from the CPDF for all federal employees; see also Falk, Appendix B). The CPDF is used to analyze S&E employment in the federal government and to note trends in the areas of recruitment, retention, and utilization. Aggregated data are compiled quarterly but only published biennially in *Occupation of Federal White and Blue Collar Workers;* special tabulations can be obtained from the CPDF to make comparisons between agencies and between S&E fields (see Appendix A, Tables 3-8, for a sample of information obtainable from the CPDF).

There is some confusion about the information contained in the CPDF as well as about the intended purposes of that data base:

- Not all federal managers and data users understand the distinction made by OPM, and reflected in the CPDF, between qualification standards and occupational standards.[4] Some agencies report that some of these standards are outdated and incorrect. However, a partially revised *Qualification Standard for*

---

[4] OPM has responsibility for the overall management of the federal government's classification and qualification systems, but "actual operation of these systems is carried out by individual federal agencies on a decentralized basis" (U.S. Merit Systems Protection Board, 1989d).

Two-Grade Interval Professional Positions was issued by OPM to all federal directors of personnel in March 1989, and OPM has completely revised the qualification standards for four broad occupational groups (professional, administrative, clerical, and technical) in order to have a generic approach that facilitates automation and accelerates the hiring process.[5] Nonetheless, many federal scientists and engineers and their supervisors seem unaware of these recent revisions, perhaps because of the difficulties in communication between scientists and engineers and federal personnel specialists.

- Similarly, many federal managers of scientists and engineers—believing that OPM equates the field of one's academic degree with his or her occupational classification—felt that misclassification occurred frequently. For instance, it was pointed out that most employees in the Water Resources Division of the U.S. Geological Survey are considered to be hydrologists, even though their degrees may be in different fields such as geochemistry. Although one usually works in the scientific or engineering field in which one has obtained a degree, that is not always the case. Thus, while OPM publishes CPDF data showing occupational classification, the CPDF could also provide tabulations by degree field (see Appendix A, Table 2).

- CPDF data can indicate more stability and less diversity than that which a division within an agency may be experiencing. For instance, BLS, the principal scientific unit in the Department of Labor (DOL), employs both statisticians and mathematical statisticians, each having different kinds of training; but because data on them is combined with data on employees in other parts of DOL, the picture drawn from OPM data might reflect what is happening in DOL overall but totally miss what is happening in BLS. Aggregated data are sometimes used by policy-makers to indicate few problems of recruitment, retention, and utilization of federal scientists and engineers in general when, in fact, there may be significant problems for specific S&E disciplines, geographic areas, or programs. Thus, scientists and engineers with whom the Committee communicated believe there is a very significant need to disaggregate data on the federal S&E work force as much and as frequently as possible—including by geographic area and by individual programs within an agency.

Although the aggregate data on retention of scientists and engineers are not very alarming—showing that, on average, less than 5 percent leave federal government employment, with about half as resignations and about half as retirements—each agency manager must be concerned within the context of his or her own operation, for turnover varies at the agency level. This fact seems to have stimulated some agencies—for example, the Naval Research Lab (NRL), the Department of Defense (DoD), and the Public Health Service (PHS)—to conduct their own research and to define problems of employee turnover, based on their needs—which are so agency-specific, especially in

---

[5] Leonard R. Klein, associate director of OPM's Career Entry and Employee Development Group, conversation with Linda S. Dix, June 26, 1990.

critical areas, that aggregated data would be of little use to a single agency. Unable to make projections based solely on the data that it sends to OPM, NRL keeps more detailed, exhaustive information, enabling the agency to compare its 1,800 scientists and engineers with those in other agencies. DoD's central data base covers every civilian and military employee of the department and enables one to distinguish between "separations with quit" (which have low rates) and "overall turbulence"--for example, moves within DoD or to another federal agency or changes in occupational titles--whose very high rates reflect the numbers of people changing jobs year to year. The PHS Historical Workforce Data File—containing information on its 7,600 civil service employees in the scientific, medical, and engineering disciplines—enables PHS to analyze the effectiveness of its recruitment and retention efforts.

2. **Managers of the federal science and engineering (S&E) work force have been unable to agree on what constitutes accurate measures of the quality of that work force. Some CPDF data can be used as proxies to input measures of quality—such as the highest academic degree conferred on an employee. In addition, OPM has recently undertaken a study of work force quality, surveying a sample of non-DoD scientists and engineers.**

Although improving the quality of the federal science and engineering work force may be the most important issue for improving the way the federal government deals with science and technology, managers of the federal S&E work force have been unable to agree on what constitutes accurate measures of its quality. Because of the nonquantifiable nature of characteristics, it was suggested that quality assessments might be accomplished through peer review or external visiting committees. It is possible, too, to look at proxies for quality of input—for example, academic grade-point averages (GPAs) and publications—to determine whether the quality of the work force differs from that of the past, an issue of concern to many managers of federal scientists and engineers.[6] This issue was examined at some length during a Conference on Workforce

---

[6] At the Committee-sponsored workshop, participants were told that NASA field center personnel officers believe they are not having greater difficulties in hiring engineers of the quality they have had in years past. According to Ray Kline, president of the National Academy of Public Administration, "Average entry-level engineers, for instance, have GPAs around 3.2, just as they did at the height of the Apollo program. NASA has seldom attracted people with GPAs in the 3.6-4.0 range, although some people use numbers like that to show declining quality." However, staff in other agencies have indicated that this revelation contradicts their own experiences. For instance, managers in federal statistical agencies decry their "inability to attract bright young technical and professional staff into our agencies, those individuals who will make a career of federal service and who will provide the basis for scientific and technical leadership and management in the future. Compared with a decade ago, we are no longer able to compete for high-quality talent being produced by the nation's universities. . . . The federal government is no longer in meaningful competition for the best and brightest. The economic basis for that is clear; it is what we hear from our applicants; and it is what we hear from faculty in the university pools of excellence from which we were able to hire in the past but cannot now" (Harry M. Rosenberg, National Center for Health Statistics, correspondence to Alan K. Campbell, March 12, 1990). The Committee notes that the difference in outlooks may be resolvable by disaggregation by degree level, an analysis that could be based on selected CPDF data.

Quality Assessment cosponsored by OPM and the U.S. Merit Systems Protection Board (MSPB) on May 8, 1989, by focusing on three questions:

- How can we best determine the quality of the federal work force?
- What measures of quality or methods of study are available?
- What problems can we expect in attempting to explore this issue? (MSPB and OPM, 1989)

As a result, a joint OPM-MSPB Advisory Committee on Federal Workforce Quality Assessment, created in early 1990, will review projects designed to assess the quality of the federal work force, assist in data interpretation and analysis, and offer advice on "strategies in response to workforce quality assessment research" (OPM, 1990).

In addition, according to Sandra Payne, chief of the Policy and Analysis Division within OPM's Career Entry and Employee Development Group, "This situation has led OPM to track and to begin to build a data base that will provide answers to questions about retention and quality. Such data are expected to assist management and policymakers in their decisions about interventions with pay or new programs enhancing performance management."[7] In fact, in early 1990 OPM began a survey of a sample of 14,500 scientists and engineers (see Appendix A, pages 70-76) in all federal agencies except DoD, which had begun a study of the quality of its own scientists and engineers in 1988.[8] The OPM survey focuses on variables used in earlier quality assessments—GPA, highest academic degree earned, major field of study, institution from which one graduated, years of professional experience, and professional achievements (awards, publications, and patents)—as well as one's most recent performance appraisal rating and individual skills and attributes (technical knowledge in specialty field, ability to apply technical skill, cross-disciplinary skills, understanding of nontechnical factors, group interaction skills, management skills, oral communication skills, initiative, creativity and ingenuity, commitment to organizational goals and objectives, and service orientation).

Management Practices Relating to the Career Work Force

3. **Perceptions about the factors affecting the federal government's ability to recruit and retain scientists and engineers have remained basically the same for the past 30 years, in spite of specific efforts by OPM and individual federal agencies to enhance such recruitment and retention.**

Many perceive that federal recruitment, retention, and utilization of scientists and

---

[7] Comments to the Committee on Scientists and Engineers in the Federal Government, November 20, 1989.

[8] Analyses of the data from the Study of Scientists and Engineers in the DoD Laboratories, conducted primarily by the Analytic Sciences Corporation and the Allen Corporation of America under contract to the Institute for Defense Analyses, have not yet been released.

engineers are frequently ineffective because of "considerable bureaucracy and limited freedom." Among the factors cited are the inability "to establish overlapping pay bands, to pay above the cap, to pay recruitment and retention bonuses, and to implement accelerated hiring or promotion procedures."[9] In addition,

> outside recruitment above the GS-11 level is constrained by the . . . lack of local direct-hire authority and the need for higher authority review and approval of advanced in-hire rates for individual candidates.[10]

Furthermore, some believe that "the Civil Service with a few exceptions is not flexible on negotiation of salary options and recruitment incentives."[11] Still another lab director pointed out that the excessive degree of control imposed on the laboratory by external sources

> impairs the laboratory's management of its financial, personnel, and physical resources, which then threatens to diminish the vitality of the technical program. The effects of this excessive control can often be delays in facility and equipment procurement that, in turn delay R&D projects, some of which are critical to urgent national security requirements; excessive personnel processing time that exacerbates the laboratory's difficulties in recruiting high-quality scientists and engineers; and inflexible financial management mechanisms. These bureaucratic constraints can threaten work quality and employee morale to the point where a high-quality researcher decides that the bureaucracy of a company or a university may look more inviting.[12]

Reinforcing that procedural delays also hinder recruitment, another federal manager added,

> It is unrealistic to expect a highly qualified scientist or engineer at the GS/GM-14/15 equivalent level to wait 4 or 5 months after a job interview takes place before a firm job offer is made. There have been several instances in the past few years where we have made a selection . . . only to have the person turn the job down at the time when we were able to officially offer the position. . . . It is estimated that we lose 50-60 percent

---

[9] William F. Raub, acting director, National Institutes of Health, to Alan Fechter, November 17, 1989. Actions available to federal agencies to counteract these negative factors are described later in this section.

[10] Marvin D. Brailsford, former commander, U.S. Army Armament, Munitions and Chemical Command, to Alan Fechter, November 20, 1989.

[11] Edward Myers, program director in the National Oceanic and Atmospheric Administration's Environmental Research Laboratories, Boulder, Colo., to Alan Fechter, November 9, 1989.

[12] Timothy Coffey, director of research, Naval Research Laboratory, to Alan Fechter, November 14, 1989.

of all outside-hire S&E candidates to whom we make offers, while awaiting final processing of [their applications].[13]

Still other factors include personnel ceilings, noncompetitive salary, inadequate fringe benefits, ethics laws, the working environment and its geographic location, and the public image of federal service (see Dix, Appendix B, and workshop proceedings, Appendix C).

OPM Initiatives

The Civil Service Reform Act of 1978 gave OPM primary responsibility for managing the federal government's S&E work force—including the effectiveness of both the relevant data systems and the administrative systems, which deal with the recruitment, utilization, and promotions of federal scientists and engineers. OPM's Central Personnel Data File can indicate the extent of turnover by government scientists and engineers as evidenced by the number of these employees who have retired or resigned and the number of new hires (see, for instance, MSPB, 1989e, and Tables 6-8 in Appendix A). OPM has taken specific action to counteract what are deemed unsatisfactory vacancy and turnover rates among scientists and engineers, although remarks by some federal managers indicate that knowledge of these interventions does not flow regularly from agency personnel offices to line managers.

Delegation of Examining and Hiring Procedures: According to MSPB (1989b),

OPM is delegating examining and hiring authorities to agencies at an accelerated rate and for a wider range of positions than previously. . . . 534 delegated examinations are in effect.

On February 2, 1990, OPM offered to delegate examining for GS-9 through GS-15 positions to agencies so they could control timeliness. However, OPM reports that few agencies have requested this authority.

In addition to authorizing agencies to develop examinations for specific positions, OPM has granted them direct-hire authority[14] (see Appendix A, Table 9). More widely implemented by OPM since July 1989, these changes "appear to offer increased opportunities to hire entry-level candidates . . . and may afford [agencies] a more competitive position in the college recruitment arena."[15] As a result of decentralization,

---

[13] Brailsford, *op. cit.*

[14] According to OPM (1990), "direct hire is based on the assumption that the limited supply of applicants and high demand for them assures that all qualified applicants will receive equivalent consideration with or without normal procedures. As an added refinement, direct hire is authorized only for applicants with numerical ratings above a predetermined score (PDS) when there are adequate numbers of basically qualified candidates but few well qualified ones."

[15] Dallas L. Peck, director of the U.S. Geological Survey, to Alan Fechter, November 27, 1989.

70 percent of all new federal employees are hired through delegation, as opposed to the 14 percent under a more centralized system in 1981. According to Palguta (see Appendixes B and C), 95 percent of scientists and engineers are employed through direct-hire authority—that is, the agencies find potential employees and hire them in order not to find themselves in the situation whereby desired individuals have taken employment elsewhere.

Special Salary Rates: Since 1955, OPM has set higher rates than available under the General Schedule of Salaries "when the government is significantly handicapped in recruiting or retaining qualified individuals."[16] The first step of a special rate range is limited to 30 percent more than the first step of the General Schedule. These special rates can be granted based on occupation, grade, and geographic location (see Appendix A, Table 10). OPM has established special rates[17] for most engineers in response to agency requests to make salaries competitive with those of the private sector. For most engineers, special rates are authorized worldwide; petroleum and mining engineers have nationwide special rates.

However, some managers of federal scientists and engineers believe that even "the special salary rates for engineers and scientists are not competitive with the private sector, particularly on the East Coast and in large metropolitan areas,"[18] citing pay differences of 20 percent at the entry level and 10-15 percent for midcareer scientists and engineers. The disparity is even greater at the senior level:

> Agencies have some hiring flexibility at the entry level—based on GPA, one can be hired at GS-7 rather than GS-5. However, when a GS-7 in a special salary rate can only be offered $27,000 by the government but can earn $40,000 in private industry, problems arise.[19]

Federal Pay Reform Act of 1990 (FPRA): Though not directed solely at scientists and engineers, this proposal of the Bush administration, introduced on May 1, is designed to retain some across-the-government discipline while still granting greater flexibility within the system. It has five objectives:

- Restructuring the pay system to reflect diverse labor markets;
- Increasing flexibilities in the pay system to adapt to special situations and circumstances;
- Strengthening the link between the performance of an employee and his or her pay;

---

[16] Barry Shapiro, deputy assistant director for pay programs in OPM's Personnel Systems and Oversight Group, conversation with Linda S. Dix, March 25, 1990.

[17] Defined as "rates which exceed normal General Schedule salaries for other employees at the same grades" (GAO, 1987).

[18] Brailsford, *op. cit.*

[19] N. L. Howton, at the Workshop.

- Instituting a credible, effective, and enduring pay adjustment process; and
- Providing immediate relief for critical pay problems.[20]

The FPRA proposes to replace the General Schedule of Salaries with two white-collar pay systems: (1) the Federal National Pay System (NS), with nationwide rates and the opportunity for added geographic differentials of up to 25 percent in exceptionally high labor cost areas with area-wide staffing problems, and (2) the Federal Locality Pay System (LS), with local rates.[21]

Key provisions of the pay reform proposal may enhance the federal government's ability to recruit and retain scientists and engineers:

- Geographic differentials of up to 8 percent for employees in New York, San Francisco, and Los Angeles;
- Pay banding of GS-16-18 positions into one senior pay range: rates will range from 120 percent of the NS-20 (current GS-15) rate to the rate for Executive Schedule, Level V; there are no steps, and progression through the rate range is based on performance;
- Staffing differentials (of up to 60 percent of basic pay) and recruitment and relocation bonuses and retention allowances (of up to 25 percent of basic pay);
- Exemption of up to 400 critical positions (in the scientific, engineering, administrative, and technical fields) from the pay ceiling: salary will be limited to Executive Schedule I ($138,900 in January 1991) unless the President, on a case-by-case basis, approves a higher salary;
- Permission for agencies to hire all grades above the minimum rate, not just GS-11 and higher positions, as by the current authority;
- Waiver of dual compensation provisions on a case-by-case basis; and
- Granting of performance-based cash awards of up to 10 percent of basic pay for ratings of Fully Successful or higher, as well as awards of up to 20 percent of basic pay in exceptional cases.[22]

Other Recruitment Initiatives: In addition, to determine other actions that the federal government could take to recruit more U.S. citizens to its employ, OPM recently completed a comprehensive study of recruitment practices of federal agencies at four-year colleges and universities. Among the survey findings are:

- 50 percent [of surveyed agencies] have no college recruiting brochure;

---

[20] "Key Features of the Federal Pay Reform Act of 1990," draft circulated to federal agencies, April 3, 1990, p. 1.

[21] However, the findings of a recent study of locality pay indicate that these differentials may be insufficient to entice individuals to work for the federal government rather than for universities or private industry (Wyatt, 1989).

[22] Information from Barbara Fiss, OPM's assistant director for pay and performance, June 26, 1990.

- 58 percent have no money budgeted for college recruiting; and
- 49 percent have no advertising budget. (National Commission on the Public Service, 1990)

As a result, OPM has recently implemented three new initiatives:

- **Career America College Hotline:** Because many students do not know how to find a federal job, in September 1989 OPM set up a college hotline. By calling 1-900-990-9200 and answering a series of questions about one's specialties, degrees, and college(s) attended, a person learns how to apply for a job and is sent the appropriate federal forms for applying. A prerecorded voice explains the process and the basics of the system. If an individual wants to find out about specific agencies, he or she may call a given number to talk to an actual recruiter.

- **Automated Applicant Referral System:** OPM has replaced the SF-171 with an automated form processed within 24 hours at its Macon, Ga., facility. The rest is left up to the individual agencies. For example, if an agency wants to recruit an engineer, it enters a specific code into this automated system; after specifying the series, grade, and specialty wanted, within minutes the agency will receive either a particular application or a referral of all the candidates who qualify for that job.

- **Federal Career Fairs:** In March 1990 OPM organized job fairs in Washington, D.C., Boston, Chicago, Denver, and San Francisco to alert the public to the kinds of jobs available in the federal government and to enable federal agencies to publicize the types of work that they perform. As a result of these two-day fairs, approximately 87,000 individuals applied for federal positions (Causey, 1990).

Agency Initiatives

In addition to OPM initiatives, most federal agencies have recognized that they themselves play an important role in the recruitment and retention of scientists and engineers (see Appendix A, Table 11, and Clark, Appendix B). They have learned not only that line managers and senior executives must go out and recruit but also that established relationships with universities continue between recruiting trips. Agencies are attempting to reach more potential employees by increasing the number and types of college campuses visited, no longer concentrating their efforts at the major research universities but pursuing candidates at other institutions such as the historically black colleges and universities.[23]

Polled informally by the Committee, college placement officers revealed that 2-20 percent of their graduating seniors are interviewed by federal agency representatives, but most placement officers expressed sentiments similar to the following:

---

[23] The Committee was told that this is done at high costs to the agencies—in terms of training staff to be recruiters, time spent by recruiters away from their "regular" assignment, and providing displays as attractive as those used by industrial recruiters.

Our graduates favor private sector employment. They are able to obtain higher salaries there and are generally impressed by the business-like approach of private sector recruiters. The regulations and paperwork involved in federal employment are seen as impediments to an easy contact: The SF-171 form is awesome to an undergraduate and it would expedite matters if an initial contact could be made on the basis of the resume alone. It is difficult to know how to direct students to contact federal agencies. Finding the correct person to talk with and obtaining any encouragement is hard. Usually the first contact with the student is with a recording machine, at a line which is continually busy!

For all of the above reasons, it is certainly recommended that hiring agencies make on-campus visits and informal presentations. These humanize federal government employment, and we are pleased to see more federal agencies on campus in recent years than ever before.[24]

Some agencies—including the Central Intelligence Agency, NASA, U.S. Air Force, Department of Energy (DOE), U.S. Patent and Trademark Office, U.S. Navy, and Army Corps of Engineers—have not only increased their on-campus recruiting but also involved practicing scientists and engineers to describe the work done by technical personnel in their agencies. The more comprehensive recruitment strategy undertaken by hiring agencies often includes "advertising in appropriate journals and newsletters; contacts at conferences; and referrals by advisory committee members and merit reviews" (National Science Foundation, 1988) as well as career days.

Other agencies develop their recruitment initiatives around educational opportunities. For instance, Morgantown Energy Technology Center (METC) has concentrated its recent efforts in this area on a cooperative education program, as have the Environmental Research Laboratories (ERL) of the National Oceanic and Atmospheric Administration (NOAA). Using a significant part of its budget, ERL has financed six joint institutes with universities. ERL not only supports postdocs and graduate students, thereby furthering research in line with NOAA's mission, but also encourages science and engineering students to choose atmospheric and oceanographic careers through joint institute funding.[25] Thus, NOAA is trying to encourage potential environmental scientists by putting more money into the universities, where the training is available and these cooperative institutes are in place. As ERL's deputy director, Robert J. Mahler, pointed out,

> This effort has resulted in our scientists updating their knowledge base, allowed university researchers to work on NOAA science problems, and expanded the educational opportunities for young scientists at the university level. We find these cooperative programs . . . to be extremely valuable for attracting scientific expertise not otherwise available to federal

---

[24] Louise Wildeman, careers services coordinator in Colorado School of Mines' Office of Career Placement, to Linda S. Dix, February 1, 1990.

[25] The number of Ph.D.s awarded by U.S. universities in environmental sciences has been steadily decreasing since 1981, from 54 to 29 in 1987 (see Coyle, S. L., and D. H. Thurgood, 1989).

laboratories, for training future scientists, and for evaluating people before hiring them into Civil Service.[26]

Similar merits of cooperative education programs were revealed in the Study of Scientists and Engineers in the DoD Laboratories (IDA, 1989a). In addition, the Statistics of Income Division of the Internal Revenue Service, which has experienced difficulties in recruiting economists and systems analysts, also highlighted the education opportunities available to government employees:

> One of the most attractive features that we indicate when recruiting is that we pay for out-service college courses related to employee's work. This is a very big incentive to attract people. Many of the graduates want to pursue further academic training; the organization benefits because the individual brings something new to the job and has a more well-rounded perspective. . . . We will lose some of the people we were able to recruit in the last two years if a way is not found to pay for training.[27]

However, it was pointed out to the Committee that cuts to agency budgets often eliminate such education opportunities.

Still other agencies have restructured their job classification system to have less trouble hiring at the entry level. For instance, the National Institutes of Health (NIH) uses a special authority of the Public Health Service Act, its enabling legislation, to bring in young scientists primarily in the biomedical area without being restricted by the civil service classification system. A tenure-type system similar to that of a university enables NIH to keep these individuals for up to seven years in a temporary appointment, and because salaries are negotiated and set administratively, supervisors feel they have more power at the entry level. At the end of seven years, either these individuals receive tenure, usually as a GS-13, or they leave; about 10 percent achieve tenure.

Finally, some federal agencies have been able to recruit high-caliber Ph.D.-level scientists and engineers in most disciplines because of concerted efforts to emphasize the "psychic income" they can provide. Among the psychic income measures stressed at NRL are "the world-renown reputation of the Laboratory, challenging R&D work, the freedom and time to pursue good research, unique facilities and equipment, opportunities for advancement, opportunities for continuing education in an area with several excellent academic institutions, a chance to utilize the skills the individual possesses."[28] As the salary disparity with the private sector widens, it can become more difficult to offset real income with psychic income, especially at entry levels.

4. **To fulfill the missions of federal agencies, science and**

---

[26] Correspondence to Alan K. Campbell, March 9, 1990.

[27] Fritz Scheuren, director of the IRS's Statistics of Income Division, to Linda S. Dix, March 7, 1990.

[28] Timothy Coffey, *op. cit.*

> engineering can be completed under a variety of scenarios—including the traditional setting within an agency, demonstration projects, federal laboratories, and managed-and-operated (M&O) facilities. Demonstration projects authorized by OPM and the contracting out of S&E work seem to have provided agencies with the flexibility deemed necessary to overcome some of the difficulties associated with recruitment, retention, and utilization of scientists and engineers.

An issue of concern to the scientific community is how to bring the best scientists and engineers to the federal government. In some instances performing S&E work in-house may be the most efficient and effective solution, but in other cases the government may gain the maximum benefit by contracting out all or part of its S&E operations. The health of the federal science and engineering and the R&D establishment centers around the question "How will federal agencies maintain the intellectual, managerial, and technical strength needed for government to do what will be required of it?" This has led to congressional examination of how government work is conducted, to questions of the role of government R&D, and to discussions of what should be done in-house versus what should be done by contractors. This section primarily summarizes findings from the Committee-sponsored workshop and the paper of Sheldon B. Clark (see Appendixes B and C).

Selected Civil Service Laboratories

As noted by Clark, some civil service laboratories,[29] tending to view the federal personnel system

> as a monolithic adversary that has little appreciation for the special needs of the research enterprise, especially its researchers and managers . . . have devised methods of overcoming particular limitations imposed by the civil service system.

Based primarily on examinations of the U.S. Army laboratory system, Clark offers the following insights about the success of federal laboratories in recruiting and retaining scientists and engineers:

- To compensate for noncompetitive salaries to new hires, one lab offers the following incentives:

    - support for participation in professional meetings,
    - liberal sabbatical policies,

---

[29] Clark defines "civil service laboratories" as "those government labs that are staffed by employees of the U.S. government who are covered by federal personnel law as contained in Title 5 of the U.S. Code."

- opportunities for advancement,
- awards programs,
- office refurbishing, and
- a "Care" program "designed to treat scientists and engineers with professional and personal dignity" and including such elements as flextime, alternative work schedules, work-at-home arrangements, and educational assistance.

• Elements of the work environment—for example, relatively stable missions and funding; national prominence; quality, quantity, and diversity of research services, equipment, and personnel; ability to focus full time on research activities; rewarding research; and freedom from grant writing—can enhance recruitment and retention (Institute of Medicine [IOM], 1988).

• Overcoming personnel ceilings, limitations on the number of full-time-equivalent personnel a lab may employ, is another method undertaken to achieve the fulfillment of a laboratory's mission. According to Clark, such ceilings pose

> a particular problem during periods of retrenchment, little growth, and/or low turnover, especially given the civil service restrictions on the lab's ability to remove the least productive personnel. Effective personnel management is hindered, since the ceilings tend to grow slower than budgets. Managers, who are best able to make decisions about how to allocate money and personnel to meet their programmatic commitments, are prevented from making the most productive decisions (IOM, 1988).

Clark found that some civil service labs have circumvented personnel ceilings "by significantly increasing their personnel pools through the use of university-based programs to bring adjunct personnel into the lab."

The study committee learned that the DoD Laboratory Demonstration Program proposes a variety of legislative and regulatory changes to enhance the recruitment, retention, and utilization of scientists and engineers in DoD.

Demonstration Projects

Under Title VI of the Civil Service Reform Act, OPM was authorized to conduct or approve alternative personnel management systems, under which certain civil service restrictions, including the following, could be waived:

- Qualification requirements;
- Classification methods;
- Compensation methods and incentive pay;
- Methods of assigning, reassigning, promoting, or disciplining employees;

- Hours of work per week;
- Methods of involving employees, unions, and employee organizations in personnel decisions; and
- Methods of reducing agency staff and grade levels. (MSPB, 1989b)

Demonstration projects enable OPM to determine the effectiveness of innovative personnel practices and have been used to test flexibilities to overcome some of the difficulties associated with recruitment, retention, and utilization of scientists and engineers. The earliest demonstration project was implemented by the Department of the Navy in 1980 at the Naval Weapons Center (NWC), China Lake, and the Naval Ocean Systems Center (NOSC), San Diego). Begun as a five-year experiment, it was extended for a second five years and now has been extended until September 1995 by congressional legislation. The authority to grant recruitment bonuses has not been used at NWC but has been used sparingly at NOSC. Both NWC and NOSC have benefited from the direct-hire authority available to any federal agency hiring in shortage categories and the authority to adjust beginning salaries within the broad pay band in order to be competitive in the marketplace. Assignment of position classification is the responsibility of line managers, with audits by the personnel department after the fact. The personnel office is supportive rather than adversarial, helping to provide better training of staff and better personnel advice to managers. In addition, NWC and NOSC employ a dual-career ladder, whereby top technical people are promoted based on their technical skills and can earn as much or more than the managers. NOSC staff attribute its low turnover rate among scientists and engineers, less than 4 percent, to its ability to offer more competitive salaries and to the quality of its work environment.

OPM has reported that the Navy demonstration project has had several measurable benefits:

- An increase in quality of people who have been recruited as indicated by managerial perceptions and increases in GPAs;
- Easier recruitment because of the ability to offer starting salaries reasonably close to the industry average;
- Adopting pay progression more similar to that employed in the private sector (start higher and advance slower);
- Pay for performance: high-quality people often are attracted by a system that will reward them differently from people performing less well;
- Satisfaction with the revised job classification system, which is as accurate as and certainly more expeditious than the old system;
- Improved attitudes of managers, who feel significantly more empowered to run the personnel system through the various flexibilities built into it; and
- Increased job satisfaction.[30]

As a result, other demonstration projects have been authorized. For example the

---

[30] Paul Thompson, at the Workshop. See also OPM (1986) and GAO (1988).

National Institute for Standards and Technology (NIST) began its personnel management demonstration project in 1988 with the following major goals:

- Improve hiring and compete more effectively for high-quality researchers through direct hiring, selective use of higher entry salaries, and selective use of recruitment bonuses;
- Better motivate and retain staff through higher pay potential and selective use of retention bonuses;
- Strengthen the line manager's role in personnel management by delegating personnel authorities; and
- Increase the efficiency of NIST personnel systems through simplification and automation.

One provision of its authorizing legislation is direct-hire authority for the whole agency, except for blue-collar workers. For occupations that have a shortage of highly qualified candidates, even a division chief can make a hire, offering what he or she thinks the market demands up to the 75th percentile of the top salary stated in the DOE salary surveys. In addition, NIST can offer $10,000 recruitment and retention bonuses and begin a new employee at any salary in the approved range. The NIST project's higher pay potential is part of a pay for performance system. Another important aspect of the demonstration project is having line managers do the classification and the qualification check, with personnel officers authorized to audit the programs. As a result, entry-level problems experienced by the National Bureau of Standards (predecessor to NIST) seem to have been resolved, as have those associated with recruiting. According to NIST staff and others such as University Research Corporation,[31] the project is successful:

> Overall, we believe the demonstration project addresses previous problems in staffing and hiring and has the potential to make NIST a better place to work. Many managers . . . feel that decentralization and streamlining of the hiring procedures enable NIST to attract individuals who might have otherwise been lost under the old, cumbersome procedures.
> NIST is able by and large to retain a majority of those individuals whom we recruit [because of] career advancement opportunities. . . . Our weakest area in retention is among the mid-level, mid-career staff, who feel the effect of the salary ceiling imposed on the Civil Service.[32]

This year OPM granted the U.S. Department of Agriculture (USDA) permission to participate in a special personnel demonstration project. The project will be conducted by two USDA research agencies, the Agricultural Research Service (ARS) and the Forest Service. The USDA demonstration is not a pay demonstration; its focus is on recruitment and selection and its only pay intervention is the authority to pay

---

[31] Public Law 99-574, which established the NIST demonstration project, requires that an outside contractor evaluate it each year. The results of the first-year evaluation are contained in U.S. Office of Personnel Management, 1989b.

[32] Raymond G. Kammer, acting NIST director, to Alan Fechter, November 20, 1989.

recruitment bonuses. However, according to H. L. Rothbart, director of the ARS North Atlantic Area,

> A major obstacle in the recruitment and retention of scientists and engineers is the federal GS salary structure. For B.S. degree holders in chemistry and engineering, beginning salaries at the GS-5-7 level are not competitive with private industry unless the applicant lacks practical research experience. When such an individual (e.g., from a smaller school with limited laboratory experience) is hired, within one year these individuals gain a sufficient amount of experience that they may then move to private industry with salary increases of $8,000 to $10,000.[33]

ARS expects the demonstration project to be flexible and responsive to local needs in order to "facilitate the attainment of a quality work force reflective of society."[34] While sharing some of the goals of earlier demonstration projects, this newly approved project also attempts to:

- Increase the reliability of the decision to grant career tenure;
- Decentralize the decision to authorize direct hire in shortage categories;
- Establish an alternative candidate assessment method which uses categorical grouping instead of numeric score;
- Provide monetary incentives for recruitment purposes; and
- Reimburse travel and transportation expenses beyond those currently authorized for travel to first post of duty.[35]

M&O Contractor Facilities

Based on his examination of 4 of the 67 M&O[36] facilities owned by the DOE but operated by a variety of contractors—private-sector firms, universities, and university consortia[37]—Clark notes that "each of the operating contracts is negotiated separately with DOE [and] personnel policies and procedures vary significantly from one installation to another." However, he points out many recruitment and retention initiatives that they share:

---

[33] Correspondence to E. E. Finney, Jr., acting area director, Beltsville Area, ARS, January 26, 1990.

[34] *Federal Register* 54(162):35134, August 23, 1989.

[35] *Ibid.*

[36] Management-and-operating (M&O) contractor scenario, formerly known as GOCO (government-owned, contractor-operated) facilities.

[37] Argonne National Laboratory managed by the University of Chicago; Sandia National Laboratories by the Sandia Corporation; Oak Ridge National Laboratory by Martin Marietta Corporation; and Oak Ridge Associated Universities by a consortium of 55 colleges and universities.

- Developing and maintaining university ties: Labs engage in "faculty and student research participation programs, consulting arrangements, lecture programs, participation in academic professional societies, and equipment-sharing programs [to] enhance the image of the lab and also its ability to recruit and retain highly qualified scientists and engineers."
- Multiple occupation-based pay schedules to reflect market rates: Clark notes that "most of the alternative personnel systems have objectives-based performance appraisals very similar in design to those required throughout the civil service, but they are generally used quite differently . . . tied to the performance appraisal systems." Before their implementation, all salary schedules and benefits programs have to be approved by DOE, however, and "individual approval is required for each salary in excess of $70,000 (but these salaries are not subject to the federal pay cap)."
- Performance bonuses.
- "A wide variety of retirement programs, ranging from those typical of large private firms to those available to employees of colleges and universities."
- Exemption from government-imposed personnel ceilings: "DOE contractors in particular can better adjust to changing or diminishing funding by shifting researchers from one program to another or, if necessary, laying people off. Unlike civil service labs, these decisions can be made entirely on the basis of skills, abilities, and performance."

As Clark concludes,

> Personnel systems need to be customized to the organizations they serve. It is not reasonable to expect that a single model will fit all organizations or that a system, once developed, can remain static. The organizations themselves and the environments in which they exist are dynamic. Every organization needs a uniqueness in its personnel system, an opportunity to mold it to its own identity, and the freedom to change it when change is needed.

5. The extent to which scientists and engineers are utilized effectively varies from agency to agency.

NOAA administers the seven ERL sites within the Department of Commerce. Responding to the Committee's query, ERL staff explained that steps are taken to utilize its work force efficiently and effectively:

> It is rare to have a scientist leave his or her area of specialty. While the mission and direction of a particular laboratory may change from time to time, the expertise of the scientist is matched to address the new directions of scientific research.

Similarly, according to Donald Feucht, former deputy director of operations, the Solar

Energy Research Institute (SERI) attributes its low annual attrition rates to the effective utilization of its work force:

> Retaining qualified scientific and engineering employees has not been a problem for SERI. Once a scientist or engineer has been hired for a specific position, SERI strives to fully utilize the talent of the technical staff as well as to provide developmental opportunities in current or new areas of research.[38]

Some federal organizations are taking steps to ensure that the skills and knowledge of their scientists and engineers are fully utilized. For instance, the Naval Ocean Systems Center recently conducted a survey to determine the extent to which its scientists and engineers were using their knowledge and skills in their work: "Most of our technically trained people, even senior managers, spend the preponderance of their time on technical matters."[39]

Discussed at some length at the Committee-sponsored workshop, however, was the emphasis on contract management by scientists and engineers employed in-house by federal agencies. The federal government clearly needs technically knowledgeable people who can interact with contractors and manage R&D contracts, but several federal scientists and engineers felt that they were required to spend an inordinate amount of time on contract matters. They would prefer to be engaged in actual S&E work and reported that disillusionment sets in among entry-level scientists and engineers when they discover that they won't be doing technical work but, rather, preparing to be contract managers because so much federal work is contracted out. The Committee learned that

> positions requiring the application of a professional knowledge of engineering or other sciences in the development or evaluation of technical requirements in connection with . . . contracts are classifiable to the Engineering Group, GS-800, or other appropriate professional or scientific series. Positions in the GS-1102 series advise and assist in developing acceptable specifications and evaluation criteria, determine the method of procurement, issue the solicitation document, and conduct the contracting process. (OPM, 1983)

Within the engineering and science groups' position classification standards, one finds that contract oversight is one of several responsibilities of scientists and engineers at the GS-11-15 levels. Thus, when disillusionment is attributed to one's being required to provide such contract management, the Committee urges that greater emphasis be placed on an employee's understanding of his or her job responsibilities before assuming a program manager's position, which requires such contract management.

---

[38] Letter to Alan Fechter, October 24, 1989.

[39] R. M. Hillyer, NOSC technical director, to Alan Fechter, November 7, 1989.

6. Many within the broader scientific and engineering community are concerned about the effects of the changing U.S. demography on the federal government's ability to recruit and retain qualified U.S. citizens, and several managers of federal scientists and engineers revealed difficulties in hiring women and minorities. CPDF data on the race/ethnicity and sex of federal employees, used by agencies such as the Equal Employment Opportunity Commission to monitor a variety of federal affirmative action programs, could also indicate where the federal government might pursue initiatives to respond to projected shortages of scientists and engineers, tapping groups currently underrepresented in the sciences and engineering.

The composition of the U.S. population has been changing dramatically since 1980. Of particular concern are the facts that the 18- to 24-year-old cohort that comprises our undergraduate population is expected to continue to decline until 1995, and the number of 16- to 24-year-old workers will drop by nearly 2 million, or 8 percent. In addition, not only are the numbers decreasing, but for the past few years the percentage of students majoring in most fields of science and engineering—traditionally, white males—has been dropping. Furthermore, projections show that the increases in the U.S. population will be greatest among ethnic groups that have not heretofore participated significantly in science and engineering. In fact, between now and the year 2000, white males are expected to comprise only 32 percent of new entrants to the labor force (U.S. Bureau of Labor Statistics, in White House Task Force, 1989).

Because the pool of talent for new scientists and engineers is comprised predominantly of females and ethnic minorities and because the federal government is the largest single employer of scientists and engineers—directly and indirectly—the White House Task Force on Women, Minorities, and the Handicapped in Science and Technology (1989) urged that the federal government pursue several actions to encourage those individuals to choose careers in science and engineering. Actions recommended to the federal government that could increase the supply of federal scientists and engineers include the following:

- Use federal R&D programs to bring about a more diverse, world-class S&E work-force;
- Collect and maintain data to evaluate the participation of minorities, women, and persons with disabilities in their federal R&D programs;
- Continue to hire and advance talented scientists and engineers, including those from underrepresented groups; and
- Provide stable and substantial support for effective intervention programs that graduate quality scientists and engineers who are members of underrepresented groups.

Another aspect of this issue is the ability of the federal government to predict its needs for scientists and engineers systemwide. The National Science Board publishes

Science & Engineering Indicators biennially, but its focus is primarily the private sector of the S&E work force. For instance, the ninth report (National Science Board, 1989) presents detailed information on labor-market indicators for S&E personnel (labor force participation rates, unemployment rates, S&E employment rates, experiences of recent S&E graduates, and employer shortages of S&E personnel) and projected demand for scientists and engineers in industry. However, the Committee learned of no government-wide mechanism by which the federal government plans to meet its own needs for scientists and engineers. Instead, some individual agencies collect and analyze their own data to make projections about their agency's needs for scientists and engineers.

7. **Government policies that limit the hiring of foreign nationals may have adverse effects on the ability of federal agencies to perform S&E work.**

Restrictions on employment of foreign-born citizens and foreign nationals often prevent their employment in federal agencies, although they comprise about 20 percent of the total S&E labor force in the United States (National Research Council, 1988). About 50 percent of engineering Ph.D.s graduating in the United States are foreign, but many federal government agencies cannot hire them as a matter of policy. The Senior Executive Service does not contain a citizenship requirement. However, separate controlling legislation of some agencies, as well as general appropriations act restrictions and individual agency restrictions, may prohibit the employment of foreign nationals. As emphasized by one college placement officer, and seconded by many workshop participants,

> At a time when so many of the nation's younger scientists are immigrants, and the government congratulates itself on its immigration policy, it is both hypocritical and absurd that the government won't hire them.[40]

In addition, this limitation skews comparisons of the federal work force with the national work force, because industry and academe generally are not prohibited from hiring foreign and foreign-born scientists and engineers.

Trends Regarding Presidential Appointments

8. **There is growing concern about the adequacy of the political appointments process and the impact of political appointees on the fulfillment of federal S&E work.**

Strong leadership—both at the science and technology policy level and within

---

[40] Robert K. Weatherall, Massachusetts Institute of Technology placement officer, to Linda S. Dix, February 8, 1990.

those federal entities employing significant numbers of scientists and engineers—is important to the recruitment, retention, and utilization of scientists and engineers with the government. As noted by Robert M. White, president of the National Academy of Engineering, "The general scientific community in the government is dependent upon the policy leadership of Presidential appointees,"[41] who by definition are supportive of the President's policies. The nature of the technical work within federal agencies requires also that they believe in their organization's mission and in the value of the work performed to accomplish it.

According to Pfiffner (Appendix B), there have been many unfilled positions at the top in departments or appointees who had no knowledge of or sympathy for science and engineering. The White House Office of Appointments attributes the vacant positions to noncompetitive pay, ethics requirements, financial disclosure, postemployment restrictions, short tenure in office, and lack of names of qualified individuals in the scientific community (see, for instance, Mackenzie, 1990).

However, members of the scientific community believe that recruitment of scientists and engineers to high-level government positions is further hindered by the President's staff establishing various ideological criteria for political appointees. The consequences can include a lengthy political appointments process[42] and short tenure of political appointees. Two particular instances in which some scientists believe this has negatively affected an agency's productivity were pointed out to the Committee: NIH and the Centers for Disease Control (CDC) have both experienced problems during the past year because of unfilled leadership positions (see Appendix C, Proceedings).[43] In addition, the process of appointing the successor to Ernest Ambler as NIST director took 10 months and included an entire budget cycle. It is important for an agency to have as its leader an individual who will serve as its advocate. However, the current system serves to deprive an agency of such advocacy. Because the average stay of a political appointee is 18-24 months, there is constant change at the top, with subsequent change in loyalty as well as reorganization.

---

[41] Remarks to the Committee on Scientists and Engineers in the Federal Government, November 20, 1989.

[42] According to the Democratic Study Group, U.S. House of Representatives, as of September 19, 1989, 178 senior positions in federal agencies had been filled by the Bush administration, but 219 remained unfilled (see *Executive Shortfall II: Continued Slow Progress in Staffing the Bush Administration*, Special Report No. 101-19).

[43] For instance, since passage of the National Cancer Act in 1972 the NIH directorship has become quite political, to the point that for almost a year NIH has had an acting director. Similarly, the directorship at the CDC, which became a political appointment about eight years ago, was unfilled for about a year, with the reported consequences including the lack of a person with the prestige of the Directorship to negotiate CDC's budget and reduced morale among careerists. As noted in Appendix A, Table 12, there have been long delays in the filling of leadership positions in other agencies such as the National Institute of Standards and Technology and Food and Drug Administration.

III. ISSUES REQUIRING FURTHER ANALYSIS

The Committee on Scientists and Engineers in the Federal Government has examined the information available to decision-makers concerned about the overall competence and capability of the federal government to attract and effectively utilize a cadre of highly qualified scientists and engineers who can develop and implement federal S&E policies. Based on this preliminary study, however, the Committee believes that many questions remain unanswered. The Committee identified the following specific issues as candidates for further analysis:

- **What mechanisms and scenarios for conducting federal S&E work could be employed on a wider basis to enhance recruitment, retention, and utilization of federal scientists and engineers?**

Within the federal government are many mechanisms, both formal and informal, to enhance the recruitment, retention, and utilization of scientists and engineers. In addition, federal S&E work is completed under a variety of scenarios. However, to the Committee's knowledge no in-depth analysis has been conducted to determine the best mechanisms for government-wide application. Individual agencies have determined the routes by which their S&E work will be accomplished, but no systemwide analysis of the effectiveness of these various scenarios in recruiting, retaining, and utilizing scientists and engineers is available. The Committee believes that a study of these mechanisms and scenarios would provide much useful information and strengthen the federal government's effectiveness. It might compare civil service laboratories with demonstration projects, with program areas, and with contract facilities (M&Os) to determine the distribution of federal S&E work to each, differences in problems faced by scientists and engineers (as well as their managers) in each scenario, and improvements to federal S&E work that might be expected if there is greater reliance on a particular scenario. In addition, such a study might answer:

- **What can be done to enhance federal recruitment of scientists and engineers, especially women and minorities at the entry level, and retention of all scientists and engineers at the midcareer level? What institutional decision-making processes should be altered and in what way? Should the relationship between OPM and the individual federal agencies be different for scientists and engineers than it is for other federal personnel?**

To more effectively recruit, retain, and utilize the federal S&E work force requires efforts both by the central personnel agency (OPM) and by the individual agencies employing scientists and engineers. Some activities must be centralized—for example, basic tools such as occupational and qualification standards. Other activities—for example, examination and hiring—should be decentralized, reflecting individual agency's needs.[44]

While agencies look to OPM for direction, it might be beneficial if they undertook self-assessments to ascertain what steps could be taken at the agency level. The Committee believes that insightful information could be gained by answering the following questions:

- What steps are (to be) taken to achieve its recruitment goal? How?
- What problems are encountered in meeting that goal? Why? What can be done to alleviate them?
- How does the agency retain its scientists and engineers, and how successful are these mechanisms?
- How are decisions made about job assignments, and how does job placement affect employee performance/productivity and morale?

A number of personnel initiatives should be encouraged, continued, and implemented more broadly. Among the possibilities are those undertaken by the military services, including career management, enlistment and reenlistment bonuses, and continuing education and training.

- **What steps must be taken to heighten the awareness within agencies of the mechanisms established by OPM to alleviate many of the problems that they encounter in recruiting and retaining scientists and engineers?**

One mechanism might be seminars designed to equip personnel officers and line managers with recruitment strategies that will attract qualified scientists and engineers; this would include clarification about direct-hire authority and the special rates approved by OPM. Another means to heighten awareness might be to exchange personnel people between agencies experiencing recruitment and retention problems and those finding it less difficult to recruit and retain scientists and engineers.

- What criteria should be used to determine effectiveness?
- What aspects of each mode of operation—such as salary, pay banding, fringe benefits, and the role of program managers—contributes to effective S&E work?
- What facilitated this effectiveness? (Why did it work?)
- How can effective aspects of recruitment, retention, and utilization be replicated systemwide?

In addition, it would seem beneficial for greater interactions to occur between agencies encountering difficulties in their utilization of scientists and engineers and those that seem to have resolved these problems.

- **How can the CPDF be more useful to agencies facing difficulties in recruiting and retaining scientists and engineers?**

---

[44]MSPB has praised OPM's efforts at decentralization (see U.S. Merit Systems Protection Board, 1989c.)

To assess the situation adequately, one must look at the agencies, their specific kinds of expertise, and what they are trying to accomplish. Agency-specific data will always be more sophisticated and more detailed, based on the agency's purposes. Nonetheless, aggregate data are useful for government-wide policy purposes. CPDF data, appropriately meshed with agency data, would enable agency people to determine whether any problems they face are systemic or unique to a specific agency. Thus, data systems on the federal S&E work force should be designed to enhance management of that work force and enable policy-makers to make sound decisions, and users of the CPDF must be made aware both of the CPDF's content and of its intended uses.

Greater collaboration and coordination between OPM and the federal agencies employing scientists and engineers should facilitate more effective management of the government's technical work force. Because the CPDF contains only those data supplied by the agencies, many of whom also collect and maintain data for their own use, discussions should center around the types of data needed by each. It is unclear whether (1) the format by which the data are collected by OPM leads to dual data systems, (2) a computer network to make the CPDF accessible to agency staff would be useful, or (3) further delineation and standardization of occupational classifications by OPM would provide more useful information both to the individual federal employers of scientists and engineers and to policy-makers. It is conceivable than an interagency group such as the Federal Coordinating Council on Science, Engineering, and Technology (FCCSET) might wish to investigate ways to make the CPDF more able to meet the needs of both OPM and the individual federal agencies employing scientists and engineers—focusing on what data are needed, the level of aggregation that should be used, and the degree of comparability of data between the public and private sectors.

- **Are there too few scientists and engineers in the federal government? Or are there too few highly qualified federal scientists and engineers?**

To answer this question, the Committee believes that there should be a more systematic assessment of requirements, available supply, and measures that can be taken to meet requirements. This might be undertaken by the FCCSET Committee on Education and Human Resources. Individual agencies should determine the number of scientists and engineers necessary for agency missions to be fulfilled, and the federal government should examine measures used by industry and academe to assess whether the quality of scientists and engineers differs significantly from that of the past. The federal government's need for scientists and engineers is part of a greater problem—the dwindling supply of U.S. scientists and engineers relative to the demand for their skills and knowledge in all sectors of the economy. But more analyses of a longitudinal nature—and perhaps different data—are needed to determine the severity of the federal government's problems in utilizing and managing its very critical human resources in comparison to the problems encountered by industry and academe. In addition, a closer examination of the different employment sectors seems warranted to answer the following questions:

- How is recruitment of scientists and engineers accomplished? If there are annual recruitment goals, how are they determined and what are they?
- What aspects of the employing organization—that is, institutional decision-

making—influence individual decisions of scientists and engineers to remain with or to leave a specific employer?
- To what extent do employers utilize scientists and engineers effectively—that is, assign responsibilities commensurate with their education and experience? How do employers respond to shifts in supply and demand?

- **What can be done to ensure that the political appointment process enhances the recruitment, retention, and utilization of scientists and engineers in the federal government?**

The Committee recommends a careful study to determine the underlying issues related to the work performed by political appointees, assessing the degree to which this work is policy oriented versus science and engineering oriented. To the extent that this work has sufficient policy content, such a study should examine

- Whether there is a need to improve the process by which individuals are recommended for political appointments;
- Whether the character of S&E work is such that using the political appointments process is inappropriate for selecting people to fill S&E policy positions in the federal government; and
- Criteria for determining how deep within each federal agency PAS (Presidential appointees requiring Senate confirmation) penetration should occur, reflecting individual agency needs.

BIBLIOGRAPHY

Carnegie Commission on Science, Technology, and Government, Task Force on Environment and Energy. 1990. *E^3: Organizing for Environment, energy, and the Economy in the Executive Branch of the U.S. Government.* New York: The Commission.

Causey, M. 1990. The federal diary: Private pay linkage. *Washington Post.* March 15, p. D2.

Committee on Army Manpower, Board on Army Science and Technology, Commission on Engineering and Technical Systems. 1983. *The Professional Environment in Army Laboratories and Its Effect on Scientific and Engineering Performance.* Washington, D.C.: National Academy Press.

Committee on Utilization of Scientific and Engineering Manpower. 1964. *Toward Better Utilization of Scientific and Engineering Talent: A Program for Action.* Washington, D.C.: National Academy of Sciences.

Coyle, S. L., and D. H. Thurgood. 1989. *Summary Report 1987: Doctorate Recipients from United States Universities.* Washington, D.C.: National Academy Press.

Dean, A. L., and H. Seidman. 1988. *Options for Organizational and Management Reform for the Intramural Research Program of the National Institutes of Health.* Washington, D.C.: National Academy of Public Administration.

Goodsell, C. T. 1985. *The Case for Bureaucracy: A Public Administrative Polemic* (2nd ed.). Chatham, N.J.: Chatham House.

Havemann, J. 1989. Senate-backed pay changes opposed as piecemeal. *Washington Post.* August 4, p. A8.

_____. 1990a. Volcker's reform: Few political appointees. *Washington Post.* April 13, p. A1.

_____. 1990b. Trying to fill the federal wage gap. *Washington Post.* May 18, p. A17.

_____, and R. J. Smith. 1989. Senate votes big boost in some pay. *Washington Post.* August 3, pp. A1, A4.

Hermann, R.J. 1982. *USDRE Independent Review of DoD Laboratories.* Washington, D.C.: Office of the Under Secretary for Defense Research and Engineering.

Hoerr, J. 1989. The payoff from teamwork. *Business Week.* July 10, pp. 56-62.

Institute of Medicine, Committee to Study Strategies to Strengthen the Scientific Excellence of the National Institutes of Health Intramural Research Program. 1988. *A Healthy NIH Intramural Program: Structural Change or Administrative Remedies?* Washington, D.C.: National Academy Press.

Institute for Defense Analysis (IDA). 1989a. *Study of Scientists and Engineers in the DoD Laboratories,* vol. I. Alexandria, Va.: IDA.

_____. 1989b. *Study of Scientists and Engineers in the DoD Laboratories,* vol. II. Alexandria, Va.: IDA.

Karl, B. 1987. The American bureaucrat: A history of a sheep in wolves' clothing. *Public Administration Review* 47(1):26-34.

Kaufman, H. 1986. Red tape: The perpetual irritant. In Francis E. Rourke (ed.),

Bureaucratic Power in National Policy Making (4th ed.), New York: Little, Brown, pp. 434-449.

Laboratory Management Task Force, U.S. Department of Defense. 1980. *Impact of Management Constraints on the DoD Laboratories.* Washington, D.C.: DoD.

———. 1982. *Study of Scientists and Engineers in DoD Laboratories.* Washington, D.C.: DoD.

Long, N. E. 1986. Power and administration. In Francis E. Rourke (ed.), *Bureaucratic Power in National Policy Making* (4th ed.), New York: Little, Brown, pp. 7-16.

Mackenzie, G. C. 1990. Appointing Mr. (or Ms.) Right. *Government Executive* **22** (4:April):30-35.

McGregor, E. B., Jr. 1988. The public sector human resource puzzle: Strategic management of a strategic resource. *Public Administration Review* **48**(6):941-950.

Millburn, G. P. 1989a. Untitled speech, Conference on Federal Workforce Quality Assessment, sponsored by the Office of Personnel Management and Merit Systems Protection Board, Washington, D.C., May 8.

———. 1989b. *Recruitment and Retention of DoD Scientists and Engineers.* Speech to Personnel Research Conference conducted by the Office of Personnel Management, Chevy Chase, Md., August 16.

National Commission on the Public Service. 1989. *Leadership for America: Rebuilding the Public Service.* Washington, D.C.: The Commission.

———. 1990. *Newsletter* **2**(3: February):2.

National Research Council. 1988. *Foreign and Foreign-Born Engineers in the United States: Infusing Talent, Raising Issues.* Washington, D.C.: National Academy Press.

National Science Board. 1989. *Science & Engineering Indicators—1989.* Washington, D.C.: National Science Foundation.

National Science Foundation. 1954+. *Scientists and Engineers in the Federal Government.* Washington, D.C.: U.S. Government Printing Office.

———. 1988. *NSF Recruitment of Scientists and Engineers: The Salary Issue.* Paper prepared for the Director and Executive Council by the Division of Personnel and Management. Unpublished.

Nelson, M. 1986. The irony of American bureaucracy. In Francis E. Rourke (ed.), *Bureaucratic Power in National Policy Making* (4th ed.), New York: Little, Brown, pp. 163-187.

Norton, R. E. 1989. Who wants to work in Washington? *Fortune* (August 14):77-80, 82.

Packard, D. 1986. The loss of governmental scientific and engineering talent. *Issues in Science and Technology* **2**(3: Spring):126-131.

Robertson, A. 1989. Internships sow seeds of Agriculture Dept. careers. *Washington Post.* August 11, p. A23.

Seidman, H., and R. Gilmour. 1986. *Politics, Position, and Power* (4th ed.). New York: Oxford University Press.

U.S. Civil Service Commission. 1964. *The Special Features of the Federal Personnel System of Interest to the Scientist and Engineer.* Washington, D.C.: U.S. Government Printing Office (out of print).

_____. 1970. *Scientists and Engineers in the Federal Personnel System.* Washington, D.C.: U.S. Government Printing Office.

_____. 1974. *Scientific and Engineering Manpower Management.* Washington, D.C.: U.S. Government Printing Office.

U.S. Congress, Joint Committee on Governmental Affairs, Subcommittee on Civil Service, Post Office, and General Services. 1986. *Alternative Pay Systems in the Federal Government.* Hearings before the subcommittee, April 15 and 30 and May 14, 1986. Washington, D.C.: U.S. Government Printing Office.

_____, Senate Committee on Governmental Affairs, Subcommittee on Energy, Nuclear Proliferation, and Government Processes. 1982. *Critical Need for Energy Research and Development: The Role of the Midwest Research Labs.* Hearing before the subcommittee, March 22, 1982. Washington, D.C.: U.S. Government Printing Office.

U.S. General Accounting Office (GAO). 1979. *Federal R&D Laboratories Directors' Perspectives on Management.* Washington, D.C.: GAO.

_____. 1984. *Federal White Collar Special Rate Program.* Report to the Subcommittee on Compensation and Benefits, House Committee on Post Office and Civil Service. Washington, D.C.: GAO.

_____. 1987. *Federal Work Force: Pay, Recruitment, and Retention of Federal Employees.* Washington, D.C.: GAO.

_____. 1988. *Federal Personnel: Observations on the Navy's Personnel Management Demonstration Project* (GAO/GGD-88-79). Washington, D.C.: GAO.

_____. 1989a. *Managing Human Resources: Greater OPM Leadership Needed to Address Critical Challenges* (GAO/GGD-89-19). Washington, D.C.: GAO.

_____. 1989b. *The Public Service: Issues Affecting Its Quality, Effectiveness, Integrity, and Stewardship* (GAO/GGD-89-73). Washington, D.C.: GAO.

U.S. Merit Systems Protection Board (MSPB). 1988. *Attracting Quality Graduates to the Federal Government: A View of College Recruiting.* Washington, D.C.: MSPB.

_____. 1989a. *Federal Personnel Management Since Civil Service Reform: A Survey of Federal Personnel Managers.* Washington, D.C.: MSPB.

_____. 1989b. *U.S. Office of Personnel Management and the Merit System: A Retrospective Assessment.* Washington, D.C.: MSPB.

_____. 1989c. *Delegation and Decentralization: Personnel Management Simplification Efforts in the Federal Government.* Washington, D.C.: MSPB.

_____. 1989d. *OPM's Classification and Qualification Systems: A Renewed Emphasis, A Changing Perspective.* Washington, D.C.: MSPB.

_____. 1989e. *Who Is Leaving the Federal Government? An Analysis of Employee Turnover.* Washington, D.C.: MSPB.

_____, and U.S. Office of Personnel Management. 1989. *A Report on the Conference on Workforce Quality Assessment.* Washington, D.C.: MSPB.

U.S. Office of Personnel Management (OPM). 1981. *Federal Personnel Manual* (Inst. 262), pp. 300-323.

_____. 1983. *FES Position Classification Standard for Contracting Series GS-1102* (TS71). Washington, D.C.: OPM

_____. 1986. *A Summary Assessment of the Navy Demonstration Project* (Management Report IX). Washington, D.C.: OPM.

_____. 1989a. Colleges say agencies need to intensify recruiting efforts. *Federal Staffing Digest* 1(2):1, 5.

_____. 1989b. *Implementation Report: National Institute of Standards and Technology Personnel Management Demonstration Project.* Washington, D.C.: OPM

_____. 1990. New group to advise on workforce quality. *Federal Staffing Digest* 2(2):5.

U.S. Office of Science and Technology Policy (OSTP). 1983. *Report of the White House Science Council's Federal Laboratory Review Panel.* Washington, D.C.: OSTP.

_____. 1984a. *Progress Report on Implementing the Recommendations of the White House Science Council's Federal Laboratory Review Panel, vol I: Summary Report.* Washington, D.C.: OSTP.

_____. 1984b. *Progress Report on Implementing the Recommendations of the White House Science Council's Federal Laboratory Review Panel, vol II: Status Reports.* Washington, D.C.: OSTP.

Waldrop, M. M. 1989. New recruits hard to find. *Science* 245(July 21):251.

Weber, M. 1986. Essay on bureaucracy. In Francis E. Rourke (ed.), *Bureaucratic Power in National Policy Making* (4th ed.), New York: Little, Brown, pp. 62-73.

White House Task Force on Women, Minorities, and the Handicapped in Science and Technology. 1989. *Changing America: The New Face of Science and Engineering* (Final Report). Washington, D.C.: The Task Force.

Wyatt Company. 1989. *Study of Federal Employee Locality Pay: Executive Summary.* Philadelphia: Wyatt.

APPENDIX A
RELATED MATERIALS

Tables

1: Science and Engineering Occupations in the Federal Government, **39**

2: Selected Data Elements in the Central Personnel Data File, **40**

3: Full-Time Permanent Scientists and Engineers, by Agency and Grade, September 1988, **41**

4: Full-Time Permanent Scientists and Engineers, by Agency and Highest Degree at Hire, September 1978 and September 1988, **42**

5: Full-Time Permanent Scientists and Engineers, by Agency and Tenure, September 1988, **43**

6: Separation Rates of Scientists, Engineers, and Computer Specialists (Full-Time Permanent, General Schedule and Equivalent), FY 1986-1988 (in percent), **44**

7: Separation Rates of Scientists, by Type (Full-Time Permanent, General Schedule and Equivalent), FY 1986-1988 (in percent), **45**

8: Turnover in Federal Science and Engineering Occupations (Full-Time Permanent, General Schedule and Equivalent), FY 1978 and 1988, **46**

9: Engineer, Scientist, and Mathematician Direct-Hire Authorities, as of April 1990, **51**

10: Special Salary Rates, as of February 1990, **52**

11: Appointments Relating to the Conduct of Federal Science and Engineering, **62**

OPM Scientists and Engineers Survey, **67**

TABLE 1: Science and Engineering Occupations in the Federal Government

Occupation		Occupation	
SOCIAL SCIENCE, PSYCHOLOGY AND WELFARE GROUP		ENGINEERING	
		801	General
101	Social Science	803	Safety
110	Economics	804	Fire Prevention
131	International Relations	806	Materials
150	Geography	808	Architecture
180	Psychology	809	Construction Control
184	Sociology	810	Civil
190	General Anthropology	819	Environmental
193	Anthropology	830	Mechanical
		840	Nuclear
COMPUTER SPECIALIST		850	Electrical
		854	Computer
BIOLOGICAL SCIENCES		855	Electronics
401	General	858	Biomedical
403	Microbiology	861	Aerospace
405	Pharmacology	871	Naval Architecture
406	Agricultural Extension	880	Mining
408	Ecology	881	Petroleum
410	Zoology	890	Agricultural
413	Physiology	892	Ceramic
414	Entomology	893	Chemical
415	Toxicology	894	Welding
		896	Industrial
AGRICULTURAL SCIENCES		PHYSICAL SCIENCES	
430	Botany		
434	Plant Pathology	1301	General
435	Plant Physiology	1306	Health Physics
436	Plant Protection and Quarantine	1310	Physics
437	Horticulture	1313	Geophysics
440	Genetics	1315	Hydrology
454	Range Conservation	1320	Chemistry
457	Soil Conservation	1321	Metallurgy
460	Forestry	1330	Astronomy and Space
470	Soil Science	1340	Meteorology
471	Agronomy	1350	Geology
475	Agricultural Management	1360	Oceanography
480	General Fish and Wildlife Admin	1370	Cartography
482	Fishery Biology	1372	Geodesy
485	Wildlife Refuge Management	1380	Forest Products Technology
486	Wildlife Biology	1382	Food Technology
487	Animal Science	1384	Textile Technology

MATHEMATICAL AND COMPUTER SCIENCES

1510	Actuarial Science	1530	Statistics
1515	Operations Research	1540	Cryptography
1520	Mathematics	1550	Computer Science
1529	Mathematical Statistics		

SOURCE: Office of Personnel Management, 1990.

TABLE 2: Selected Data Elements in the Central Personnel Data File

---

Agency Code and Subelement
Current Appointment Authority
Effective Date of Personnel Action
Professional, Administrative, Technical, Clerical, Other Category
Functional Classification of Scientists and Engineers

Position Occupied
General Schedule Equivalent Grade
Step/Rate
Salary
Type of Appointment

Tenure
Geographic Location of Duty Station
Metropolitan Statistical Area
Occupational Series
Performance Level

Supervisory Status
Civil Service Retirement System Coverage
Federal Employee Retirement System Coverage
Data of Birth
Citizenship Status

Race and National Origin
Sex
Social Security Number
Academic Discipline
Year Degree Attained
Education Level and Degree at Hire

SOURCE: U.S. Office of Personnel Management

TABLE 3: Full-Time Permanent Scientists and Engineers, by Agency & Grade, September 1988

Agency	GS Level 5-7	9-12	13-15	16-18	ST Level 16-18	SES	Other*	Total
All Scientists and Engineers								
Defense	4696	56081	34406	7	22	720	3660	99592
Agriculture	1944	19168	6021	7	19	150	86	27395
Interior	524	8700	4457	4	25	83	2	13795
HHS	195	2515	3159	1	2	113	2	5987
Commerce	470	2886	3157		24	209	1227	7973
NASA	208	2902	8330	4	6	366	5	11821
Transportation	307	1490	3372		2	92	13	5276
Other	782	8348	12392	63	1	602	1494	23682
All	9126	102090	75294	86	101	2335	6489	195521
Scientists								
Defense	4150	47165	31655	74	86	1255	3721	88106
Agriculture	893	12951	8344	4	17	354	1464	24027
Interior	1828	17312	5349	7	16	147	83	24742
HHS	433	6825	3561	4	25	79	1	10928
Commerce	173	2398	2918	1	2	112	2	5606
NASA	454	2797	2866		22	196	864	7199
Transportation	5	168	1244	2	3	49	1	1472
Other	6	81	406			11		504
Other	358	4633	6967	56	1	307	1306	13628
Engineers								
Defense	4976	54925	43639	12	15	1080	2768	107415
Agriculture	3803	43130	26062	3	5	366	2196	75565
Interior	116	1856	672		3	3	3	2653
HHS	91	1875	896			4	1	2867
Commerce	22	117	241			1		381
NASA	16	89	291		2	13	363	774
Transportation	203	2734	7086	2	3	317	4	10349
Other	301	1409	2966		2	81	13	4772
Other	424	3715	5425	7	2	295	188	10054

* Pay plans other than GS, ST, or SES, including demonstration projects.
SOURCE: Central Personnel Data File, U.S. Office of Personnel Management.

TABLE 4: Full-Time Permanent S&Es, by Agency & Highest Degree at Hire, 1978 and 1988

Agency	1978				1988			
	BS	MS	PHD	Unspec.	BS	MS	PHD	Unspec.
All Scientists and Engineers								
Defense	45080	13532	3655	6693	69411	20767	5399	
Agriculture	16730	4065	2961	8	18090	4530	3110	2
Interior	7946	2957	1397	430	7970	3586	1600	8
HHS	3081	1561	1030		2618	1458	1511	6
Commerce	3817	2000	1333	4	3805	2014	1470	2
NASA	7463	2788	1059		7386	2998	1408	
Transportation	3539	1020	255	8	3530	1093	162	
Other	9482	5403	3741	627	11098	7175	4694	7
All	97138	33326	15431	7770	123908	43621	19354	25
Scientists								
Defense	40675	18548	13320	2131	44773	22070	16303	22
Agriculture	9085	4882	2735	1384	12080	6627	3904	
Interior	14463	3660	2846	7	16073	4150	2992	2
HHS	5554	2601	1347	315	5725	3112	1541	7
Commerce	2792	1459	1014		2385	1353	1483	6
NASA	3340	1747	1231	4	3408	1803	1344	2
Transportation	1066	582	611		447	301	721	
Other	197	262	163	2	168	216	104	
	4178	3355	3373	419	4487	4508	4214	5
Engineers								
Defense	56463	14778	2111	5639	79135	21551	3051	3
Agriculture	35995	8650	920	5309	57331	14140	1495	
Interior	2267	405	115	1	2017	380	118	
HHS	2392	356	50	115	2245	474	59	1
Commerce	289	102	16		233	105	28	
NASA	477	253	102	397	211	126		
Transportation	6397	2206	448	6939	2697	687		
Other	3342	758	92	6	3362	877	58	
	5304	2048	368	208	6611	2667	480	2

SOURCE: Central Personnel Data File, U.S. Office of Personnel Management.

TABLE 5: Full-Time Permanent S&Es, by Agency and Tenure, September 1988

Agency	Career	Career Conditional*	Total
All Scientists and Engineers			
Defense	80084	19508	99592
Agriculture	24302	3093	27395
Interior	12516	1279	13795
HHS	5004	983	5987
Commerce	6689	1284	7973
NASA	9937	1884	11821
Transportation	4456	820	5276
Other	19209	4473	23682
All	162197	33324	195521
Scientists			
Defense	20212	3815	24027
Agriculture	21849	2893	24742
Interior	10014	914	10928
HHS	4697	909	5606
Commerce	6058	1141	7199
NASA	1294	178	1472
Transportation	467	37	504
Other	11207	2421	13628
	75798	12308	88106
Engineers			
Defense	59872	15693	75565
Agriculture	2453	200	2653
Interior	2502	365	2867
HHS	307	74	381
Commerce	631	143	774
NASA	8643	1706	10349
Transportation	3989	783	4772
Other	8002	2052	10054
	86399	21016	107415

* Individuals having 3 years or less service in the federal government.
SOURCE: Central Personnel Data File, U.S. Office of Personnel Management.

TABLE 6: Separation Rates of Scientists, Engineers and Computer Specialists (Full-Time Permanent, General Schedule and Equivalent), FY1986-1988 (in percent)

Type	Average Employment (No.)	Quits	Retirements	Transfers	Other Separations*	Total
FY 1986						
Scientists	83337	2.7	2.6	0.7	6.6	5.9
Engineers	97740	2.9	2.3	1.1	6.9	5.7
Total S&E	181077	2.8	2.5	0.9	6.7	5.8
Computer Specialists**	38831	2.7	2.1	2.0	7.3	5.3
FY 1987						
Scientists	83335	2.4	1.9	0.9	5.8	4.9
Engineers	100765	2.5	1.9	1.2	6.1	4.8
Total S&E	184100	2.5	1.9	1.1	5.9	4.9
Computer Specialists**	40817	2.2	1.7	2.1	6.5	4.4
FY 1988						
Scientists	83912	2.3	1.8	0.8	5.4	4.6
Engineers	103341	2.6	2.5	1.1	6.5	5.5
Total S&E	187253	2.5	2.2	1.0	6.0	5.1
Computer Specialists**	42887	2.4	2.8	2.2	7.8	5.6

NOTE: Excludes placements in nonpay status and demonstration pay plans.
* Includes agency-controlled removals, terminations, and discharges as well as reductions in force and deaths.
** Includes analysts and programmers (occ. series 0334) who may or may not be involved in scientific or engineering applications. Computer scientists (occ. series 1550) are included in the "Scientist" category.

SOURCE: Occupational Series Dynamics Report - FY 1986, 1987, 1988, from OPM's Central Personnel Data File.

TABLE 7: Separation Rates of Scientists, by Type (Full-Time Permanent, General Schedule and Equivalent), FY1986-1988 (in percent)

Type	Average Employment (No.)	Quits	Retirements	Transfers	Other Separations*	Total
FY 1986						
Physical	29814	2.3	2.9	0.7	6.2	5.5
Math/Stat/ Computer	11645	3.8	1.8	1.0	6.9	5.9
Biological/ Agricultural	30311	2.4	3.0	0.5	6.5	6.0
Social/ Psychological	11567	3.7	2.0	1.0	7.3	6.3
FY 1987						
Physical	29408	2.1	2.2	1.0	5.8	4.8
Math/Stat/ Computer	11697	3.2	1.1	1.2	5.8	4.6
Biological/ Agricultural	30691	1.9	2.2	0.5	5.0	4.5
Social/ Psychological	11539	3.9	1.5	1.2	7.6	6.3
FY 1988						
Physical	28932	2.1	2.0	0.7	5.2	4.4
Math/Stat/ Computer	11757	2.9	2.0	1.0	6.3	5.2
Biological/ Agricultural	31544	1.8	1.7	0.6	4.4	3.8
Social/ Psychological	11679	3.9	1.7	1.4	7.5	6.1

NOTE: Excludes placements in nonpay status and demonstration pay plans.
* Includes agency-controlled removals, terminations, and discharges as well as reductions in force and deaths.
SOURCE: Occupational Series Dynamics Reports - FY 1986, 1987, 1988, from OPM's Central Personnel Data File.

TABLE 8: Turnover in Federal Science and Engineering Occupations (Full-Time Permanent, General Schedule and Equivalent), FY 1978 and 1988

	Occ Series	Total Pop	% Change	Empl Controlled Resign (No.)	Transfer (No.)	Agency Controlled* (No.)	Other** (No.)
	GS-100 **Social Science, Psychology, and Welfare Group**						
1978	101	2397		64	22	2	53
1988		2602	8.55	73	45	9	67
	110	4568		172	105	3	45
		4468	-2.19	242	79	4	77
	131	48		3	0	0	1
		61	27.08	2	2	0	3
	150	165		6	1	0	0
		255	54.55	9	1	0	1
	180	2939		101	14	6	45
		3011	2.45	112	18	3	79
	184	88		1	1	0	0
		56	-36.36	7	1	0	3
	190	47		0	0	0	1
		41	-12.77	1	0	0	0
	193	221		6	2	0	0
		504	128.05	10	12	0	5
	GS-400 **Biological Sciences Group** **Biological Scientists**						
	401	3363		58	47	3	37
		4341	29.08	91	39	0	72
	403	1506		49	8	0	20
		1655	9.89	73	19	0	33
	405	272		0	5	0	2
		299	9.93	12	2	0	7
	406	67		2	1	0	2
		48	-28.36	1	0	0	3
	410	104		0	2	0	0
		96	-7.69	1	1	0	3
	413	323		4	0	0	10
		371	14.86	13	4	0	8

414	727	-10.04	5	2	0	10
	654		2	2	0	29

Agricultural Scientists

430	123		1	2	0	1
	147	19.51	2	0	0	4
434	308		2	0	2	1
	286	-7.14	3	1	0	9
435	246		0	0	1	4
	273	10.98	6	1	0	12
436	862		8	1	0	15
	1151	33.53	20	7	1	14
437	78		1	0	0	1
	106	35.90	1	5	1	1
440	211		5	1	0	0
	264	25.12	1	0	0	6
454	1007		25	25	0	9
	1205	19.66	15	12	1	18
457	4411		74	17	5	98
	4639	5.17	77	16	5	89
460	5495		45	35	1	73
	5903	7.42	33	22	0	129
470	1809		39	16	2	25
	1696	-6.25	31	7	0	53
471	313		2	2	0	7
	303	-3.19	6	1	10	18
475	2880		107	7	3	58
	3737	29.76	131	11	0	59
480	179		1	1	2	4
	159	-11.17	1	2	0	8
482	1162		11	14	0	6
	1287	10.76	12	8	0	31
485	433		2	1	0	3
	575	32.79	5	2	0	6
486	949		8	10	0	6
	1479	55.85	6	21	0	24
487	104		3	1	0	2
	101	-2.88	0	0	0	5

Occ Series	Total Pop	% Change	Empl Controlled Resign (No.)	Transfer (No.)	Agency Controlled* (No.)	Other** (No.)
GS-800						
Engineering and Architecture Group/Engineers						
801	16388		207	157	25	364
	18302	11.68	283	190	8	888
803	574	-3.14	15	18	3	7
	556		22	6	1	17
804	107	22.43	3	3	0	3
	131		2	8	0	3
806	828	44.57	10	6	2	20
	1197		29	9	1	34
808	1434	20.50	32	34	2	27
	1728		47	47	1	55
810	14282	5.03	284	191	20	230
	15000		380	173	5	390
819	1076	154.00	13	12	0	3
	2733		194	29	4	43
830	9066	45.06	213	113	15	174
	13151		411	127	11	309
840	2022	40.21	67	29	0	12
	2835		92	17	2	31
850	3405	35.51	89	71	7	61
	4614		136	74	5	120
855	19536	39.16	395	170	16	162
	27186		619	237	17	643
858	132	79.55	5	2	0	0
	237		13	3	0	0
861	8180	6.36	101	38	8	135
	8700		140	44	3	298
871	1027	23.17	26	9	1	15
	1265		35	17	1	18
880	479	-12.32	4	3	1	9
	420		6	6	0	11
881	380	-90.67	9	3	0	4
	4641		7	4	0	20
890	433	-9.47	6	0	1	9
	392		7	1	0	13

48

892	53		2	1	0	1
	63	18.87	3	1	0	2
893	1294		28	12	1	21
	1624	25.50	63	10	5	37
894	65		3	1	0	2
	88	35.38	2	2	0	2
896	2019		39	59	5	35
	3050	51.06	104	52	4	93

GS-1300
Physical Sciences Group/Physical Scientists

130	4467		49	25	10	89
	4896	9.60	131	50	5	139
1306	420		17	7	0	6
	545	29.76	24	17	0	16
1310	4914		92	23	8	84
	3768	-23.32	53	15	1	135
1313	493		9	9	1	5
	564	14.40	9	3	0	11
1315	1811		18	7	1	17
	2198	21.37	55	12	0	40
1320	7433		135	52	9	138
	6626	-10.86	167	51	5	198
1321	563		12	1	0	16
	314	-44.23	6	1	1	14
1330	527		2	1	0	6
	457	-13.28	9	1	0	5
1340	2074		8	10	0	38
	2206	6.36	29	10	0	54
1350	2155		33	25	3	30
	2351	9.10	43	17	0	54
1360	747		14	25	4	35
	718	-3.88	18	7	1	11
1370	3070		20	9	2	47
	4333	41.14	57	27	0	30
1372	281		2	1	2	1
	344	22.42	3	2	0	3
1382	178		2	3	0	4
	265	48.88	8	0	1	8
1384	97		2	1	0	2
	91	-6.19	3	2	0	3

Occ Series	Total Pop	% Change	Empl Controlled Resign (No.)	Empl Controlled Transfer (No.)	Agency Controlled* (No.)	Other** (No.)
1386	84		4	1	0	3
	47	-44.05	1	0	0	6
GS-1500 Mathematics and Statistics Group/Mathematics and Computer Scientists						
1510	114		3	2	0	4
	129	13.16	6	3	0	2
1515	2960		72	60	0	36
	3742	26.42	73	38	2	133
1520	3824		110	40	7	29
	2639	-30.99	56	6	3	68
1529	949		31	23	2	15
	991	4.43	40	11	0	12
1530	2551		78	48	3	41
	2544	-0.27	79	33	5	45
1540	11		2	1	0	1
	1	-90.91	0	0	0	1
1550	127		6	1	0	2
	2308	1717.32	116	27	7	15
Total 1978	188794					
1988	231129					

NOTE: Identification of the individual occupational series is given in Table 1 of this appendix.
* Removals, terminations, discharges.
** Other includes voluntary and involuntary retirements, disability retirements, reductions in force, and deaths.

SOURCE: Occupational Series Dynamics Reports - FY 1978 and 1988, from OPM's Central Personnel Data File.

TABLE 9: Engineer, Scientist, and Mathematician Direct-Hire Authorities, as of April 1990

Region	Engineers	Scientists	Mathematicians
ATLANTA REGION (AL, FL, NC, SC, GA, MS, TN, VA)	All agencies, specialties and locations, GS-5 through 15	All agencies, specialties and locations, GS-5 through 15	All agencies, specialties and locations, GS-5 through 15
CHICAGO REGION (IL, IN, IA, KS, KY, MI, MN, MO, NE, ND, OH, SD, WV, WI)	All Agencies, specialties and Locations, GS-5 through 12.	Chemist, Geodesist, Health Physicist, Land Surveyor, Metallurgist, Oceanographer, all agencies and locations, GS-5/7. (Other specialties at GS-5/7 must have OPM rating.) Case-by-case basis for GS-9 and above.	All specialties at GS-5/7 must have OPM rating. Case-by-case basis for GS-9 and above.
DALLAS REGION (AR, AZ, CO, LA, MT, NM, OK, TX, UT, WY)	All agencies, specialties and locations, GS-5/7. Case-by-case basis for GS-9 and above.	Astronomer, Health Physicist, Land Surveyor and Oceanographer, all agencies and locations, GS-5/7. Other specialties at GS-5/7 must have OPM rating. Case-by-case basis for GS-9 and above.	All agencies, specialties and locations, GS-5/7. Case-by-case basis for GS-9 and above.
PHILADELPHIA REGION (CT, DE, ME, MD, MA, NH, NJ, NY, PA, PR, RI, VT, VI)	All agencies, specialties and locations, GS-5 through 11.	All agencies specialties and locations, GS-5/7. Case-by-case basis for GS-9 and above.	All agencies, specialties and locations, GS-5/7. Case-by-case basis for GS-9 and above.
SAN FRANCISCO REGION (AK, CA, HI, ID, NV, OR, WA, Pacific Overseas)	Alaska: All GS-5/12; case-by-case GS-13/15 California, Hawaii, Nevada, Washington: All GS-5/15 Idaho and Oregon: All GS-5/7 only.	Alaska, Hawaii, Idaho, Oregon and Washington: All GS-5/7 only. California and Nevada: All, GS-5/15.	California and Nevada: All GS-5/15. Alaska, Hawaii, Idaho, Oregon and Washington: All GS-5/7 only.
WASHINGTON AREA SERVICE CENTER (Washington, DC metro area, Atlantic Overseas)	All agencies, locations and specialties, GS-5/11; Case-by-case basis, GS-12/15	All agencies, locations and specialties, GS-5/7. Case-by-case basis GS-9 and above.	All agencies, locations and specialties, GS-5/15

SOURCE: Office of Personnel Management, Staffing Operations Division.

TABLE 10: Special Salary Rates as of February 1990

Occupation	Location	Agency/Org	Grade	Step 1	Step 10
GS-0180 Psychologist	1				
	Texas	Justice	11	$36863	$45827
	Lackland AFB	Air Force	12	42989	53735
			13	46861	59641
	Oklahoma	Justice	11	36863	45827
	El Reno		12	41795	52541
			13	45441	58221
	Connecticut	Justice	11	38855	47819
	Danbury		12	42989	53735
	New York		13	46861	59641
	New York City				
GS-0457 Soil Conservationist	2	USDA	9	29649	37065
			11	34363	43336
			12	38637	49392
GS-0470 Soil Scientist	2	USDA	9	29649	37065
			11	34363	43336
			12	38637	49392
GS-0800 Engineer, Optics	New Mexico	Air Force	9	31490	38762
	Kirkland AFB		11	36144	44937
			12	39807	50355
			13	44551	57079
GS-0801 Engineer, Gen	Worldwide	3	5	21201	26097
			7	26252	32309
			9	31490	38762
			11	33846	42639
			12	36645	47193

GS-0803 Engineer, Safety	Worldwide	3	5	21201	26097
			7	26252	32309
			9	31490	38762
			11	33846	42639
	5		12	36645	47193
GS-0804 Engineer, Fire Prevention	Worldwide	3	5	21201	26097
			7	26252	32309
			9	31490	38762
			11	33846	42639
	5		12	36645	47193
GS-0806 Engineer, Materials	Worldwide	3	5	21201	26097
			7	26252	32309
			9	31490	38762
			11	33846	42639
	5		12	36645	47193
GS-0807 Landscape Architect	Worldwide	3	5	21201	26097
			7	26252	32309
			9	31490	38762
			11	33846	42639
	5		12	36645	47193
GS-0808 Architect	Worldwide	3	5	21201	26097
			7	26252	32309
			9	31490	38762
			11	33846	42639

GS-0810 Engineer, Civil	Worldwide	3	5	21201	26097
			7	26252	32309
			9	31490	38762
			11	33846	42639
			12	36645	47193
		5			
GS-0819 Engineer, Environmental	Worldwide	3	5	21201	26097
			7	26252	32309
			9	31490	38762
			11	33846	42639
			12	36645	47193
		5			
GS-0830 Engineer, Mechanical	Worldwide	3	5	21201	26097
			7	26252	32309
			9	31490	38762
			11	33846	42639
			12	36645	47193
		5			
GS-0840 Engineer, Nuclear	Worldwide		5	21201	26097
			7	26252	32309
			9	31490	38762
			11	34363	43156
			12	38637	49590
		5			

GS-0850 Engineer, Electrical	Worldwide	4	5 7 9 11 12	21201 26252 31490 34363 38637	26097 32309 38762 43156 49590
GS-0854 Engineer, Computer	Worldwide	4	5 7 9 11 12	21201 26252 31490 34363 38637	26097 32309 38762 43156 49590
GS-0855 Engineer, Electronics	Worldwide	4	5 7 9 11 12	21201 26252 31490 34363 38637	26097 32309 38762 43156 49590
GS-0858 Engineer, Biomedical	Worldwide	3	5 7 9 11 12	21201 26252 31490 33846 36645	26097 32309 38762 42639 47193
GS-0861 Engineer, Aerospace	Worldwide	3	5 7 9 11	21201 26252 31490 33846	26097 32309 38762 42639

GS-0871 Naval Architect	Worldwide	3		5	36645	47193
			5	21201	26097	
			7	26252	32309	
			9	31490	38762	
			11	33846	42639	
			12	36645	47193	

GS-0880 Engineer, Mining	Nationwide	USDA	5	18017	22175
		Army	7	22326	27483
		Energy	9	27305	33605
		Fed Energy Reg	11	31349	38972
		Interior			
		Labor			
		Treasury			
		DoD			

GS-0881 Engineer, Petroleum	Nationwide	Army	5	20780	25577
		Energy	7	25739	31679
		EPA	9	30571	37627
		Fed Energy Reg	11	33044	40667
		Justice	12	37573	46717
		NTSB			
		DOT			
		DoD			
		Interior			
		Export-Import Bk			

GS-0890 Engineer, Agricultural	Worldwide	3	5	21201	26097
			7	26252	32309
			9	31490	38762
			11	33846	42639

GS-0892 Engineer, Ceramics	5	Worldwide	3	5 7 9 11 12	21201 26252 31490 33846 36645	26097 32309 38762 42639 47193
GS-0893 Engineer, Chemical	5	Worldwide	3	5 7 9 11 12	21201 26252 31490 33846 36645	26097 32309 38762 42639 47193
GS-0894 Engineer, Welding	5	Worldwide	3	5 7 9 11 12	21201 26252 31490 33846 36645	26097 32309 38762 42639 47193
GS-0896 Engineer, Industrial	5	Worldwide	3	5 7 9 11 12	21201 26252 31490 33846 36645	26097 32309 38762 42639 47193

GS-1310 Physicist, Optics	New Mexico Kirkland AFB	Air Force	9 11 12 13	31490 36144 39807 44551	38762 44937 50355 57079

GS-1320 Chemist	Nationwide	Justice Treasury DoD	5 7 9 11	21201 26252 28001 31883	26097 32309 35417 40847

GS-1321 Metallurgist	Nationwide	Air Force Army Interior NTSB Navy Smithsonian Commerce	5 7 9 11	19805 24532 27705 30725	24377 30193 34635 39266

GS-1370 Cartographer	Washington, DC MSA	Commerce DoD Interior USDA State	5 7 9 11	21201 26252 28825 32879	26097 32309 36241 41843

GS-1382 Food Technologist		USDA	7 8 9 10	22887 25351 27177 29020	28944 32065 34593 37183

GS-1510 Actuary	Washington, D.C. Illinois Chicago Missouri Kansas City New York	DoD Energy GAO Labor OPM PensBenftGuar	5* 7* 9* 11 12 13	20113 24906 30473 36863 39407 44021	25009 30963 37889 45827 50153 56801

	New York City	RR Retirement Bd			
	<u>Ohio</u>	Treasury			
	Dayton	VA			
	<u>Pennsylvania</u>	Air Force			
	Philadelphia	USDA			
	<u>Utah</u>	HUD			
	Salt Lake City				
GS-1515	<u>California</u>	Navy	5	20113	25009
Operations Research			7	24906	30963
Analyst			9	30473	37889
			11	33875	42839
			12	37019	47765
GS-1520	<u>California</u>	Army	5	20113	25009
Mathematician			7	24906	30963
			9	30473	37889
			11	33875	42839
			12	37019	47765
GS-1529	<u>Washington, D.C.</u>	USDA	5	20178	24840
Mathematical		Commerce	7	23067	28827
Statistician		DoD	9	28220	35276
		Education	11	32243	40775
		Energy			
		EPA			
		EEOC			
		Interior			
		Labor			
		DOT			
		Treasury			
		VA			
		Pension Benft Guar			
		HHS			
		Justice			

	OMB		
California	VA		
Palo Alto		9	30473	37889
		11	32879	41843
Marin Co.	USDA		
		5	20113	25009
		7	24906	30963
		9	30473	37889
		11	33875	42839
		12	37019	47765

GS-1550
Computer Scientist

Pennsylvania	Navy			
Warminster		5	20780	25577
		7	25739	31679
		9	29140	36223
		11	31449	40026
California	Interior			
San Francisco Co		5	20113	25009
San Mateo Co		7	24906	30963
		9	30473	37889
		11	33875	42839
		12	37019	47765
Washington, DC MSA	Commerce			
Maryland	DoD	5	21201	26097
Annapolis	HHS	7	26252	32309
Patuxent River	NASA	9	28272	35544
Virginia	Treasury			
Dahlgren	Justice			
Connecticut	Navy			
New London		5	20780	25577
Rhode Island		7	25739	31679
Newport		9	29738	37073
		11	32547	41412
		12	38124	48555

* These salaries also apply to HHS personnel in Baltimore, Md.
SOURCE: Office of Personnel Management, Hours of Duty, Pay and Leave, Annotated (Federal Personnel Manual System Supplement 990-2), OPM: Washington, D.C.: February 2, 1990.

1. Arizona: Phoenix; California: Boron, Los Angeles, Term Island; Georgia: Atlanta; Kansas: Leavenworth; New York: Otisville, Raybrook; Pennsylvania: Loretto; South Dakota: Yankton; Texas: Texarkana; West Virginia: Morgantown.

2. Connecticut; Maryland: Montgomery Co; Massachusetts; New Hampshire: Hillsboro Co, Rockingham Co, Stafford Co; New Jersey: Bergen Co, Essex Co, Hudson Co, Hunterdon Co, Mercer Co, Middlesex Co, Monmouth Co, Morris Co, Passaic Co, Somerset Co, Sussex Co, Union Co, Warren Co; New York: Nassau Co, Rockland Co, Suffolk Co, Westchester Co; Rhode Island.

3. USDA, Air Force, Army, Consumer Product Safety Commission, Energy, EPA, Federal Energy Regulatory Commission, GSA, HHS, Interior, Justice, Labor, NASA, National Transportation Board, Navy, DOT, Treasury, VA, Voice of America, DoD, Export-Import Bank, HUD, Smithsonian Institution, Commerce, SBA, U.S. Courts, Architect of the Capitol, State, U.S. Soldiers/Airmens Home.

4. USDA, Air Force, Army, Consumer Product Safety Commission, Energy, EPA, Federal Energy Management Agency, GSA, HHS, Interior, Justice, Labor, NASA, National Transportation Safety Board, Navy, DOT, Treasury, VA, DoD, Smithsonian Institution, Commerce, Architect of the Capitol, State, U.S. Soldiers/Airmens Home.

5. At Ft. Irwin, Calif., the Army has been authorized to grant special rates as follows:

Grade	Step 1	Step 10
9	32121	39537
11	34843	43636
12	37840	48388

TABLE 11: Appointments Relating to the Conduct of Federal Science and Engineering

POSITION	DEPT/INCUMBENT	TYPE OF APPT
	I. Executive Office of the President	
	The White House Office	
Asst for National Security Affairs	Colin L. Powell	PA
Deputy Assistant	Robert M. Gates	PA
	Council of Economic Advisers	
Chairman	Michael Boskin	PAS
Members	John Taylor	PAS
	Richard Schmalensee	PAS
	Council on Environmental Quality	
Chairman	Michael Deland	PAS
	Office of Management and Budget	
Director	Richard Darman	PAS
Deputy Director	William Diefenderfer	PAS
Chief Economist	Ahmad Al-Saammarie	
Associate Director		
Natural Resources, Energy & Sci	Robert Grady	SES
Human Resources, Veterans & Labor	Thomas Scully	SES
National Security & Intl. Affairs	Robert Howard	SES
Administrator, Office of Info and Regulatory Affairs	act: James Macrae	PAS
	Office of Science and Technology Policy	
Director	D. Allan Bromley	PAS
Associate Director	James Wyngaarden	PAS
	Thomas Ratchford	PAS
	act: Wm. Phillips	PAS
	act: Eugene Wong	PAS
	II. Executive Departments	
	Department of Agriculture	
Assistant Secretary		
Economics	Bruce L. Gardner	PAS
Food & Consumer Services	Catherine Bertini	PAS
Science & Education	Charles Hess	PAS
Natural Resources & Environment	John Evans	PAS
	Department of Commerce	
Assistant Secretary		
Technology Policy	Deborah Wince-Smith	PAS
Nat'l Telecommunications & Info	Janice Obuchowski	PAS
Economic Development	act: James Perry	PAS
<u>Nat'l Oceanic and Atmospheric Admin.</u>		
Under Secretary/Admin.	John Knauss	PAS

Assistant Secretary	Joy Wilson	PAS
Chief Scientist	vacant	PAS
<u>Patent and Trademark Office</u>		
Assistant Secretary & Commissioner	act: Jeff Samuels	PAS
Deputy Commissioner	act: Michael Kirk	PAS
Asst Commissioner		
Patents	act: Jim Denny	PAS
Trademarks	Jeff M. Sammuels	PAS
Director, Bureau of the Census	Barbara E. Bryant	PAS
Director, Natl Institute of Standards and Technology	John Lyons	PAS

Department of Defense

Under Secretary		
Defense Policy	Paul Wolfowitz	PAS
Acquisition		PAS
Assistant Secretary		
International Security Policy	Stephen J. Hadley	PAS
International Security Affairs	Henry S. Rowen	PAS
Special Operations & Low Intensity Conflict	act: Jas. R. Locher	PAS
Atomic Energy	Robert B. Barker	PAS
Production & Logistics	Jack Katzen	PAS
Command Control, Communications, & Intelligence	Duane P. Andrews	PAS
Health Affairs	act: Dav. Newhall	PAS
<u>Office of Defense Research and Engineering</u>		
Director	vacant	PAS
Deputy Director		
Resrch & Advanced Technology	George P. Milburn	SES
Test & Evaluation	Robert C. Duncan	SES
Strategic & Theatre Nuclear Forces	act: George Scheider	SES
Director, Defense Advanced Research Projects Agency	act: Victor Reis	SES
<u>U.S. Air Force</u>		
Assistant Secretary		
Readiness Support	vacant	PAS
Acquisition	John J. Welch, Jr.	PAS
<u>U.S. Army</u>		
Assistant Secretary		
Installations & Logistics	Susan Livingston	PAS
Civil Works	Robert W. Page	PAS
Research, Development, & Acquisition	Stephen Conver	
<u>U.S. Navy</u>		
Assistant Secretary		
Shipbuilding & Logistics	act: F. Swofford	PAS
Research, Engineering, & Systems	act: Richard Rumpf	PAS

Department of Education

Assistant Secretary, Educational Research & Improvement	Christopher Cross	PAS
Commissioner, Center for Education Statistics	Emerson Elliott	PAS

Department of Energy

Under Secretary	John C. Tuck	PAS
Assistant Secretary		
Int'l Affs & Energy Emergencies	John J. Easton, Jr.	PAS
Environment, Safety & Health	act: Peter N. Brush	PAS
Conservation & Renewable Energy	J. Michael Davis	PAS
Defense Programs	Victor Stello, Jr.	PAS
Nuclear Energy	William Young	PAS
Fossil Energy	act: Michael McElwrath	PAS
Director		
Civilian Radioactive Waste Mgmt.	act: Samuel Rousso	PAS
Office of Alcohol Fuels	David M. L. Lindahl	PAS
Office of Energy Research	act: James Decker	PAS
Administrator		
Economic Regulatory Administration	Chandler van Orman	PAS
Energy Information Administration	H. A. Merklein	PAS

Department of Health and Human Services

Assistant Secretary		
Human Development	Mary Gall	PAS
Health	James Mason	PAS
Surgeon General	Antonia Novello	PAS
Administrator		
Alcohol, Drug Abuse, & Mental Health Administration	Frederick K. Goodwin	PAS
Director		
Centers for Disease Control	William Roper	PAS
National Institutes of Health	act: William Raub	PAS
Public Health Service	James Eagen	PAS
National Cancer Institute	Vincent DeVita, Jr.	PAS
Nat'l Institute for Occupational Safety & Health	J. Donald Millar	SES
Commissioner		
Food & Drug Administration	act: James Bensen	PAS

Department of the Interior

Assistant Secretary		
Fish, Wildlife, & Parks	Constance Harriman	PAS
Water & Science	John Sayre	PAS
Land & Minerals Management	David C. O'Neal	PAS
Director		
U.S. Fish & Wildlife Service	John F. Turner	PAS
Bureau of Mines	Thomas S. Ary	PAS
U.S. Geological Survey	Dallas L. Peck	PAS
Office of Surface Mining	Harry Snyder	PAS
Commissioner, Bureau of Reclamation	Dennis Underwood	PAS

Department of Labor

Assistant Secretary		
Policy	Jennifer Dorne	PAS
Occupational Safety and Health	Alan McMillan	PAS
Mine Safety & Health	David O'Neal	PAS

Commissioner, Bureau of Labor Statistics	Janet L. Norwood	PAS
Director, Women's Bureau	Bonnie Friedman	PAS

Department of State

Under Secretary		
Economic Affairs	Richard T. McCormack	PAS
Security Assistance, Science		
& Technology	Edward J. Derwinski	PAS
Assistant Secretary		
Oceans & Int'l Environmental &		
Scientific Affairs	Curtis Bohlen	PAS

Department of Transportation

Administrator		
Federal Aviation Administration	James B. Busey	PAS
Federal Highway Administration	Thomas Larson	PAS
Federal Railroad Administration	Gilbert Carmichael	PAS
Natl Highway Traffic Safety Admin	Jerry Ralph Curry	PAS
Urban Mass Transit Admin	Brian W. Clymer	PAS
Maritime Administration	Warren Labeck	PAS
Resrch & Special Programs Admin	Travis Dungan	PAS

Department of the Treasury

Asst Secretary, Economic Policy	Sidney L. Jones	PAS

III. Independent Agencies and Government Corporations

Board of Governors of the Federal Reserve System

Chairman	Alan Greenspan	PAS
Vice Chairman	Manuel H. Johnson	PAS
Governors	Ed. W. Kelley, Jr.	PAS
	Wayne D. Angell	PAS
	Martha R. Seger	PAS
	John P. LaWare	PAS
	vacant	PAS

Consumer Product Safety Commission

Chairman	Jacqueline Jones-Smith	PAS
Commissioners	Anne M. Graham	PAS
	Carol G. Dawson	PAS
	vacant	PAS
	vacant	PAS

Environmental Protection Agency

Administrator	William K. Reilly	PAS
Deputy Administrator	F. Henry Habich	PAS
Assistant Administrator		
Policy, Planning, & Evaluation	Clarence Davies	PAS
Water	Lajuana Wilcher	PAS
Solid Waste & Emergency	Donald Clay	PAS
Air & Radiation	William Rosenberg	PAS
Pesticides & Toxic Substances	Linda J. Fisher	PAS
Research & Development	Erich Bretthauer	PAS

Federal Energy Regulatory Commission

Chairman	Martin L. Allday	PAS
Commissioners	Charles A. Trabandt	PAS
	Charles G. Stalon	PAS
	Elizabeth Moler	PAS
	vacant	PAS

Federal Maritime Commission

Chairman	act: James J. Carey	PAS
Vice Chairman	vacant	PAS
Commissioners	William D. Hathaway	PAS
	Francis J. Ivancie	PAS
	vacant	PAS

Agency for International Development

Assistant Administrator		
Program & Policy	Reginald J. Brown	PAS
Science & Technology	act: Richard Bissell	PAS

National Aeronautics and Space Administration

Administrator	Richard H. Truly	PAS
Deputy Administrator	James R. Thompson	PAS
Associate Administrator		
Aeronautics & Space Technology	Arnold D. Aldrich	SES
Space Science & Applications	Lennard A. Fisk	SES

National Science Foundation

Director	Erich Bloch	PAS
Deputy Director	Frederick Bernthal	PAS
Assistant Director		
Geosciences	Robert Corell	SES
Biological, Behavioral, & Social Sciences	Mary Clutter	SES
Mathematical & Physical Sciences	act: Kent Wilson	SES
Education & Human Resources	Luther Williams	SES
Engineering	John White	SES
Scientific, Technological, & Internationl Affairs	F. Karl Willenbrock	SES

Nuclear Regulatory Commission

Chairman	Kenneth M. Carr	PAS
Commissioners	Thomas M. Roberts	PAS
	James R. Curtiss	PAS
	Kenneth C. Rogers	PAS
	Forrest J. Remick	PAS

NOTES: Only full-time positions that are compensated are listed. "Acting" usually means that a career employee holds the position temporarily until the political appointment process is worked through; "vacant" means that no one, appointed or career, is now in that position: PA = Presidential appointment; PAS = Presidential appointment, by and with the advice and consent of the Senate; SES = Senior Executive Service.

SOURCE: *United States Government Policy and Supporting Positions,* published by the U.S. Government Printing Office for the House of Representatives Committee on Post Office and Civil Service (data verified on May 25, 1990).

SCIENTISTS AND ENGINEERS SURVEY

United States Office of Personnel Management

DO NOT FOLD, STAPLE, TEAR OR PAPER CLIP THIS FORM.
DO NOT SUBMIT PHOTOCOPIES OF THIS FORM.

We can process this information only if you:
1) Use a number 2 lead pencil.
2) Completely blacken each oval you choose.
3) Completely erase any mistakes or stray marks.

PRINT YOUR RESPONSE IN THE BOXES AND BLACKEN THE APPROPRIATE OVALS.

USE NO. 2 PENCIL ONLY

EXAMPLES

SOCIAL SECURITY NUMBER: 1 6 7 - 4 6 - 0 2 4 8

4. What was your undergraduate overall class standing?
   - ☐ Top 1%
   - ☐ Top 5%
   - ● Top 10%
   - ☐ Top 25%
   - ☐ Top 50%
   - ☐ Lower 50% to 26%
   - ☐ Lower 25% to 1%
   - ☐ Unknown

   Mark the highest percentage group that applies to your class standing.

Please Print Last Name First
NAME: _____ DATE: _____

---

1. SOCIAL SECURITY NUMBER

Educational Background

2. What is the **HIGHEST DEGREE** you have earned, and when was it awarded?
(Note: If you have two equivalent degrees e.g., 2 masters or 2 Ph.Ds, please indicate the highest degree that was most recently earned.)

- A. ○ High School Diploma
- B. ○ Associate's Degree
- C. ○ Bachelor's Degree
- D. ○ Master's Degree
- E. ○ Doctorate Degree

Year Highest Degree Awarded? ➔ 19 ___

IF YOUR ANSWER TO QUESTION 2 WAS "A" OR "B", SKIP TO QUESTION 8, OTHERWISE, CONTINUE ON TO QUESTION 3.

3. In what year was your bachelor's degree awarded? ➔ 19 ___

4. What was your undergraduate overall class standing?
- ○ Top 1%
- ○ Top 5%
- ○ Top 10%
- ○ Top 25%
- ○ Top 50%
- ○ Lower 50% to 26%
- ○ Lower 25% to 1%
- ○ Unknown

Mark the highest percentage group that applies to your class standing.

5. What was your overall undergraduate grade point average (GPA)?

Your GPA in your major field of study?

Your GPA for your last two years?

NOTE: A = 4.0
B = 3.0
C = 2.0

GPA OVERALL | GPA IN MAJOR | JUNIOR/SENIOR GPA

○ Unknown ○ Unknown ○ Unknown

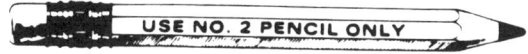

0000455

Page 1   E-895, March 1990

6 What was your major as an undergraduate? Enter the three digit code from the list in the instructions.

7 From what institution was your **HIGHEST DEGREE** awarded? Enter the three-digit identifying code for your institution from the list provided in the instructions.

Specify: _____ ← ○ Other Not Listed

8 During the past 12 months, were you enrolled in a university-sponsored course(s) for the purpose of expanding your professional skill?
○ Yes   ○ No

If **YES**, were these course(s) any of the following?
	YES	NO
Technical Course(s)	○	○
Degree-Oriented Course(s)	○	○

9 How many university courses have you completed since earning your highest degree?
○ 0   ○ 4
○ 1   ○ 5 to 10
○ 2   ○ 11-15
○ 3   ○ More than 15

10 Since receipt of your highest degree, approximately how much time do you devote per year to formal technical training that is related to your occupational specialty?
○ Less Than 1 Week Per Year   ○ 5-8 Weeks
○ 1 Week Per Year   ○ 2-4 Months
○ 2-4 Weeks   ○ More than 4 Months

11 Since receipt of your highest degree, approximately how much time do you devote per year to training in supervisory, management, and executive skills?
○ Less Than 1 Week Per Year   ○ 5-8 Weeks
○ 1 Week Per Year   ○ 2-4 Months
○ 2-4 Weeks   ○ More than 4 Months

IF YOU HAVE A GRADUATE DEGREE, ANSWER THE FOLLOWING QUESTION; OTHERWISE, SKIP TO QUESTION 13.

12 While earning your highest degree, what was your **PRIMARY** source of financial support? Select only **ONE** source of support from the entire list.

OWN/FAMILY RESOURCES
○ Own Earnings   ○ Family Contributions
○ Spouse's Earnings

UNIVERSITY-RELATED
○ Teaching Assistantship   ○ College Work-Study
○ Research Assistantship   ○ Co-op
○ University Fellowship   ○ Other

12 Continued.
STUDENT LOANS
○ Guaranteed Student Loan   ○ Other Loan
○ National Direct Student Loan

FEDERAL SUPPORT
○ NIH Traineeship   ○ Graduate & Professional
○ ADAMHA Traineeship   Opportunities Program
○ ADAMHA Fellowship   Fellowship (G*POP)
○ Other HHS   ○ Other Dept of Ed
○ NSF Fellowship   ○ Veterans Administration
○ NDEA Fellowship   (e.g., G.I. Bill)
○ Title VI Foreign Language ○ Active Duty Military
  & Area Studies Fellowship ○ Other Federal

U.S. NATIONALLY COMPETITIVE FELLOWSHIPS (NON-FEDERAL)
○ Ford Foundation   ○ Other Fellowship
○ Rockefeller Foundation

OTHER SOURCES
○ Business/Employer Funds (not earnings)
○ Other

■ Employment Information

13 For what agency do you work? (Refer to instructions for agency codes.)

14 What is your civil service **JOB CLASSIFICATION CODE**? (Refer to the instructions for 4-digit codes.)

15 Is your civil service job classification code in a field closely related to your **HIGHEST** degree?
○ Yes   ○ No

16 If you are an **ENGINEER**, what is your professional status?
○ Registered Professional Engineer
○ Engineer-In-Training/Engineering Intern
○ Not Registered or Certified

17 What is your civil service functional classification? (Refer to the instructions for definitions of functional classifications. Select only **one** of the options given below.)
○ Development
○ Design
○ Installations, Operations, Maintenance
○ Test and Evaluation
○ Production
○ Research
○ Data Collection, Processing, Analysis
○ Other, Not Provided on List

18 What is your current OR equivalent grade and step/level?

TYPE	GRADE	STEP/SES LEVEL
○ GS	○ 5	○ 1
○ GM	○ 7	○ 2
○ SES	○ 9	○ 3
○ Other	○ 11	○ 4
	○ 12	○ 5
	○ 13	○ 6
	○ 14	○ 7
	○ 15	○ 8
	○ 16	○ 9
	○ 17	○ 10
	○ 18	

19 In what year did you enter **FEDERAL GOVERNMENT SERVICE** as a scientist or engineer, and what was your entry-level type and grade?

YEAR	TYPE	GRADE	STEP/SES LEVEL
○ 0	○ GS	○ 5	○ 1
○ 1	○ GM	○ 7	○ 2
○ 2	○ SES	○ 9	○ 3
○ 3	○ Other	○ 11	○ 4
○ 4		○ 12	○ 5
○ 5		○ 13	○ 6
○ 6		○ 14	○ 7
○ 7		○ 15	○ 8
○ 8		○ 16	○ 9
○ 9		○ 17	○ 10
		○ 18	
○ Unknown			○ Unknown

20 In what year did you join your **CURRENT AGENCY** as a scientist or engineer, and what was your entry-level type and grade?

YEAR	TYPE	GRADE	STEP/SES LEVEL
○ 0	○ GS	○ 5	○ 1
○ 1	○ GM	○ 7	○ 2
○ 2	○ SES	○ 9	○ 3
○ 3	○ Other	○ 11	○ 4
○ 4		○ 12	○ 5
○ 5		○ 13	○ 6
○ 6		○ 14	○ 7
○ 7		○ 15	○ 8
○ 8		○ 16	○ 9
○ 9		○ 17	○ 10
		○ 18	
○ Unknown			○ Unknown

21 How many total full-time equivalent (FTE)* years of professional experience have you had in each of the following employment sectors? (Round to the nearest year and indicate 0 if less than 6 months.)

*FTE to include **TOTAL years of ALL professional experience** (e.g., years of teaching and military service) but to **EXCLUDE** time as a student.

CIVILIAN GOVERNMENT YEARS	ACTIVE DUTY MILITARY YEARS	PRIVATE SECTOR YEARS	OTHER YEARS
⓪⓪	⓪⓪	⓪⓪	⓪⓪
①①	①①	①①	①①
②②	②②	②②	②②
③③	③③	③③	③③
④④	④④	④④	④④
⑤⑤	⑤⑤	⑤⑤	⑤⑤
⑥	⑥	⑥	⑥
⑦	⑦	⑦	⑦
⑧	⑧	⑧	⑧
⑨	⑨	⑨	⑨

22 How many FTE years of professional experience have you had in jobs using the knowledge, skills, and abilities in which you were formally trained?

YEARS
⓪⓪
①①
②②
③③
④④
⑤⑤
⑥⑥
⑦⑦
⑧⑧
⑨⑨

23 Did you enter the Federal workforce as a participant in:
○ Co-op Program ○ Internship Program
○ Other Special Program ○ Post-Doctoral Program

24 Within six months of attaining your highest degree, how many formal offers of employment did you receive?
○ 0 ○ 2 ○ 4 ○ More than 5
○ 1 ○ 3 ○ 5 ○ N/A (Did not seek employment)

25 Which of the following factor(s) were most influential in your decision to accept **YOUR CURRENT JOB**? (Multiple answers acceptable.)
○ Geographic location of employment
○ Proximity to public transportation
○ Proximity to other industry/Government
○ Proximity to universities
○ Cost of living in locality
○ Salary, earning potential
○ Benefits
○ Opportunity for professional achievement
○ Opportunity for advancement
○ Facilities/equipment
○ Job security
○ Type of work (e.g., challenging work)
○ Lack of other job offers
○ Reputation of organization
○ Reputation of colleagues
○ Reputation of the Civil Service
○ Training opportunities
○ Financial support for continuing education
○ Opportunity to contribute to national priorities and issues

26 In your current position, how many hours are in your typical work week? (Include both your regular hours and additional time beyond your regular weekly hours.)
○ 40 or less ○ 51-55
○ 41-45 ○ 56-60
○ 46-50 ○ More than 60

27 Were you employed by an academic institution (in a teaching capacity) secondary to your full-time job during the past 3 years?
○ Yes ○ No

▪ Interest in Job Change

28 During the past 12 months, did any representative of an outside company or government agency contact you regarding an offer of professional employment?
○ Yes ○ No

29 During the past 12 months, did you express interest in or explore the possibility of a new job?
○ Yes ○ No

IF YOU ANSWERED "NO" TO QUESTION 29, SKIP TO QUESTION 32, OTHERWISE GO ON TO THE NEXT QUESTION.

30 Where was the job(s) for which you applied? (Multiple answers acceptable.)
- In the Federal Government
- In State or Local Governments
- In the Private Sector

31 Which of the following factor(s) were MOST important in your interest in leaving or decision to leave your current position? (Multiple answers acceptable.)
- Better pay
- Better benefits
- More affordable cost of living
- Greater opportunity for professional achievement
- Greater opportunity for professional advancement
- More challenging work
- Greater satisfaction with job responsibilities
- Seeking fewer bureaucratic constraints
- Freedom from extensive contract monitoring
- More educational opportunities
- More intellectually stimulating colleagues
- Better reputation of employer/organization
- More recognition for professional contributions
- Change in technical area
- More clerical/technical support
- Better facilities/equipment
- More job security
- Shorter working hours
- Geographic location of new employer
- Impact of ethics and procurement rules or laws

32 Of those scientists and engineers whom you know personally, which of the following reason(s) were MOST important in their decision to voluntarily leave their Federal position to accept non-Federal employment? (Multiple answers acceptable.)
- Better pay
- Better benefits
- More affordable cost of living
- Greater opportunity for professional achievement
- Greater opportunity for professional advancement
- More challenging work
- Greater satisfaction with job responsibilities
- Seeking fewer bureaucratic constraints
- Freedom from extensive contract monitoring
- More educational opportunities
- More intellectually stimulating colleagues
- Better reputation of employer/organization
- More recognition for professional contributions
- Change in technical area
- More clerical/technical support
- Better facilities/equipment
- More job security
- Shorter working hours
- Geographic location of new employer
- Impact of ethics and procurement rules or laws
- Do not personally know any departed scientists or engineers

▪ Professional Society Participation

33 In how many professional societies or associations do you hold membership? (Indicate for your specialty field only.)

	0	1	2	3	4	5-9	10+
International	○	○	○	○	○	○	○
National	○	○	○	○	○	○	○
State	○	○	○	○	○	○	○
Local	○	○	○	○	○	○	○

34 Do you now hold office or chair a committee in one or more professional societies/associations?
- Yes
- No

35 During your professional career, have you been selected as a fellow or a member in any of the following societies?

	FELLOW	MEMBER
Professional Society or Association		
National Academy of Sciences		
National Academy of Engineering		

▪ Professional Achievements

36 Have you received any of the following awards during the past 12 months or prior to that period? (If so, mark all that apply.)

	PRIOR TO PAST 12 MONTHS	THE PAST 12 MONTHS
Performance Cash/Award, including PMRS		
Beneficial Suggestion Award		
Special Act or Service Award		
President's Award for Distinguished Federal Service		
Quality Step Increase		
Sustained Superior Performance		
SES Distinguished Presidential Rank Award		
SES Meritorious Presidential Rank Award		
Professional Society Award		
Foundation Award		
Foreign Government Award		
Citation in Who's Who		
Arthur S. Fleming Award		
Other		

SPECIFY:

37 How many publications have you had in each of the following categories during the past five years?

TOTAL NUMBER OF PUBLICATIONS DURING THE PAST FIVE YEARS

	0	1	2	3	4	5+
Books	○	○	○	○	○	○
Chapters in Books	○	○	○	○	○	○
Monographs	○	○	○	○	○	○
Technical Reports	○	○	○	○	○	○
Articles	○	○	○	○	○	○
Book Reviews	○	○	○	○	○	○
Conference Papers/Presentations	○	○	○	○	○	○
Other	○	○	○	○	○	○

38 How many patents have you applied for or had granted in the past 12 months and prior to that period?

NUMBER OF PATENTS

	0	1	2-4	5-9	10-19	20+
Applied for in the past 12 months	○	○	○	○	○	○
Granted in the past 12 months	○	○	○	○	○	○
Applied for prior to the past 12 months	○	○	○	○	○	○
Granted prior to the past 12 months	○	○	○	○	○	○

Job Responsibilities

39 Which of the following BEST describes your current supervisory/managerial responsibilities? (Mark only one.)
- ○ Little or no supervisory responsibilities
- ○ Team leader or program manager providing only technical direction
- ○ Directly supervise engineers, scientists, and/or technicians
- ○ Directly supervise only non-technical staff (e.g., clerical/support personnel)
- ○ General managerial responsibilities (includes oversight of units of technical and non-technical personnel, with units run by supervisory personnel)

40 What is the total number of employees (technical and/or non-technical) that you supervise/manage?
- ○ 0
- ○ 1 or 2
- ○ 3 or 4
- ○ 5 to 7
- ○ 8 to 20
- ○ 21 to 50
- ○ 51 to 100
- ○ 101 to 1000
- ○ More than 1000

41 Please rate each of the following work related factors in terms of how they facilitate efficient and effective completion of your work/products.

	GREATLY HINDERS TIMELY COMPLETION		NEITHER FACILITATES NOR HINDERS		GREATLY FACILITATES TIMELY COMPLETION
Facilities (e.g. space, equipment)	①	②	③	④	⑤
Technical support	①	②	③	④	⑤
Clerical support	①	②	③	④	⑤
Proximity of work group	①	②	③	④	⑤
Availability of good information	①	②	③	④	⑤
Knowledge/skills of co-workers	①	②	③	④	⑤
Quality of new hires	①	②	③	④	⑤
Personal knowledge and skills	①	②	③	④	⑤
Independence in setting goals, schedules, priorities	①	②	③	④	⑤
Administrative paperwork	①	②	③	④	⑤
Supervisory expectations	①	②	③	④	⑤
Regulations and procedures related to contracts/purchasing	①	②	③	④	⑤
Personal initiative/motivation	①	②	③	④	⑤

42 Please rate your satisfaction with each of the following factors:

	VERY DISSATISFIED	DISSATISFIED	NEITHER SATISFIED NOR DISSATISFIED	SATISFIED	VERY SATISFIED
Your job	①	②	③	④	⑤
Challenge/interest associated with your work	①	②	③	④	⑤
Your pay	①	②	③	④	⑤
Your productivity	①	②	③	④	⑤
Output of your working group	①	②	③	④	⑤
Your interest in meeting organizational objectives	①	②	③	④	⑤
Quality of new hires	①	②	③	④	⑤
Your group's interest in meeting organizational objectives	①	②	③	④	⑤
Your progress within the organization	①	②	③	④	⑤
Your potential for advancement	①	②	③	④	⑤
Training opportunities provided by your employer	①	②	③	④	⑤
Your immediate supervisor	①	②	③	④	⑤
Your overall supervision	①	②	③	④	⑤
Your organization's receptivity to new technology/ideas	①	②	③	④	⑤
Your organization's interest in employee welfare/satisfaction	①	②	③	④	⑤
Working conditions	①	②	③	④	⑤
Working for the Federal Government compared to the private sector	①	②	③	④	⑤
Working for your agency compared to other Federal departments	①	②	③	④	⑤
The service orientation of your work group	①	②	③	④	⑤

QUESTIONS 43 TO 49 ARE TO BE ANSWERED BY SUPERVISORS/ MANAGERS OF SCIENTIFIC/ENGINEERING PERSONNEL ONLY. IF YOU HAVE NO SUPERVISORY/MANAGERIAL RESPONSIBILITIES OR SUPERVISE/MANAGE NON-TECHNICAL STAFF ONLY, SKIP TO QUESTION 50.

43 In general, how many months of in-house, on-the-job training are required for entry-level scientists and engineers (S/Es) before they can function productively in your organization?
- Less than 3 months
- 4 to 6 months
- 7 to 9 months
- 10 to 12 months
- 13 to 15 months
- 16 to 18 months
- More than 18 months

44 What skills and attributes, if any, do you believe current entry-level S/Es in your organization are lacking? (Mark all that apply.)
- Technical knowledge in specialty field
- Ability to apply technical skill
- Cross disciplinary skills
- Understanding of non-technical factors (i.e., costs, marketing)
- Group interaction skills
- Management skills
- Oral communication skills
- Written communication skills
- Initiative
- Creativity and ingenuity
- Commitment to organizational goals and objectives
- Service orientation
- Other
  Specify: _____
- None

45 For each of the following time periods, how do you think the typical entry level S/E recruited by your organization compares in overall quality to the typical candidate in the potentially available S/E applicant pool? ("Top 25," for example, would mean that you believe the typical entry level new hire was among the top 25% in the potentially available applicant pool.)

NEW S/E RECRUIT COMPARED WITH AVAILABLE S/E POOL

	1970's	1980's
Top 25%	○	○
Top 50%	○	○
Lower 50%	○	○
Lower 25%	○	○
Don't know	○	○

46 How do you think the overall quality of the typical S/E in your organization compares with the national S/E population during the last two decades?

TYPICAL S/E COMPARED WITH S/E POPULATION

	1970's	1980's
Top 25%	○	○
Top 50%	○	○
Lower 50%	○	○
Lower 25%	○	○
Don't know	○	○

47 Which of the following factor(s) affect the decisions made by S/Es in your organization regarding employment (i.e., to accept employment, not to accept, to leave, and/or to remain)? (Multiple answers acceptable.)

	ACCEPT	DON'T ACCEPT	LEAVE	REMAIN
Geographic location of employment	○	○	○	○
Proximity to public transportation	○	○	○	○
Proximity to other industry/government	○	○	○	○
Proximity to universities	○	○	○	○
Cost of living in locality	○	○	○	○
Salary, earning potential	○	○	○	○
Benefits	○	○	○	○
Opportunity for professional achievement	○	○	○	○
Opportunity for professional advancement	○	○	○	○
Facilities/equipment	○	○	○	○
Job security	○	○	○	○
Type of work (e.g., challenging work)	○	○	○	○
Lack of other job offers	○	○	○	○
Reputation of organization	○	○	○	○
Reputation of colleagues	○	○	○	○
Reputation of the Civil Service	○	○	○	○
Training opportunities	○	○	○	○
Financial support for continuing education	○	○	○	○
Opportunity to contribute to important national objectives	○	○	○	○

48 What is your estimate of the quality of S/Es that left your agency during the 1970's and 1980's? Of those who left, estimate the percentage falling into each of the three quality levels shown. Your percentages should total 100 for each time period.

1970's			1980's		
TOP QUARTER	MIDDLE 50%	BOTTOM QUARTER	TOP QUARTER	MIDDLE 50%	BOTTOM QUARTER
__%	__%	__%	__%	__%	__%

(Digits 0–9 bubbles for each column)

49 Are you able to recruit and hire S/Es of comparable quality to replace those S/Es who leave your organization?
- Yes
- Yes, but it's becoming more difficult
- No
- Sometimes

Performance Appraisal

50 Did you write your most recent performance plan, did your supervisor write it, or was it written jointly?
- ○ I wrote it
- ○ My supervisor wrote it
- ○ My supervisor and I wrote it
- ○ Don't have a performance plan
- ○ Don't know

51 Was your performance plan for this year entirely new, was it modified from last year, or was last year's plan used again?
- ○ Developed new
- ○ Modified
- ○ Last year's plan used
- ○ Haven't been here two years
- ○ Don't know

52 Overall, would you say your current performance plan is:
- ○ Only a little challenging
- ○ Moderately challenging
- ○ Very challenging
- ○ Nearly impossible to achieve
- ○ Don't know

53 Please indicate whether you agree or disagree with each of the following statements using the 5 point scale below.

	STRONGLY DISAGREE	DISAGREE	NEITHER AGREE NOR DISAGREE	AGREE	STRONGLY AGREE
My current performance plan helps me to set priorities for my job	①	②	③	④	⑤
My current performance plan accurately represents the most important parts of my job	①	②	③	④	⑤
My performance plan takes into account the creativity and innovativeness in my job	①	②	③	④	⑤
My job does not translate well into a written performance plan	①	②	③	④	⑤
My performance plan helps me to understand what is expected of me	①	②	③	④	⑤

54 What was the month and year of your most recent formal performance appraisal?

Enter 95 if you have not been with your agency long enough to have a performance appraisal. Please do not answer the remaining questions if 95 has been entered.

YEAR: ○ Jan ○ Feb ○ Mar ○ Apr ○ May ○ Jun ○ Jul ○ Aug ○ Sep ○ Oct ○ Nov ○ Dec

55 What was the overall rating you received at that time?
- ○ Unsatisfactory
- ○ Minimally successful
- ○ Fully successful
- ○ Exceeds fully successful
- ○ Outstanding
- ○ Don't know

56 Confidentially, did you think that this rating was:
- ○ Too high
- ○ Accurate
- ○ Too low
- ○ Don't know

57 In your most recent appraisal, did you have any discussion with your supervisor?
- ○ Yes ○ No ○ Don't know

58 Did you feel that discussion was:
- ○ A full discussion
- ○ Somewhere in between
- ○ A minimal discussion
- ○ Don't know

59 Was that discussion before, after, or at the same time as the final rating?
- ○ Before
- ○ After
- ○ At the same time
- ○ Before and after
- ○ Don't know

60 Do you feel that your most recent performance appraisal accurately assessed:

	YES	NO	DON'T KNOW
The quality of your work	○	○	○
The quantity of your work	○	○	○
The timeliness of your work	○	○	○
The innovativeness of your work	○	○	○

61 Please indicate whether you disagree or agree with each of the statements, using the five-point scale.

	STRONGLY DISAGREE	DISAGREE	NEITHER AGREE NOR DISAGREE	AGREE	STRONGLY AGREE
My most recent performance appraisal was mostly based on my performance plan	①	②	③	④	⑤
My supervisor did not give a fair hearing to my views when doing my appraisal	①	②	③	④	⑤
My supervisor considers the performance appraisal of subordinates to be an important part of his or her duties	①	②	③	④	⑤
Performance appraisals influence personnel actions taken in this agency	①	②	③	④	⑤
Performance appraisal is unfair because the scores are forced into a given distribution with "quotas"					
My supervisor evaluates my performance on things that are not part of my job	①	②	③	④	⑤

APPENDIX B
COMMISSIONED PAPERS

- *Recruitment, Retention, and Utilization of Scientists and Engineers in the Federal Government: Results of a Literature Review* by Linda S. Dix   77

- *Quantitative Inputs to Federal Technical Personnel Management* by Charles E. Falk   95

- *Meeting Federal Work Force Needs with Regard to Scientists and Engineers: The Role of the U.S. Office of Personnel Management* by John M. Palguta   111

- *Differences in Recruitment, Retention, and Utilization Processes: A Comparison of Traditionally Operated Federal Laboratories, M&O Facilities, and Demonstration Projects* by Sheldon B. Clark   121

- *The Political Appointments Process and the Recruitment of Scientists and Engineers* by James P. Pfiffner   133

RECRUITMENT, RETENTION, AND UTILIZATION OF SCIENTISTS AND ENGINEERS IN THE FEDERAL GOVERNMENT: Results of a Literature Review

Linda S. Dix
Staff Officer
Office of Scientific and Engineering Personnel

Introduction

One activity to be undertaken under the aegis of the Committee on Scientists and Engineers in the Federal Government was a literature review to determine what earlier research had revealed about the ability of the federal government to recruit, retain, and utilize scientific and engineering talent effectively. The following summarizes information compiled from sources listed in the bibliography. The most recent studies of this issue, focusing on specific agencies, are the 1988 examination of the intramural program at the National Institutes of Health (Institute of Medicine, Committee to Study Strategies, 1988) and a three-year effort conducted by the Institute for Defense Analysis (IDA), studying 25,000 scientists and engineers in 66 Department of Defense (DoD) laboratories. Although the DoD data are still being analyzed, preliminary findings are included here (see also IDA, 1989a and 1989b; Millburn, 1989a and 1989b). Furthermore, the usefulness of data collected in that study has led the Office of Personnel Management (OPM) to design a survey questionnaire to be mailed to a representative sample of scientists and engineers in all other federal agencies.

In spite of efforts of the past two decades to encourage U.S. scientists and engineers to consider federal employment, some federal agencies have been unable to employ the numbers considered essential for completion of their missions, leading some within the science policy community to conclude:

> The federal system plods along for the most part, fostering mediocrity and lacking the means to attract or encourage the genius needed for technical inspiration and organizational leadership. (Packard, 1986)

A recent General Accounting Office (GAO, 1989a) study found that federal operations are so affected by serious human resource problems that the government cannot meet the needs of its citizens. From surveys of installation heads, personnel directors, personnel officers, and OPM in 1989, GAO found that 40-71 percent had greater difficulty in hiring good employees than in 1984 and 40-77 percent said that retention had worsened. (In contrast, only 2-20 percent of those interviewed felt recruitment and retention had improved between 1984 and 1989.) This is particularly true in technical fields and seems to occur at all civil service levels. But of particular concern is the fact that many experienced and competent senior executives are leaving federal service for employment in the private sector. In fact,

Among the very best—those who have won presidential merit awards—the average quit rate in 1986 and 1987 ran at 24% annually, with 75% of the departees going to industry. (Norton, 1989)

A similar assessment was made by federal lab directors. Less than 10 percent "think that salaries or bonuses are good enough. One half of the directors say that pay is too low and is not competitive with industry, and one half say that bonuses are too small" (IDA, 1989a). As a result, GAO has delineated specific areas that federal agencies should examine closely to encourage more scientists and engineers to engage in federal employment: (1) recruitment and staffing practices, (2) salary and benefits, and (3) planning for the types and numbers of people needed. Perhaps the major problem facing those who pursue federal employment, at least in Washington, D.C., is that they must put their lives and finances "on public display in the fishbowl-on-the-Potomac" (Norton, 1989).

Recruitment of Scientists and Engineers

Both the number of vacancies and the level of recruitment difficulty vary within and between federal agencies, (e.g., see Frascinella, 1989). For instance, the Environmental Protection Agency (EPA) has "experienced problems hiring and retaining sufficient numbers of technical personnel to implement the Superfund program" (GAO, 1989a) because of high employee turnover, inadequate pay, and insufficient training of staff. Recruitment difficulties have also been experienced at the National Institutes of Health (NIH), which has been "unable to hire a single senior biomedical research scientist from industry or academe in the past ten years" (Norton, 1989). Similar problems have been reported by the following agencies (GAO, 1987 and 1989b):

- Social Security Administration
- Internal Revenue Service
- National Science Foundation, particularly in scientific and engineering occupations, since 1985
- Department of the Army (electronics engineers, general engineers, physicists, computer scientists, and research psychologists)
- Bureau of Oceans and International Environment and Scientific Affairs, Department of State
- National Institute of Standards and Technology
- Office of Energy Research, Department of Energy
- National Oceanic and Atmospheric Administration
- Department of Health and Human Services
- National Aeronautics and Space Administration (NASA)

However, other federal agencies fill vacancies in scientific and engineering disciplines quite easily or encounter problems sporadically. When directed by an executive order of the President (December 1985) to provide information about problems that they have encountered in recruiting and retaining scientists and engineers, three agencies (the U.S. Geological Survey, the National Science Foundation, and the Department of

Transportation) noted no significant problems. In addition, within a federal organization, the significance of the difficulty of recruiting qualified scientists and engineers sometimes varies; the Department of the Army was cited to illustrate this point. In its 1982 study, the Laboratory Management Task Force noted that

> [DoD] departure rates seem to be reasonable. Because of the substantial populations of GS-12 and -13, the majority of attrition occurs at these levels. As a result, there are significant losses at these critical levels which are hard to replace.

That study further showed that in 1981 the 7.4 percent increase in the number of DoD scientists and engineers at GS-5-15 almost balanced the 6.4 percentage who left. However, a more recent study shows serious shortages in five fields at DoD labs—artificial intelligence, computer engineering, computer networking, signal processing, and systems engineering—with recruitment difficulties also experienced in acoustics, biomechanics, ceramics, control system engineering, digital communications, fiber optics, human factors, robotics, and weapons design (IDA, 1989a). Thus, GAO (1987) has concluded that "some agencies are experiencing difficulty in recruiting and retaining scientists and engineers while others are not." Nonetheless, it has been shown that "weaknesses in the government's recruitment and hiring processes have been major impediments to obtaining quality people" (GAO, 1989a) and often result in agencies having "to choose between accepting a less qualified candidate or leaving a position vacant" (Packard, 1986).

Retention of Scientists and Engineers

Attrition of scientists and engineers from the federal government has been a major issue of the 1980s. For instance, between 1981 and 1984 the Air Force

TABLE 1: Quit Rates for DoD Engineers (in percent)

Fiscal Year	Quit Rate	Fiscal Year	Quit Rate
1975	1.8	1981	2.3
1976	1.5	1982	2.2
1977	2.0	1983	3.2
1978	2.4	1984	3.3
1979	2.5	1985	3.6
1980	2.4		

SOURCE: General Accounting Office, *Federal Work Force: Pay, Recruitment, and Retention of Federal Employees* (GAO/GGD-87-37), Washington, D.C.: GAO, 1987.

experienced a 164 percent increase in the number of resignations of civilian scientists and engineers, with resignations occurring at all grade levels (Packard, 1986). This is compounded by the fact that in a recent year only 1,792 of 2,445 vacant engineering positions in the Air Force were filled, after 2,737 job offers were made for them (recruitment success rate of 73.3 percent) (GAO, 1987). The overall quit rate for engineers in DoD averaged 2.47 percent for the period 1975-1985 (see Table 1). Although the average annual DoD quit rate was 2.1 percent for the 1975-1982 period, it has remained around 3.4 percent since then, but staff have found no reason for this jump.

Factors Affecting Recruitment and Retention of Scientists and Engineers

Several organizational, personal, and economic factors influence one's decision not to work for a federal agency or to leave federal employment: noncompetitive federal salaries, advancement opportunities, the nature of the work, geographic location of work, etc. In addition, exogenous factors affect attrition: "the state of the labor market, the particular occupation, and the age, sex, and education of employees" (GAO, 1987).

Several of the studies examined revealed that the changing demography of the U.S. work force, together with competition from the private sector for high-quality scientists and engineers, hinders the ability of the federal government to recruit and retain the quality needed to be effective. Several other reasons have been given for the current situation:

- Restrictions imposed not only by budgetary constraints but also by personnel ceilings
- Salary increases determined more by length of service rather than by quality of one's performance
- Noncompetitive federal salaries for scientists and engineers. (Packard, 1986)

These factors received regular attention in studies that zeroed in on the inflexibility of the civil service system, as shown in the report following a comprehensive examination of the Army laboratories:

> The personnel policies and procedures of a laboratory and its parent organization are important in attracting and retaining good scientists and engineers and in providing them rewarding careers. Undue bureaucratic complications and delays in recruiting, for example, can put a laboratory at a serious disadvantage in competing for talented science and engineering graduates. Uncompetitive salaries and benefits, of course, also impede recruiting and retaining good personnel. Laboratories must provide opportunities for advancement and increased responsibilities. Similarly, their promotion and termination procedures and practices must be regarded as straightforward and fair. (Committee on Army Manpower, 1983)

Further, the 1983 White House Science Council[1] report (Office of Science and Technology Policy, 1983) concurred on the widespread nature of the problem:

> Almost all of the Federal laboratories . . . suffer serious disadvantages in their abilities to attract, retain, and motivate scientific and technical personnel required to fulfill their missions. The principal disadvantage is the inability of the Federal laboratories, particularly those under the Civil Service system, to provide scientists and engineers with competitive compensation. . . . Furthermore, cumbersome procedures for hiring new staff make it hard to bring in new talent even when other obstacles have been overcome.
>
> The rigidity of the Civil Service promotion and salary system limits rewards for outstanding scientists and engineers. . . . Promotion is linked to management responsibilities, and current rules do not allow for adequate recognition of scientific performance alone. Recent personnel ceilings imposed strictly on a numerical basis without distinguishing among types of staff have adversely affected the laboratories' R&D activities. . . . This personnel situation leaves the Federal laboratories vulnerable to weak scientific leadership if senior qualified personnel cannot be replaced and to declining quality of research because of inadequate infusion of young talent.

Thus it was not surprising to read the conclusion of a report assessing the ability of NIH to recruit and retain scientists:

> The combination of increasingly burdensome and unnecessary constraints along with lower salaries and less flexible administrative policies creates justified concern about NIH's ability to continue its past successes in building the staff necessary to sustain the quality and vitality of the intramural program. (Committee to Study Strategies, 1988)

Personnel Ceilings

The 1979 GAO study of federal laboratories reports that "the directors were concerned over the adverse effect of personnel ceilings on their operations, [advocating for themselves] more personnel control, including hire and fire authority." Although 51 percent of the managers surveyed had control over the type of people hired and in what disciplines, the other 49 percent said that they must "get approval or operate within parameters set by higher organizational levels." Following close on the heels of the GAO study, DoD's Laboratory Management Task Force (1980) focused two of its five major recommendations on the issue of personnel ceilings: stabilize laboratory personnel ceilings and repeal high grade ceilings. Similar recommendations came from both the U.S. Defense Research and Engineering Independent Review of DoD

---

[1] A 1983 panel of distinguished scientists, chaired by David Packard, studied five aspects of federal laboratories—mission; personnel; funding; management; and interaction with universities, industry, and users of research results—operated by the six agencies receiving the largest portion of federal R&D funding (NASA and the departments of Defense, Agriculture, Commerce, Energy, and Health and Human Services).

Laboratories (Hermann, 1982) and the Laboratory Management Task Force's 1982 study of scientists and engineers in DoD laboratories, the latter finding that

> Ceilings by themselves are not an intrinsic barrier to maintenance of an effective S&E [science and engineering] work force beyond a critical mass required to operate a laboratory. What does appear to be important is the maintenance of a stable ceiling consistent with workload to facilitate planning and management within the DoD labs. . . . The majority of Technical Directors did report significant adverse impacts of . . . total ceilings including reduced ability to meet mission requirements, deletion of specific technologies that should be addressed, reduced ability to hire and promote experienced and deserving personnel as well as overall reduced quality of work.

Still other adverse effects of personnel ceilings that hinder recruitment of scientists and engineers include inadequate staffing levels, increased contracting out of agency work and subsequent reduction of in-house expertise, inability to respond to requests for work, increased S&E workload, and increased use of temporaries (IDA, 1989a).

Noncompetitive Salaries

Among the stipulations of Section 5305 of the U.S. Code of Federal Regulations is the requirement that unless the President and Congress agree on alternative pay rates,

> Federal white-collar employees' salaries under the General Schedule are to be adjusted each year to maintain comparability with private sector salaries for similar levels of work. (GAO, 1987)

However, beginning in 1979, such adjustments have not been made. The result is that by 1987, federal employees received salaries averaging 23.8 percent less than their counterparts in private industry (GAO, 1987). In fact, the salaries for federal employees in the upper echelons "have sunk far below the norms of corporate America" (Norton, 1989) during the past decade.

Data obtained in 1987 by GAO from OPM as well as from the two federal agencies employing the most scientists and engineers—DoD and NASA—show that scientists and engineers, like many other employees in the federal government, are paid lower salaries than their counterparts in the private sector. Of the seven occupations examined by GAO (1987), three are relevant to this study of scientists and engineers in the federal government: chemists, engineers, and computer specialists (Table 2). However, these data show no relationship between the pay gap and quit rate in these occupations.

In a later report, GAO (1989) noted that the differences in salary for federal employees and their private-sector counterparts ranged from 26 percent on the General Schedule of Salaries to 65 percent for senior executives. Salary discrepancies are particularly prevalent for scientists and engineers, but such discrepancies depend on one's place of employment. In general, a federal scientist earns about $3,000 **more** than his counterpart in business and industry, whereas a federal engineer earns $700 **less** than

TABLE 2: 1985 Pay Gaps and Quit Rates (in percent)

Occupation	Pay Gap Range	Quit Rate
Chemist	27.9-50.7	2.3
Accountant	27.2-46.0	2.3
Engineer	19.4-46.0	3.3
Buyer	24.7-34.9	3.2
Computer specialist	5.9-29.1	2.8
Clerk-typist	10.1-11.1	13.8
Secretary	4.0-9.3	6.9
All General Schedule workers	19.2	5.2

SOURCE: General Accounting Office, *Federal Work Force: Pay, Recruitment, and Retention of Federal Employees* (GAO/GGD-87-37), Washington, D.C.: GAO, 1987.

his peer in the private sector (IDA, 1989b). However, at EPA salaries for chemists and engineers "trailed private sector pay by $7,800 to $41,300, or 25 to 68 percent" (GAO, 1989a). In addition, a recent comparison of salaries found that a DoD scientist earns an average of $5,000 **more** than the national average but a DoD engineer earns about $1,000 **less** than the national average (IDA, 1989b). In 1986, when federal laboratories received $18 billion (or one-third) of the federal R&D budget and employed about one-sixth of all U.S. research scientist and engineers, David Packard, chairman of Hewlett-Packard Company, warned:

> At the heart of the problem is pay, with rigidity and inertia of the personnel administration system being a less important but contributing factor. . . . The [pay] problem is particularly acute in the scientific and engineering fields, where industrial pay scales have risen faster than the rest. [Because Congress links congressional and civil service pay and hesitates to raise its own pay], the result is not only lower federal salaries but also severe salary compression at the senior levels. (Packard, 1986)

From information provided by 13 federal organizations in response to a December 1985 executive order of the President, GAO (1987) reported that 11 of these organizations experienced recruitment and retention problems because of the noncompetitive nature of federal salaries. Such problems tended to be agency-specific:

- The U.S. Geological Survey noted its inability to hire about 10 percent of their "prime candidates" in engineering positions (3-4 from a vacancy pool of 40) each year.
- The Department of Transportation cited recruitment difficulty only for entry-level

technician positions in the Boston area, where competition with high-technology industry is great.
- Both the National Bureau of Standards (now the National Institute of Standards and Technology) and NASA cited noncompetitive salaries as a major contributor to the loss of technical, scientific, and engineering candidates.
- NASA noted that from FY1983 to FY1985, its scientist and engineer losses, other than retirement, increased from 294 to 361 employees.

The salaries that B.S. engineers can draw from industry particularly affect NASA's ability to recruit them:

> Top pay for a beginning engineer at NASA is $25,000—that includes a 30% premium for hard-to-fill jobs like those in engineering and medicine. Top graduates . . . can command up to $40,000 in business. (Norton, 1989)

Similarly, the effect of the federal pay schedule on the retention of high-level talent was keenly noted in a study of the 118 doctoral scientists and engineers at the U.S. Army's Waterways Experiment Station in Vicksburg, Miss. During the period January 1980 to June 1987, 32 doctorates (or 27 percent) left WES:

> Those who left did so primarily for a higher salary. The private sector attracted 41 percent, universities 22 percent, and other Federal agencies 16 percent. (Vincent, 1987)

GAO's 1989(b) study, which looked at all scientists and engineers (as opposed to the 1987 examination of chemists, engineers, and computer specialists), found that "noncompetitive compensation further exacerbates the problem by creating higher rates of turnover, which, in turn, create the need for more recruiting by federal agencies." Because low salaries were making recruitment and retention of highly capable scientists and engineers difficult for the national labs, the Committee on Army Manpower (1983) recommended higher starting salaries for "new graduates possessing unique and needed skills so that these salaries are competitive," and Packard (1986) urged Congress "to act quickly to halt the erosion of scientific talent before the vitality of the laboratories is seriously undermined." Thus it was with much backing of the scientific community that adjustments were made to the General Schedule of Salaries to enable supervisors to hire engineers in entry and mid-level grades at "rates which exceed normal General Schedule salaries for other employees at the same grades" (GAO, 1987). Nonetheless, it is felt by many that "our lack of pay comparability with the private sector means that we are becoming less able to compete for the shrinking pool of citizen S&E graduates" (Millburn, 1989b). In fact, the Committee to Study Strategies to Strengthen the Scientific Excellence of the National Institutes of Health Intramural Research Program (1988) urged increasing

> NIH's flexibility in pay . . . so that it may compete more effectively for people critical to the continued success of the various programs and otherwise to administer more effectively its public responsibilities.

The committee also noted that although "there is merit in the claim that an unfavorable pay disparity exists and is growing," the magnitude of the problem may be overstated.

Inadequate Fringe Benefits

Several studies of federal compensation have shown that "the federal government's pay and benefits structure has serious implications for the quality of the federal workforce" (GAO, 1989b). The low level of fringe benefits provided by federal employers contributes to a number of resignations by scientists and engineers, particularly at grades GS-13 and above (Laboratory Management Task Force, 1982). In fact, Packard (1986) stated, "Federal health and life insurance provisions and annual and sick leave allowances are far less generous than those offered by many private companies and universities." Furthermore, the Office of Science and Technology Policy and the Office of Management and Budget urged "legislative action to permit continuity of pension plans for scientists and engineers who move between Federal laboratories and universities" (OSTP, 1984a). On the other hand, some attribute low attrition among federal employees in general to this very "lack of portability of civil service retirement benefits" (GAO, 1987), implying that the loss of federal scientists and engineers could be compounded by a change in retirement programs.

Other Factors

Still other factors influencing federal recruitment and retention of scientists and engineers have been noted not only in earlier studies but also recently by the press, including weak leadership within federal agencies, ownership of intellectual property, and ethics laws.

Weak Agency Leadership: Several studies have focused on the leadership in national laboratories, but in some instances the assessment of problems encountered by the labs can apply more broadly to other federal agencies. The Committee on Army Manpower (1983) noted that

> The quality and stability of its own leadership over the years is a primary factor in determining the laboratory's reputation in its field. It is also a primary factor in maintaining talented and productive scientific and engineering personnel.

But for one to lead an agency effectively—that is, use employees effectively and efficiently—he or she must thoroughly understand the mission of the agency, a task complicated by several factors. First, the missions of agencies frequently change:

> The great national research centers financed by the government utilize large numbers of scientists and engineers. The missions of some of them, especially of those related to defense, have changed since their establishment. It is important that their present and future missions be clear-cut and of high priority, and that their use of scientists and engineers be unmistakably in the national interest. In maintaining these major

considerations of manpower, the government has a special responsibility to appraise them in terms of both their contributions to urgent government needs and their impact on the overall utilization of scientists and engineers, taking into consideration the needs of the private sector of the economy. (Committee on Utilization of Scientific and Engineering Manpower, 1964)

As agency missions change, trying to effect the change is a large task. For instance, in 1989 EPA's Science Advisory Board suggested that the agency

beef up its research program . . . by doubling its funding of environmental research in the next 5 years, putting more emphasis on investigator-initiated projects, and creating a new institute for environmental research which would focus on novel, preventive, and anticipatory research. (Marshall, 1989a)

Second, the mission statements are sometimes unclear. In such cases the result can be

lack of overall technical objectives and guidance for the laboratories. . . . Without explicit policy direction and commitments, even with the management autonomy the directors appear to have, it is difficult to assure that the projects selected are part of an integrated program or that program progress is being attained. It is even more difficult to prevent short-term influences from controlling the laboratory agenda. . . . if the Federal laboratory role is to continue and be an effective use of resources, close scrutiny of the policy framework and resource support is warranted now. (GAO, 1979)

Thus the Committee on Army Manpower (1983) recommended that each federal agency

should provide its directors, as well as its scientists and engineers, with consistent objectives that are both achievable and specific . . . and delegate the necessary responsibility to allow them to perform the creative and innovative research and development required to meet these goals.

Another problem contributing to weak leadership and inadequate management is increased politicization. Agency leadership is increasingly determined by political appointments, a policy that can not only hinder mission accomplishment but also make it difficult to maintain competent and stable leadership. One way of strengthening agency leadership, according to GAO (1987), is participation in the training prescribed for Senior Executive Service (SES) candidates and incumbents. However, GAO found that only 48 percent of all SES members had received annual training for the two previous years and that the average annual training time per executive was only 52 hours. Earlier studies also have shown that agency leadership is strengthened when

Federal managers . . . know how many and what types of people they need to accomplish their programs' objectives. Linking mission accomplishment with personnel requirements requires good planning systems and sound workforce information. (GAO, 1989b)

Ethics Laws: The possibility of conflicts of interest arises when scientists and engineers are privy to certain information because of their employment by the federal government. As a result, Congress has been most interested in this issue in recent years, leading to reports by GAO on how the postemployment provisions of the Ethics in Government Act of 1978 (Public Law 95-521) have been implemented. GAO (1989b) found that "application of the Ethics Act's postemployment conflict of interest provisions is governed in large part by how a former employee's agency has been compartmentalized."[2] To make DoD managers and employees aware and knowledgeable of ethical issues, Secretary of Defense Richard B. Cheney has proposed creation of an ethics council composed of top agency leaders that would develop an ethics program (Moore, 1989).

Numerous senior executives have recently quit, reportedly because of tighter interpretations of P.L. 100-679, passed by Congress in 1988 (Norton, 1989; Marshall, 1989b). Among the senior executives who recently left federal employment after as much as 18 years of service are William Ballhaus, Jr., director of NASA's Ames Research Center; Noel W. Hinners, NASA's associate deputy administrator and chief scientist; H. Robert Heller, former Federal Reserve Board governor; and 18 other senior technical employees at NASA, including Robert Aller, chief of the office of space operation; E. Ray Tanner, deputy director of space station operations; John Thomas, director of the shuttle booster redesign program; and James Odom, associate administrator, and Thomas Moser, acting associate administrator, for the space station. Had these senior executives remained with the government, the new ethics code would have forced them to sell stock in companies in which their employing agencies did business, to sever "professional and social as well as financial connections with their past" (Norton, 1989), and to resign from business and even nonprofit directorships. Richard Truly, NASA administrator, feels that the new ethics code will have a strong negative impact on that agency: "When ten senior executive service people leave you, they take with them 250 to 300 years of government leadership and experience" (Marshall, 1989b).

Although P.L. 100-679 permits federal employees to provide scientific advice, as long as it is not used on contract negotiations, Norman R. Augustine, CEO of Martin Marietta, has concluded:

> There's no way I can serve in the government. [The conflict-of-interest laws are] sufficiently vague and subject to ex post facto interpretation. They've got criminal sanctions. No one wants to be the test case ten years down the road. I certainly don't. (Norton, 1989)

---

[2] Compartmentalization is "the process by which agencies are divided into designated subunits for application of the 1-year no-contact restriction contained in the Ethics Act. The restriction prohibits former senior-level employees from contacting their former agencies on particular matters either before the agency or in which the agency has a direct and substantial interest" (GAO, 1989b).

DoD also experienced resignations upon passage of P.L. 100-679. If proposed legislation passes, further limiting postemployment activities (e.g., banning work for any major defense contractor until at least two years after working for DoD), other DoD employees may resign. Congressman Les AuCoin has said that the proposed legislation is designed to attract managers "who are more interested in the national interest than their own career interest" (Norton, 1989). However, the problem of retaining senior employees is so significant that it

> threatens to affect the continuity and institutional memory needed to resolve various administrative and programmatic problems. . . . In fiscal year 1985, 615, or 9.9 percent, of career SES members left SES. The majority . . . took another paid position in business, industry, or consulting. Nearly half reported increases in their salaries. (GAO, 1989b)

Conflicts of interest can have different effects on scientific productivity. A recent case in point was the controversy centering around accusations that "a top-secret Star Wars project was hyped to key people in government by famed physicist Edward Teller and a young protege" (Dworkin, 1988). According to Dworkin, because of the action taken by Teller, Roy Woodruff, associate director of that laboratory for defense systems, "resigned in protest."

Ownership of Intellectual Property: A fundamental question encountered not only by scientists and engineers employed by the federal government, but also by their counterparts in other sectors is "Who has rights of ownership in science, under what circumstances, and how free are they to convey the 'owned' intellectual property to others?" This unresolved question has been perceived by many as a deterrent to federal employment:

> Government controls on the communication of scientific and technical information involve the collision of basic First Amendment issues and government's rights to limit access, where that is deemed in the national interest. In practice, governmental agencies have at times overclassified such information ostensibly to protect national security or national economic competitiveness and have also leaked such information when that was thought useful. . . . It may be that the U.S. government has recently become particularly intent on using legislation, designed originally for other purposes, to control the flow of scientific information. (Zuckerman, 1988)

Thus Congress considered legislation whereby scientists and engineers working in federal laboratories and cooperating with private industry could market their inventions that did not apply directly to the mission of the particular lab. This legislation was viewed as necessary because few federal scientists and engineers patent their work, yet they often publish their research. As a result, "the Soviets and Japanese take best advantage of federal research," according to Eugene Stark, industrial initiatives officer at Los Alamos National Laboratory (Hyatt, 1986). Hyatt reported that many felt that passage of this legislation would enable labs focusing on areas such as health, agriculture, and defense to be "a seedbed for innovative products and new companies." He cited Oak Ridge National Laboratory as an example of one federal laboratory where such commercialization has been in effect for some time; in 1985 "the lab spent about $250,000 polishing up eight new technologies for private industry . . . and spawned four start-ups."

However, other researchers have noted that recent laws and decisions by the U.S. Supreme Court have examined but not satisfactorily answered the question "What are appropriate controls on the dissemination of scientific and technical information?" Furthermore, a number of government actions have curtailed dissemination of scientific and technical information:

> Government initiatives include moves to expand the government classification system; to require prepublication review agreements from government grantees, contractees, and employees; and to invoke statutes such as the Espionage Act, the Invention Secrecy Act, and Export Control Laws to prevent or punish disclosure of scientific and technical information. Government actions invoking the Export Laws have interfered with presentations of papers at scientific society meetings and personal contacts between foreign scholars and American scientists. Under the Espionage Act, a government employee has been prosecuted for disclosing classified information, an action ordinarily not punishable as a crime. (Weil, 1988)

Such restrictions have negative impacts on both the individual scientist or engineer and the general public. According to Weil, scientists tend to avoid controversy "that may deflect them from scientific work" or lead to "loss of access to information or loss of grants or employment." Thus scientific inquiry may be stymied. Furthermore, "when government employees, contractees, or grantees give up the right to inform the public, the public is the loser" (DuVal, 1986).

Two of the factors often cited as affecting the federal government's ability to recruit scientists and engineers are more tangible than others but appear to be just as difficult to correct: the geographic location of employment and quality of the working environment.

Geographic Location of Employment: In considering whether to work for a federal agency, it is not unusual for an individual to consider the cost of living near the place of employment. Recruiting new hires as well as replacements for employees who leave can be quite difficult. For instance, NASA has encountered problems in replacing its senior employees:

> Potential candidates to manage the space station program are balking at the high cost of living in Washington, D.C. As a result, the agency is having a hard time selling its openings. . . . Without some special action of Congress, moreover, the government has no legal way to offer a bonus to people who make the move. (Waldrop, 1989)

Although the government does provide pay differentials in some regions of the country, the findings of a recent study of locality pay indicate that these differentials may be insufficient to entice individuals to work for the federal government rather than universities or private industry (Wyatt, 1989).

Quality of Working Environment: The impact of the working environment on one's productivity and performance has been assessed many times. In fact, 26 years ago, a committee of the National Academy of Sciences recommended that this issue not be ignored:

> The Civil Service Commission should . . . carefully review government personnel policies to determine which ones have or can have a significant effect on the environment in which research and development is carried out in government laboratories. Where changes in such policies seem advisable, authority to make them should be promptly sought. At the same time, the commission should aid and encourage agency heads and lab directors fully to use all existing authority to improve working environments. (Committee on Utilization of Scientific and Engineering Manpower, 1964)

Nonetheless, a later survey of 192 laboratories directed by 8 federal agencies found that "deteriorating facilities and equipment" was one of five major problem areas affecting recruitment and retention of scientists and engineers (GAO, 1979). This was subsequently confirmed in the Committee on Army Manpower's 1983 study of "shops, libraries, laboratory supplies and equipment, computer facilities, and other resources."

Other aspects of the work environment, besides the physical, are program content, stability, and impact. The Committee on Army Manpower found that

> Laboratory scientists and engineers are highly motivated by challenging and important work. If they feel that their work is irrelevant to their clients or that their clients fail to take full advantage of the laboratory's results, they may seek other employment. This applies particularly to more talented and highly motivated individuals whom the Army can least afford to lose.

Negative Public Image of Federal Service: Added together, the many factors cited above contribute to a negative public image of federal service, and at the same time the public has a poor image of scientists and engineers (Office of Scientific and Engineering Personnel, 1989). The National Commission on the Public Service (1989) stated this succinctly:

> It is evident that public service is neither as attractive as it once was nor as effective in meeting perceived needs. No doubt, opposition to specific policies of government has contributed to a lack of respect for the public servants who struggle to make the policies work. This drives away much of our best talent which can only make the situation worse.

As noted in recent survey of selected college and university deans and placement officers, 75 percent considered the negative image of federal service a significant obstacle to the ability of federal agencies to recruit college graduates (U.S. Merit Systems Protection Board, 1988). This has, in turn, "demoralized federal employees and hindered recruitment" to the extent that, in one survey of Senior Executive Service members, only 13 percent reported that they would advise someone to pursue a career in public service. The National Commission on the Public Service (1989) cautioned,

> One need not search far to see grounds for concern. Crippled nuclear weapons plants, defense procurement scandals, leaking hazardous waste dumps, near-misses in air traffic control, and the costly collapse of so many savings and loans have multiple causes. But each such story carries some similar refrains about government's inability to recruit and retain a talented work force: the Department of Defense is losing its top procurement specialists to contractors who can pay much more; the FAA is unable to hold skilled traffic controllers because of stress and working conditions; the EPA is unable to fill key engineering jobs because the brightest students simply are not interested.

Summary

During the past 25 years, numerous studies of the federal scientific and technical work force have been conducted. Some have been narrowly focused on a particular agency while others have examined a specific issue across agencies. Although consensus is apparent on some issues, for others the study findings offer conflicting data. For example, most studies of the overall federal S&E work force note that recruitment and retention are adversely affected by such factors as personnel ceilings, salaries confined by civil service regulations, fringe benefit packages less attractive than those offered by other employment sectors, weak agency leadership, ethics laws, regulations governing ownership of intellectual property, geographic location of employment, quality of working environment, and the negative public image of federal service. However, there is often disagreement about the magnitude of the effects that these factors have on recruitment and retention. The degree of difficulty in recruiting and retaining scientists and engineers is usually agency- and discipline-specific. Furthermore, differences in degree often occur *within* agencies.

Many steps have been taken to facilitate recruitment and retention of scientists and engineers by federal agencies. For instance, personnel demonstration projects, now at 10 sites, have been shown to have positive effects on recruitment and retention. Other mechanisms to encourage federal employment and to lower turnover rates among scientists and engineers include special rates for certain position classifications and pay schedules based on locality of employment. However, studies indicate that other organizational and decision-making processes within the federal government sometimes outweigh the mechanisms designed especially to enhance recruitment and retention.

Bibliography

Committee on Army Manpower, Board on Army Science and Technology, Commission on Engineering and Technical Systems. 1983. *The Professional Environment in Army Laboratories and Its Effect on Scientific and Engineering Performance.* Washington, D.C.: National Academy Press.

Committee on Utilization of Scientific and Engineering Manpower. 1964. *Toward Better Utilization of Scientific and Engineering Talent: A Program for Action.* Washington, D.C.: National Academy of Sciences.

Committee on the Utilization of Young Scientists and Engineers in Advisory Services to Government. 1972. *The Science Committee.* Washington, D.C.: National Academy of Sciences.

Committee to Study Strategies to Strengthen the Scientific Excellence of the National Institutes of Health Intramural Research Program, Institute of Medicine. 1988. *A Healthy NIH Intramural Program: Structural Change or Administrative Remedies?* Washington, D.C.: National Academy Press.

Dworkin, P. 1988. Long knives in the laboratory: In-fighting by scientists at the Lawrence Livermore National Laboratory. *U.S. News & World Report* **104**(February 29):16-18.

DuVal, B. S., Jr. 1986. Enforcing Security at the Source: Secrecy and the Government Employee, Contractee, and Grantee. Paper presented at the annual meeting of the American Association for the Advancement of Science, Philadelphia, Penn., May 1986.

Frascinella, J. 1989. Working for the government. *Washington Post,* July 12, 1989, p. G11.

Hermann, R. J. 1982. *USDRE Independent Review of DoD Laboratories.* Washington, D.C.: Office of the Under Secretary for Defense Research and Engineering.

Hyatt, J. 1986. Federal labs may open for business. *Inc.* **8**(April):22.

Institute for Defense Analysis (IDA). 1989a. *Study of Scientists and Engineers in the DoD Laboratories,* vol. I. Alexandria, Va.: IDA.

_____. 1989b. *Study of Scientists and Engineers in the DoD Laboratories,* vol. II. Alexandria, Va.: IDA.

Laboratory Management Task Force, U.S. Department of Defense. 1980. *Impact of Management Constraints on the DoD Laboratories.* Washington, D.C.: DoD.

_____. 1982. *Study of Scientists and Engineers in DoD Laboratories.* Washington, D.C.: DoD.

Marshall, E. 1989a. EPA drafts new research agenda. *Science* **244**(June 10):1253.

_____. 1989b. Top talent leaving NASA. *Science* **245**(July 21): 251.

Millburn, G. P. 1989a. Untitled speech, Conference on Federal Workforce Quality Assessment, sponsored by the Office of Personnel Management and Merit Systems Protection Board, Washington, D.C., May 8.

_____. 1989b. Recruitment and Retention of DoD Scientists and Engineers. Speech to Personnel Research Conference conducted by the Office of Personnel Management, Chevy Chase, Md., August 16.

Moore, M. 1989. Cheney seeks $30 billion savings in purchase system: Proposal includes streamlining operations, cutting payroll costs, increased computerization. *Washington Post,* July 11, 1989, p. A8.

National Commission on the Public Service. 1989. *Leadership for America: Rebuilding the Public Service.* Washington, D.C.: The Commission.

Norton, R. E. 1989. Who wants to work in Washington? *Fortune* (August 14): 77-80, 82.

Office of Scientific and Engineering Personnel. 1989. *Responding to the Changing Demography: Women in Science and Engineering.* Internal report. Washington, D.C.: National Academy of Sciences.

Packard, D. 1986. The loss of governmental scientific and engineering talent. *Issues in Science and Technology* 2(3: Spring):126-131.

U.S. Civil Service Commission. 1970. *Scientists and Engineers in the Federal Personnel System.* Washington, D.C.: U.S. Government Printing Office.

_____. 1974. *Scientific and Engineering Manpower Management.* Washington, D.C.: U.S. Government Printing Office.

_____. 1964. *The Special Features of the Federal Personnel System of Interest to the Scientist and Engineer.* Washington, D.C.: U.S. Government Printing Office (out of print).

U.S. Congress, Joint Committee on Governmental Affairs, Subcommittee on Civil Service, Post Office, and General Services. 1986. *Alternative Pay Systems in the Federal Government.* Hearings before the subcommittee, April 15 and 30 and May 14, 1986. Washington, D.C.: U.S. Government Printing Office.

_____, Senate Committee on Governmental Affairs, Subcommittee on Energy, Nuclear Proliferation, and Government Processes. 1982. *Critical Need for Energy Research and Development: The Role of the Midwest Research Labs.* Hearing before the subcommittee, March 22, 1982. Washington, D.C.: U.S. Government Printing Office.

U.S. General Accounting Office (GAO). 1979. *Federal R&D Laboratories Directors' Perspectives on Management.* Washington, D.C.: U.S. GAO.

_____. 1984. *Federal White Collar Special Rate Program.* Report to the Subcommittee on Compensation and Benefits, House Committee on Post Office and Civil Service. Washington, D.C.: U.S. GAO.

_____. 1987. *Federal Work Force: Pay, Recruitment, and Retention of Federal Employees.* Washington, D.C.: U.S. GAO.

_____. 1989a. *Managing Human Resources: Greater OPM Leadership Needed to Address Critical Challenges* (GAO/GGD-89-19). Washington, D.C.: GAO.

_____. 1989b. *The Public Service: Issues Affecting Its Quality, Effectiveness, Integrity, and Stewardship* (GAO/GGD-89-73). Washington, D.C.: GAO.

U.S. Merit Systems Protection Board. 1988. *Attracting Quality Graduates to the Federal Government: A View of College Recruiting.* Washington, D.C.: MSPB.

U.S. Office of Science and Technology Policy (OSTP). 1984a. *Progress Report on Implementing the Recommendations of the White House Science Council's Federal Laboratory Review Panel, vol I: Summary Report.* Washington, D.C.: OSTP.

_____. 1984b. *Progress Report on Implementing the Recommendations of the White House Science Council's Federal Laboratory Review Panel, vol II: Status Reports.* Washington, D.C.: OSTP.

_____. 1983. Report of the White House Science Council's Federal Laboratory Review Panel. Washington, D.C.: OSTP.

Vincent, M. K. 1987. *Loss of Doctorates from WES, 1980-1987* (Miscellaneous Paper

0-87-2). Vicksburg, Miss.: Army Engineer Waterways Experiment Station, Office of Technical Programs and Plans.

Waldrop, M. M. 1989. New recruits hard to find. *Science* **245**(July 21):251.

Weil, V. 1988. Policy incentives and constraints on scientific and technical information. *Science, Technology, & Human Values* **13**(1&2):17-26.

Weisbrod, B. A. 1989. Rewarding performance that is hard to measure: The private nonprofit sector. *Science* **244**:541-545.

Witham, F. 1970. *Scientists and Engineers in the Federal Government, Personnel Bibliography Series Number 30.* Washington, D.C.: U.S. Government Printing Office.

Wyatt Company. 1989. Study of Federal Employee Locality Pay: Executive Summary. Wyatt: Philadelphia.

Zuckerman, H. A. 1988. Introduction: Intellectual property and diverse rights of ownership in science. *Science, Technology, & Human Values* **3**(1&2):7-16.

QUANTITATIVE INPUTS TO FEDERAL TECHNICAL PERSONNEL MANAGEMENT

Charles E. Falk
National Science Foundation
(retired)

Opinions may differ on the key requirements for effective management systems; however, everyone seems to agree that adequate information input is an absolute necessity. This axiom applies also to the federal government's management of its science and engineering work force. This paper deals with the quantitative information that is, or certainly should be, used in the management of this critical resource. Failure to do so can produce not only management in a vacuum but, even worse, actions based on incorrect anecdotal information. Thus any evaluation of the effectiveness of the federal technical personnel management system should assess both the adequacy of available data and whether such data are being used by those who operate and manage the system. To assist this facet of the study, this paper will explore the types of information required, briefly describe the data systems that provide this information, analyze some pertinent data readily available at this time, and finally make some recommendations related to the development and use of quantitative information on federal scientists and engineers.

Data Categories

Work Force Characteristics

Personnel data requirements can be broken down into two major categories: descriptive and dynamic. The first, descriptive of the existing or prospective work force, should place the federal technical work force into proper perspective with respect to the overall national pool of scientists and engineers to ascertain whether acquisition of new personnel is likely to be restricted by supply shortages. It should also depict the characteristics of the work force, including demographic characteristics such as age, sex, and race (the first to provide indicators of likely attrition and the other two to show to what extent major human resource pools are used). Educational data such as highest degree obtained should be available to show what specific educational pools will have to be tapped. Grade-level data can be used as a surrogate to experience and level of expertise and responsibility. Finally, information on the type of primary work activity—such as R&D, operation, or management—provides important information on the types of training and experience required.

All descriptive data should be presented by occupation and agency so that specific requirements can be identified. The agency data and information on the number and characteristics of scientists and engineers engaged in work related to various areas of critical national interest—such as defense, energy, or environment—provide insight into how changes in national priorities are likely to influence future requirements for specific occupations. Comparisons with similar characteristics of technical personnel in other employment sectors such as industry or academe can identify the relatively unique needs of the federal sector.

All of the data mentioned thus far are quantitative—that is, they deal with the number of individuals having specific characteristics. Another class of information probably of equal importance in determining the effectiveness of programs is the quality of the individuals involved. Although it is difficult to develop quantitative quality indicators, educational attainment—that is, highest degree and grade level—data—can be used at least as partial quality indicators.

Dynamic Data

One of the most important aspects of personnel management involves the dynamics of the work force. Related data provide information on the magnitude and characteristics of new hires. Furthermore, other data (e.g., on separations and length of government service) can be used as indicators of work satisfaction. Data elements required for a good understanding of the dynamics include the following:

- Turnover data—that is, information on length of service, both in the federal government and in a specific agency, coupled with separation rates—provide information on job satisfaction. Data on types of separation provide important information on inability to retain personnel. Moreover, data on job satisfaction of the total work force, based on such information as a recent survey of the Senior Executive Service personnel, provide important insights.
- Salary comparisons with other agencies and, especially, other employment sectors are unquestionably one of the most important sets of potential dissatisfaction indicators. However, such data must be presented with sufficient detail to make meaningful comparisons possible. Thus it is essential to know the age and occupation distributions of the personnel involved, for a younger work force is likely to be at a lower pay level while certain occupations such as engineering, even at a given age, require higher rates of pay.
- Data on career patterns of scientists and engineers within the government can be compared with patterns in other employment sectors to illuminate potential sources of work dissatisfaction. Although it may be possible to generate such data from the federal employment base, for the federal government is a single employer, it may be difficult to obtain similar data for comparisons with other employment sectors.

Quantitative Information Sources

Human resource data are generally developed from two sources: employers and employees. Although employer-based data usually are limited because they are derived from personnel files, this is not the case for the federal government.

Descriptive Data

Office of Personnel Management: OPM maintains an extensive data bank based on the periodic reports (monthly, quarterly, or at pay-period intervals) it receives from most federal agencies and departments. The principal omissions are the National Security Agency, the Central Intelligence Agency, the Postal Service, the Tennessee Valley Authority, and the uniformed military. Among the 58 data elements of the system are most of the descriptive data requirements mentioned above—namely age, sex, race, citizenship, educational level, occupational classification, functional classification, salary, and grade. Summary statistical tables of occupations by sex, salary, and grade are published biennially by OPM in the report *Occupations of Federal White-Collar and Blue-Collar Workers.* The National Science Foundation (NSF) uses OPM data to produce an annual set of detailed statistical tables called *Federal Scientists and Engineers: 19--.* These reports present annual snapshots of the federal science and engineering work force and contain such descriptive data as occupation, agency, sex, highest degree level, primary work activity, management or supervisory status, median salary, and years of service.

Thus between these two reports there exist regularly published statistics that cover most of the required descriptive data. Some of the tabulations needed for sophisticated analyses such as median salary by age and occupation, necessary for salary comparisons between agencies or other employment sectors, can in principle be derived but are not available on a regular basis or sometimes not at all.

The principal advantage of the OPM data base is that it includes information on almost every federal employee who is classified in a science or engineering occupation; there is no sampling. An advantage of the published NSF data is that they show OPM data in compilations compatible with NSF data from other employment sectors. A disadvantage of the NSF tables is that NSF's definitions of scientist and engineer changed in 1984. Prior to this date individuals were included regardless of their highest academic degree; subsequently, only those with at least a baccalaureate degree have been included. Although this makes time-series analysis difficult, this deficiency is probably not serious except for engineers and computer specialists.

National Science Foundation: Descriptive data also can be obtained from the reports of the NSF's Scientific and Technical Personnel Data System (STPDS). These data are based on information specially generated for NSF from the decennial census, supplemented by information from regular surveys of the S&E work force identified in the census and of new S&E baccalaureate, master's, and doctorate recipients. The principal advantage of these data are better functional detail and classification by areas of critical national interest. Another possible advantage is that the information is provided by the individuals involved and thus may be more accurate. A major disadvantage is that the information is derived from a sample (about 3-4 percent in the case of most groups, 13 percent in the case of new doctorates). Thus small data cells will have relatively large sampling errors.

National Research Council: With the support of several federal agencies, the Research Council's Office of Scientific and Engineering Personnel collects and analyzes data on the nation's science and engineering doctorates biennially. Data elements are generally the same as those in the NSF surveys, but the NRC survey involves a sample that is somewhat larger than those in the above-mentioned NSF surveys.

Others: The Department of Defense (DoD) is in the midst of a survey of its S&E work force. The survey questions cover characteristics, possible quality indicators (college grade-point average, class standing, patents granted, publications, and awards), and job satisfaction.

The OPM data base does not cover the same universe as NSF's STPDS or the doctorate surveys of the NRC. OPM data identify individuals who are working in S&E occupations and can independently identify individuals by their academic discipline. The NSF system is based on adherence to 2 out of 3 criteria (field of degree, occupation, and self classification); the NRC system uses field of degree as its inclusion criterion. Consequently, the NSF system also covers individuals who have degrees in science and engineering but are not working in science and engineering occupations.

Dynamic Data

Information on the dynamics of the federal work force can be derived from the OPM data base. OPM data, which are collected monthly and compiled quarterly, include accession and separation rates. The latter provide information on different types of separation, such as resignations, retirement, discharge, and death. Accession data cover new hires and transfers. Accession and separation rates are reported on a fiscal year basis, and OPM officials indicate that these data are used primarily by federal central management agencies such as OPM and the Office of Management and Budget. Although specific operational agencies provide the data, they seldom request summaries or special compilations from OPM.

Mobility data developed periodically, but relatively infrequently, by NSF cover mobilities between sectors of employment, field of degree, and occupation. Information on mobility between federal agencies could be produced by OPM.

Projections

Estimates of likely future supply and demand relationships are extremely important for federal policies that can affect either one. For example, direct educational support can boost supply, and increases in highly technical programs such as those of the National Aeronautics and Space Administration (NASA) can stimulate demand. Although periodic projections are made by the Department of Labor, these generally cover all occupations and so provide a limited amount of detail on scientists and engineers. Several divisions of NSF produce more detailed projections of demand and supply of scientists and engineers, although some are limited to doctorates. A problem with the NSF projections is their relative infrequency, some being published as many as 8-10 years apart.

The NSF and especially the OPM data can be used by individual agencies to obtain an overall picture of the federal S&E work force, to obtain information about their own corps of scientists and engineers, and to compare themselves with other agencies and sectors of employment. However, it is important to determine whether these data are made readily available to the agencies and whether the agencies use them. Certainly some of the descriptive data are published biennially by NSF and OPM. However, operating agencies seem to seldom make use of the dynamic data collected by OPM, data that one might consider the most important for personnel management. Furthermore, it is not clear how useful such relatively highly aggregated data are for agencies' personnel management. Of course, it is possible that agencies themselves compile their own personnel data or develop projections of their own S&E demand and then relate them to the broader national projections produced by the NSF and the Department of Labor. Clearly any future study of the processes of federal S&E personnel management should examine these possibilities.

Descriptive Data

The numerical information shown below comes from NSF reports that compile OPM data in a form compatible with other NSF human resource data.

Overall Magnitude

The federal government is the largest single employer of scientists and engineers in the United States. NSF indicates that in 1988 there were 411,800 federally employed scientists and engineers, who constituted 7.5 percent of the total U.S. science and engineering work force. This is somewhat lower than the 10 percent reported in 1976. The NSF data indicate that in 1987 there were 27,532 federally employed S&E doctorates, accounting for about 6.6 percent of the national total.

Occupational Fields

OPM reports that in 1988 engineers were by far the largest group, accounting for 50 percent of the total federal scientists and engineers (Figure 1). The relative occupational distributions essentially have not changed from 1978 but those for doctorates are significantly different. Physical scientists made up the largest proportion (36 percent of doctorates), followed by life scientists (26 percent), engineers (14 percent), psychologists (10 percent), social scientists (7 percent), and mathematicians and computer scientists (6 percent).

Agency Distribution

In 1988, as reported by OPM, DoD employed the largest proportion (49 percent) of federal scientists and engineers, followed by the Department of Agriculture (USDA, 12.8 percent), Department of Interior (6.8 percent), NASA (5.5 percent), Department of Health and Human Services (HHS, 3.9 percent), and Department of Commerce (3.7 percent). This relative distribution has remained essentially unchanged since 1978, except that the domination by DoD was somewhat smaller that year, only 44 percent compared with the 49 percent reported in 1988. However, relative increases in the total number of scientists and engineers varied greatly by agency. Thus the number

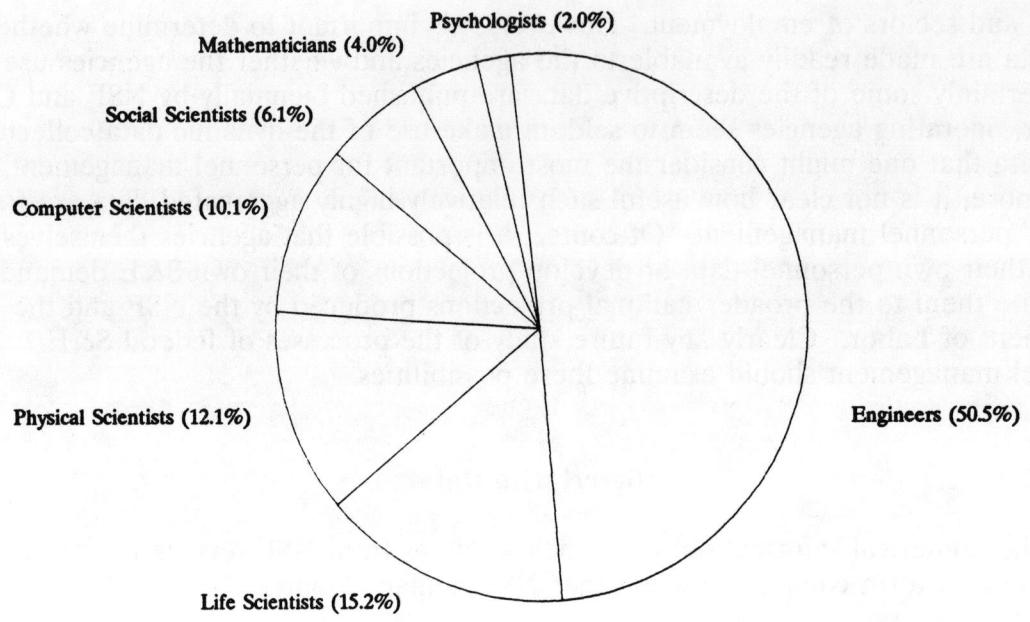

SOURCES: National Science Foundation, *Federal Scientists and Engineers: 1988*, Washington, D.C.: U.S. Government Printing Office; OPM data.

Figure 1. Federal scientists and engineers, by occupation, 1988.

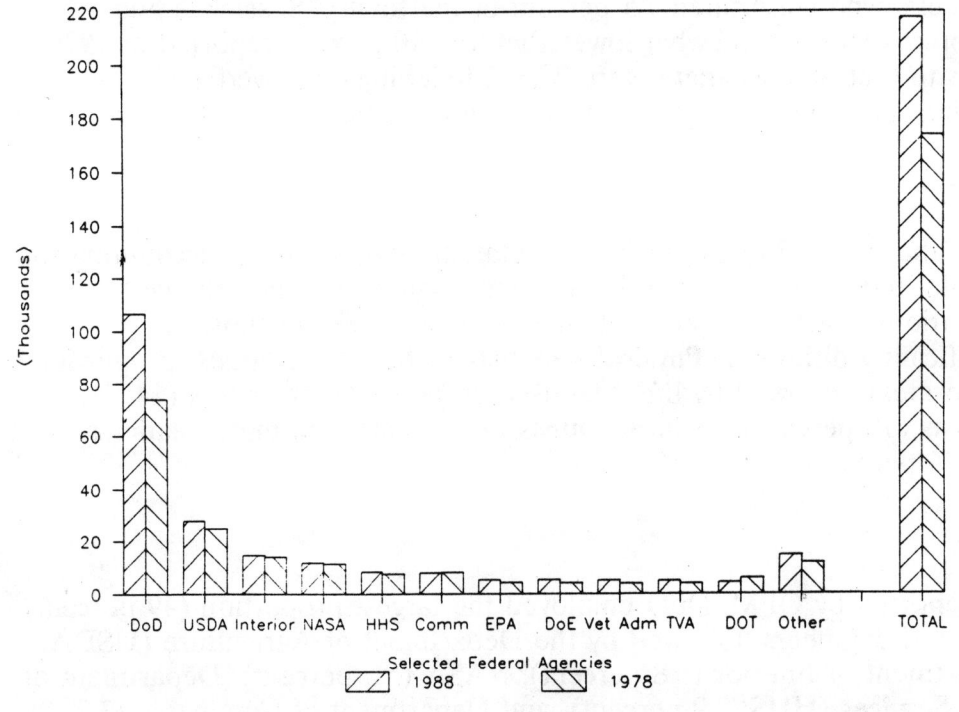

SOURCES: National Science Foundation, *Federal Scientists and Engineers: 1988* and *Federal Scientific and Technical Personnel: 1976, 1977, and 1978*, Washington, D.C.: U.S. Government Printing Office; OPM data.

Figure 2. Federal scientists and engineers, by agency, 1978 and 1988.

of S&E employees in DoD increased by 44 percent during that period, while in the Veterans Administration, Department of Energy, Department of Transportation, and Environmental Protection Agency increases were only in the 20-30 percent range (Figure 2). The Department of Commerce actually experienced a decrease of 2 percent.

Agency distributions by occupation are not too different from the overall distribution. DoD is still the leader in terms of engineers (67 percent), physical scientists (32 percent), mathematicians (56 percent), computer scientists (53 percent), and social scientists (33 percent). Only in the life sciences and psychology are other agencies ahead, led by USDA (63 percent) and the Veterans Administration (51 percent), respectively.

Because several agencies may work on a single issue of national concern, one cannot assume that distribution by agency reflects national interest or priority. For example, although EPA ranks only seventh among the agencies in terms of total S&E employment, the proportion of federal scientists and engineers who engage in environmentally related activities ranks second (Figure 3).

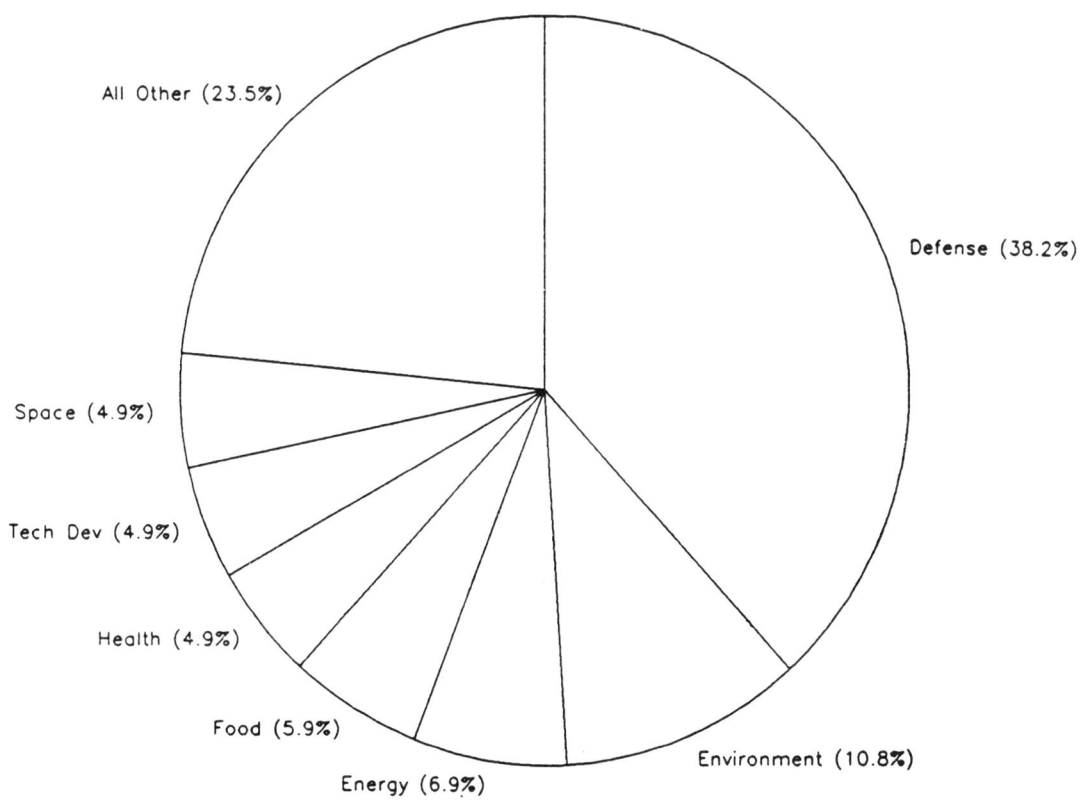

SOURCE: National Science Foundation, *Federal Scientists and Engineers: 1986*, Washington, D.C.: U.S. Government Printing Office, 1987.

Figure 3. Federal scientists and engineers, by area of national interest, 1986.

Areas of National Interest

To assess future federal requirements for scientists and engineers, it is useful to know what proportions are working now in areas of national interest. This will permit the development of some first-order dollar/manpower relationships. Of course, the substantive nature of future expansions of specific areas also has a major influence on future S&E requirements. Not surprisingly, NSF-generated data show that in 1986 defense activities used by far the greatest proportion of federal scientists and engineers (39 percent); this is true for scientists (26 percent) as well as for engineers (50 percent). Environmentally oriented activities were in second place, making up 11 percent of the total, and were also in second place with respect to scientists (16 percent) but in third place with respect to engineers (6 percent). Second place among engineers was the area of energy (9 percent), although with respect to all scientists and engineers, energy came in third (7 percent). Among scientists, food accounted for third place (11 percent).

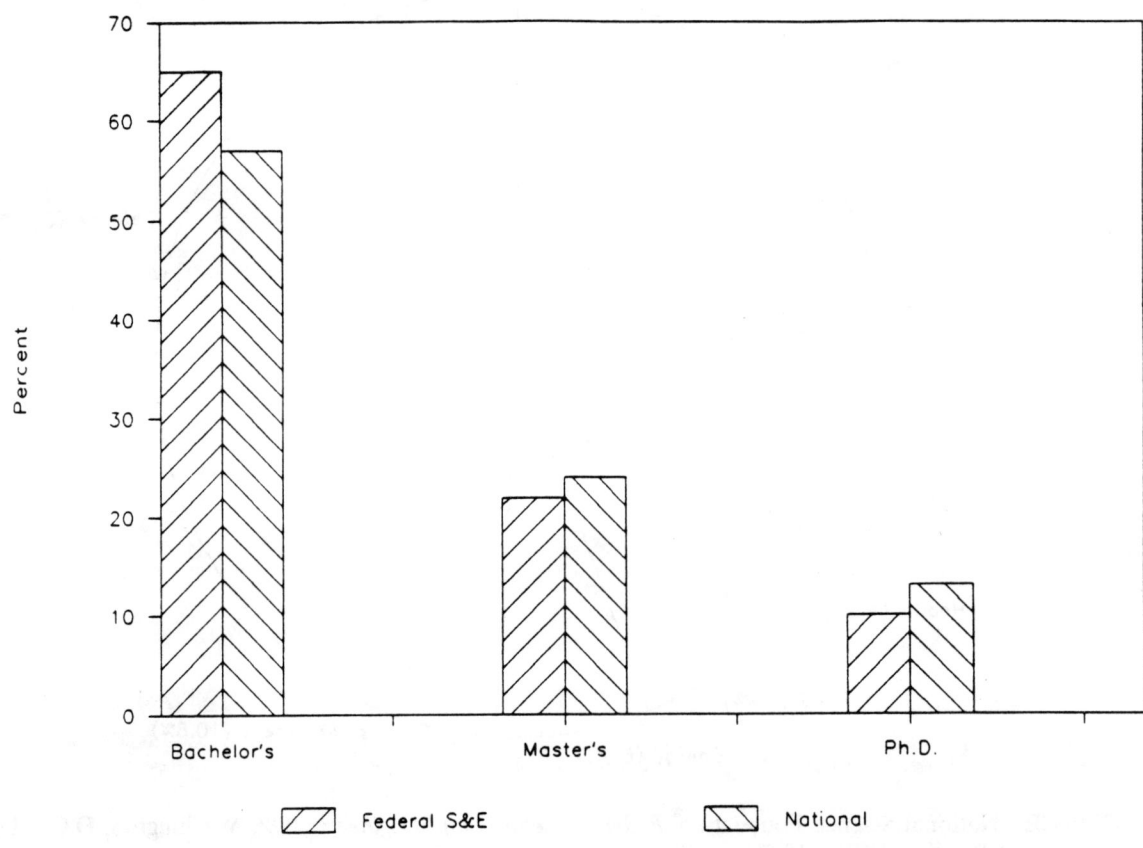

SOURCE: National Science Foundation, *Federal Scientists and Engineers: 1988*, Washington, D.C.: U.S. Government Printing Office, 1989.

Figure 4. Federal scientists and engineers, by highest academic degree earned, 1988 (in percent).

Highest Degree

The distribution of federal scientists and engineers by highest academic degree earned, as reported by OPM, is not too different from the national distribution derived from NSF data (Figure 4). Exceptions are that the proportion of baccalaureates is about 15 percent higher in the federal government, whereas the proportion of doctorates is lower by about 23 percent. These figures are not too surprising if one considers that academe, which constitutes about 15 percent of the national S&E work force, concentrates heavily on doctorates.

Academic degree distributions of scientists and engineers do vary considerably by occupation. For instance, 69 percent of the psychologists and 29 percent of the physical scientists in the federal government are Ph.D.s. The highest baccalaureate proportions are found in the computer sciences (78 percent) and life sciences (62 percent).

Primary Work Activity

Federal scientists and engineers are similar to the national total in that about 25 percent were engaged in R&D in 1988, about 6 percent were primarily engaged in management, and less than 1 percent were in R&D grant and contract administration (Figure 5).

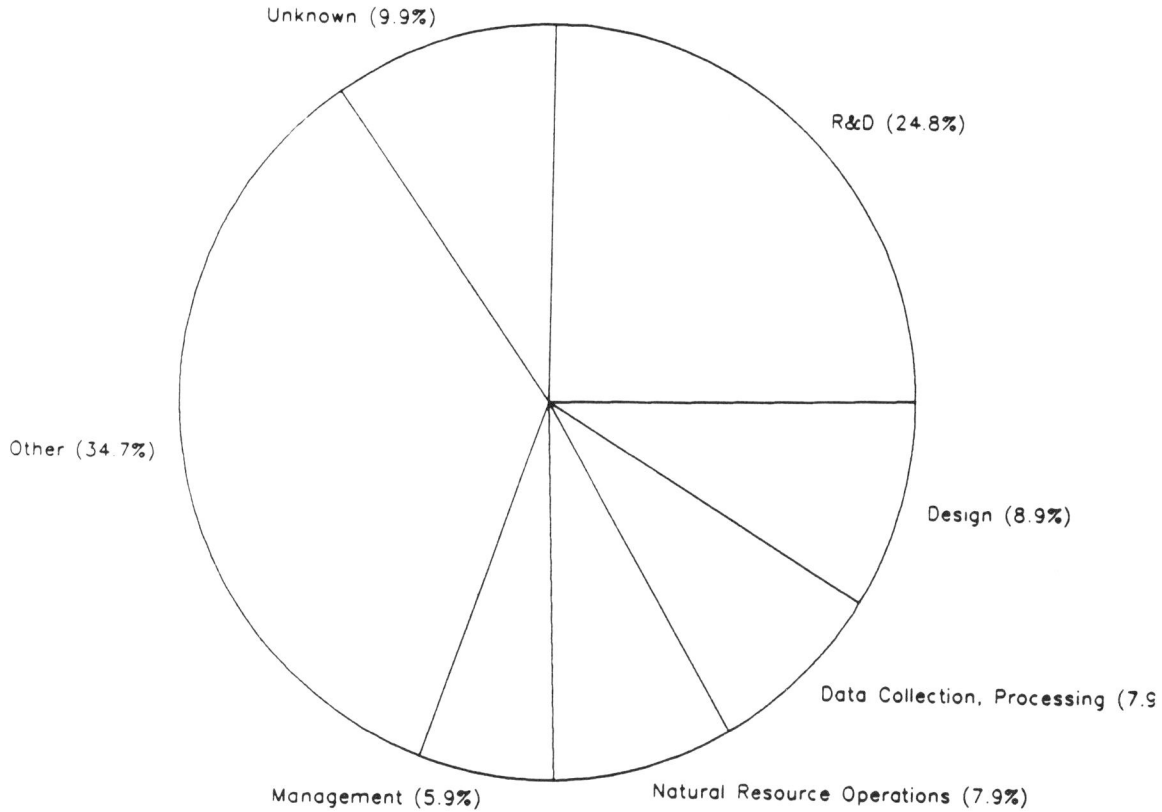

SOURCE: National Science Foundation, *Federal Scientists and Engineers: 1988*, Washington, D.C.: U.S. Government Printing Office, 1989.

Figure 5. Federal scientists and engineers, by primary work activity, 1988.

Sex and Race

In 1988 about 14 percent of federal scientists and engineers were female, and about 7 percent were black or Hispanic. These percentages are about the same as the national proportions. These relatively low figures have important implications for the future if the federal government or the nation should have difficulties in attracting sufficient numbers of scientists and engineers into their respective work forces.

Salary

The salaries of federal scientists and engineers, compared with those in other employment sectors, can be an important indicator of the federal government's competitiveness in the human resources marketplace. If one examines average salaries, developed from NSF surveys, the government seems to be at just about the same level as industry or academe, but this is not the case when an analysis is made by major occupational groups (Table 1). In the case of engineers, the average government salary is 2-5 percent lower than those of the other two sectors; for social scientists the federal figure is up to 40 percent higher. These data, which are so different from anecdotal information, are really not too meaningful. Further analyses are needed in terms of age and academic degree distributions. Although these data are in the NSF data bank, no published information is available.

One set of data that offers some insight at a more meaningful comparable level was provided by NSF's Surveys of Recent Science and Engineering Graduates. Table 2 shows such information for 1986. Compared to industry, the federal government does not seem to have very competitive salaries among new master's graduates in all fields

TABLE 1. Average Salary of Scientists and Engineers, by Sector of Employment and Occupation, 1986

Occupation	Federal Government	Industry	Four-Year College or University
Physical scientists	$39,000	$41,500	$40,800
Environmental scientists	40,100	37,700	40,800
Life scientists	33,300	33,300	34,700
Psychologists	39,300	32,200	39,400
Social scientists	40,700	28,700	39,600
Engineers	40,500	41,200	42,500
TOTAL	$39,800	$39,600	$39,200

SOURCE: National Science Foundation, *U.S. Scientists and Engineers: 1986,* Washington, D.C.: U.S. Government Printing Office, 1987.

TABLE 2. Median Salaries of Recent Science and Engineering Graduates, by Sector of Employment and Occupation, 1986

Occupation	Federal Government		Industry		Four-Year College or University	
	B.S.	M.S.	B.S.	M.S.	B.S.	M.S.
Scientists	$22,500	$26,300	$23,600	$34,000	$19,100	$22,600
Environmental scientists	18,400	26,300	21,600	31,000	17,000	17,000
Life scientists	18,600	*	18,000	*	16,000	*
Engineers	28,500	34,000	30,000	36,300	19,600	29,700
TOTAL	$27,300	$30,000	$29,100	$35,000	$19,100	$22,900

NOTE: The federal government employs too few physical scientists, psychologists, and social scientists for comparisons to be made with industry and academe.
* Too few federally employed master's degree recipients to compare sectors.
SOURCE: National Science Foundation, *Characteristics of Recent Science and Engineering Graduates: 1986*, Washington, D.C.: U.S. Government Printing Office, 1987.

for which data exist. For new baccalaureates the situation is somewhat different. At the overall level the government seems to be competitive. However, a field analysis shows that this must be attributable to favorable situations in the physical sciences, psychology, or the social sciences, because in the environmental sciences, engineering, and the life sciences the government was about 15 percent below industrial salaries. Interestingly, the narrowest gaps were in engineering at both the baccalaureate and the master's levels.

Age

Age distribution, particularly the proportion of those beyond the age of 55, will have a significant impact on the federal government's requirements for S&E replacements during the next decade. The 1986 distribution, compiled from OPM data, shows that 14 percent of the S&E work force are older than 55. Furthermore, there seems to be no significant variation in age distributions among the agencies that employ the greatest number of scientists and engineers.

Dynamic Data

Although considerable dynamic data are collected by OPM, very few compilations are made or published.

Length of Government Service

Length-of-service data published by OPM may provide some insight to what extent fresh

TABLE 3: Federal Scientists and Engineers in Selected Agencies, by Length of Service, 1988 (in percent)

Agency	Years			
	Less than 5	5-14	15-24	More than 25
Defense	25	34	24	16
Agriculture	16	36	28	21
Interior	14	43	27	17
NASA	20	24	20	36
Health & Human Services	26	31	29	14
Commerce	18	33	30	19
TOTAL	22	34	25	17

SOURCE: National Science Foundation, *Federal Scientists and Engineers: 1988,* Washington, D.C.: U.S. Government Printing Office, 1989.

points of view are injected into governmental science and technology activities. The data in Table 3 show that 17 percent of all government scientists and engineers have more than 25 years of federal service, and 22 percent have less than 5 years. These proportions do not seem excessive, but there are variations among agencies. NASA, for instance, seems to have an unusually large group, 36 percent, in the greater-than-25-years category; however, this is not attributable to a relatively small less-than-5-years group but rather to a considerably smaller 5-24-years group. The Interior Department has a relatively small group, 14 percent, in the less-than-5-years category because its 5-24-years group is unusually large.

Accession and Separation

These are probably two of the most important data elements that are not made available in regularly published form but that can be accessed by agencies. One might argue that there is no need to publish these data since they are mostly used for internal personnel management. On the other hand, such publicly available compilations (for example, by occupation and agency) would be useful for external reviews of the federal S&E work force as well as for studies by academics and other interested groups. Although accession and separation data usually can be generated on request, this often involves delays and expense to the user. A fringe benefit of published data would be the feedback received from users which, if acted upon, could make the data even more useful to analysts.

The following example derived from a special OPM run involves resignation rates, which can be indicative of job satisfaction. In 1988 the resignation rate of federal scientists and engineers was 2.1 percent, compared to 2.0 percent in 1978. This rate is fairly small, although the change may indicate some increase of unrest. In 1988 computer scientists had the highest resignation rate (3 percent). However, the resignation rates of physical scientists showed the greatest change from 1978 to 1988—from 1.4 percent to 2.1 percent.

Separation Reasons and Job Satisfaction

When separation rates are too high, especially among high-quality or high-grade personnel, it seems important to know the reasons for such separations. Furthermore, to prevent high separation rates or to improve effectiveness and efficiency, it is useful to know more about specifics of job dissatisfaction. No published compilations on job satisfaction were found, with the exception of a summary of a 1988 survey of former members of the Senior Executive Service. More than half of the Senior Executives surveyed left their jobs, in part, for monetary reasons: 57 percent because of the possibility of continued ceilings on executive salaries, 35 percent to obtain higher pay outside the government, and 42 percent because of possible changes in the retirement system. Also almost half gave one of the following nonmonetary reasons: criticism of federal workers (47 percent), politicalization of their agency (44 percent), knowledge and skills not being used appropriately (42 percent), and incompetence of immediate supervisors (39 percent).

Quality Indicators

It is extremely difficult to develop indicators that reflect the quality of personnel, especially of more experienced employees. For scientists and engineers engaged in fundamental research, bibliometric data could be a quality indicator. For newly graduated applicants, one could examine their SAT or GRE scores as well as the distribution of newly hired recent graduates of quality-rated universities. As for newly hired mature scientists and engineers, the quality of their previous employer and their position in their previous organization could possibly provide some insights into the quality question. As indicated earlier, DoD and OPM are experimenting with surveys that may provide data that could be used to develop some quality indicators.

Findings and Questions

Use of Data

A valuable data resource exists in OPM's Central Personnel Data File. Although OPM uses such data to develop pay policies, it is not clear to what extent this information is being used by other centralized units responsible for policies and practices that affect scientists and engineers in all federal agencies. Moreover, a cursory examination of the system seems to indicate that personnel units in individual agencies are not using this available central resource, and the reasons for this should be explored. Any future examination of the personnel management of federal scientists and engineers should evaluate the extent to which these data are being used or, in the case of individual agencies, possibly being duplicated.

Development of Quantitative Information

Any more detailed study of federal S&E personnel management should investigate the extent to which individual agencies are maintaining summaries of the descriptive and dynamic characteristics of their own S&E work force and have developed projections of their future needs.

Publication of Dynamic Statistics

Evaluations should be made of the need for periodical published compilations of data from OPM's Central Personnel Data File.

Missing Quantitative Information

Some data important to evaluating the effectiveness and efficiency of the federal S&E work force do not exist. Efforts should be made periodically to generate quantitative information on job satisfaction, reasons for separations, and quality of newly hired as well as experienced scientists and engineers. The current experimental efforts of the DoD and OPM are steps in the right direction.

Analyses of Future Federal S&E Personnel Needs

Analyses of personnel needs caused by changes in national priorities must not use agencies as surrogates for areas of national interest, for activity in such areas often is widely dispersed among many agencies. For example, the EPA is the seventh largest employer of scientists and engineers, yet the number of federal S&E employees who report environment as their primary area of involvement is the second largest group.

Occupation

Similarly, care has to be taken not to assume concentration of particular occupations on the basis of agency missions. For example, the largest number of life scientists are employed by the departments of Agriculture and Interior, not HHS. Also the largest number of psychologists are in the Veterans Administration, not HHS.

Salary Data

These data should always be reported by occupation, age, and highest degree. Failure to do so—that is, to report just median or average salaries only by agency or occupation—is likely to lead to misleading comparisons among sectors of employment, agencies, or occupations.

Projections

Federal agencies that develop national projections of the demand and supply of scientists and engineers should be encouraged to update and publish them more frequently.

Bibliography

National Science Foundation. 1981. *Federal Scientific and Technical Personnel: 1976, 1977, and 1978.* Washington, D.C.: U.S. Government Printing Office.

_____. 1987. *Characteristics of Recent Science and Engineering Graduates: 1986.* Washington, D.C.: U.S. Government Printing Office.

_____. 1987. *Federal Scientists and Engineers: 1986.* Washington, D.C.: U.S. Government Printing Office.

_____. 1987. *U.S. Scientists and Engineers: 1986.* Washington, D.C.: U.S. Government Printing Office.

_____. 1988. *Doctoral Scientists and Engineers: A Decade of Change.* Washington, D.C.: U.S. Government Printing Office.

_____. 1989. *Federal Scientists and Engineers: 1988.* Washington, D.C.: U.S. Government Printing Office.

U.S. Department of Labor. 1989. *Occupational Outlook Handbook: 1988/89.* Washington, D.C.: U.S. Government Printing Office.

U.S. Merit Systems Protection Board (MSPB). 1989. *The Senior Executive Service--Views of Former Federal Executives.* Washington, D.C.: MSPB.

U.S. Office of Personnel Management (OPM). 1987. *Occupations of Federal White-Collar and Blue-Collar Workers.* Washington, D.C.: OPM.

MEETING FEDERAL WORK FORCE NEEDS WITH REGARD TO SCIENTISTS AND ENGINEERS: THE ROLE OF THE U.S. OFFICE OF PERSONNEL MANAGEMENT

John M. Palguta
Deputy Director, Office of Policy and Evaluation
U.S. Merit Systems Protection Board

The Environment

The concept of work force management encompasses a number of related tasks. Recruiting, training, motivating, and retaining employees and planning for future work force needs are all part of the picture. Management of the approximately 2.2 million members of the federal civilian work force (not counting the U.S. Postal Service) is especially challenging given the worldwide scope and impact of government operations, the wide diversity in its various tasks and missions, and the massive number of highly skilled employees and occupations required to accomplish the goals and objectives of government.

Created under the Civil Service Reform Act of 1978 (CSRA), the U.S. Office of Personnel Management (OPM) was assigned major, but by no means sole, responsibility for federal work force management. Indeed, a major thrust of the Reform Act was to provide greater flexibility and creativity to federal personnel management. This flexibility is achieved in part through greater delegation of personnel management authority and responsibility to each federal agency. Congress continues to play a major role in providing the framework of civil service law within which work force management in the executive branch must operate.

The CSRA also established the U.S. Merit Systems Protection Board (MSPB) as the successor agency to the U.S. Civil Service Commission. MSPB serves as part of the checks and balances built into the federal merit system by the CSRA. In addition to government-wide responsibility for adjudication of employee appeals, MSPB is charged with the conduct of special studies of the civil service system and annual oversight reviews of OPM. Reports of these studies are addressed to the President and Congress.

Many of the MSPB studies over the last 10 years have dealt with the issue of recruitment and selection. This is one of the more crucial components of effective work force management inasmuch as each new federal employee serves as a building block upon which so much of the success of government must depend. Entry-level recruitment—that is, recruitment of employees at the start of a career ladder—represents an especially important element in this process because it involves the potential of a long-term mutual commitment and investment. Indeed, the realization that government and the nation are best served by employees selected for their ability to do the job led to the establishment, more than a century ago, of a merit-based civil service system through passage of the Civil Service Act of 1883.

The importance of an effective recruitment program for scientists and engineers was recently underscored by an MSPB study of federal employee turnover. In its report of that study, MSPB (1989a) notes that turnover rates vary widely based on occupation, agency, geographic location, and employee demographics, yet overall turnover among many engineering and scientific occupations is lower than the government-wide average. For example, only about 5 percent (or less) of all engineers, computer specialists, chemists, physicists, and geologists left the government during 1987 compared to an average turnover rate of 9 percent for government as a whole. Further, almost half of the turnover among these engineers and scientists was attributable to retirement rather than resignation. The point is that, so far, the federal government has been able to retain its engineers and scientists at a reasonable rate once it recruits them. This further accentuates the need to be concerned about the initial intake of these individuals to assure that high-quality candidates are available and selected. A high retention rate is of little value if the individuals being retained are only marginally adequate.

The duties performed by federal engineers and scientists can greatly affect the quality of our national defense, environment, and health. The effectiveness of these individuals depends in part on the training and developmental opportunities they are provided, the quality of their supervision, the ability of their organizations to make good use of their skills, and their willingness to remain with the government long enough to make a significant contribution. It also depends, of course, on what they bring into government in the way of fundamental skills, knowledge, and abilities. The government's skill as a recruiter, therefore, has a major impact on the competency level of its work force.

The Federal Government as Recruiter

In its 1988 report on the federal government's ability to attract college graduates to employment, MSPB found that:

> The Government is not perceived as an "employer of choice" by many graduates of some of the country's most highly rated academic institutions. Furthermore, even among those graduates who have a positive view of the Government as an employer, many are perplexed by the "civil service hiring labyrinth" and find little active encouragement on the part of most federal agencies. This raises concerns about the future quality of the federal work force and its ability to effectively and efficiently carry out the necessary functions of Government."

Part of that report dealt with the perceptions of deans or college placement officials from nine highly rated schools of engineering with regard to the attitudes and experiences of the students within the engineering curriculum. Engineering positions account for one of the ten most populous occupational areas in the federal government typically staffed with recent college graduates at the career entry level. Furthermore, although the total number of federal employees has remained remarkably stable for more than 20 years, the number and thus the proportion of employees who are in engineering and scientific occupations has steadily increased. From 1965 to 1985 the number of engineers employed by the federal government increased by 50 percent to approximately 103,000. To maintain a viable work force of scientists and engineers, normal attrition alone requires that several thousand new engineers and scientists be hired each year. For example, in 1985 there were approximately 87,500 employees in the six most populous engineering disciplines and approximately 5,000 hires into entry-level (GS-5 and -7) positions in those occupations. (The total number of positions in each of the six most populous engineering disciplines were electronics engineers, 24,033; general engineers, 19,569; civil engineers, 16,755; mechanical engineers, 13,583; aerospace engineers, 8,700; and electrical engineers, 4,810.)

Despite the relatively large numbers, federal agencies to date have been able to fill most of their scientific and engineering vacancies. Unfortunately, numbers do not tell the whole story. The MSPB study also found that the government's ability to hire its "fair share of the best and brightest" is, for the most part, severely limited. This limitation appears to be most strongly linked to perceptions of noncompetitive salaries and a poor public image of the federal government as an employer.

Although the federal government's ability to systematically assess the quality of its employees is rather rudimentary, there is enough anecdotal evidence to cause concern. For example, in his prepared testimony in March 1986 before the House Subcommittee on Science, Research, and Technology of the Committee on Science and Technology, David Packard, chairman of the board of Hewlett-Packard and a former deputy secretary of defense, noted that:

> Defense Department data show that the aptitude scores of newly hired [DoD] scientists and engineers are declining relative to national norms, [and that] faced with problems in recruiting, federal agencies often have to choose between accepting a less qualified candidate or leaving a position vacant.

Given that 70 percent of all federal engineers work for the Department of Defense, this is a worrisome finding. Nor is this an isolated perception. In a 1986 MSPB survey returned by a representative cross-section of more than 16,000 federal employees, the Board asked supervisors whether the quality of applicants for different categories of job vacancies in their work group had improved, remained the same, or worsened during the previous four years. Commenting on the quality of the applicants for GS-5-7 entry-level professional or administrative positions, more than a third (36 percent) of the supervisors thought that applicant quality had declined. Three years later, a similar MSPB survey revealed that 42 percent of all supervisors who tried to fill GS-5-7 entry-level professional or administrative positions believed that applicant quality had declined.

Obstacles to Effective Recruitment

If the federal government is not recruiting a sufficient number of well-qualified engineers and scientists, the question remains "Why not?" Effective recruitment of well-qualified candidates requires that at least three interdependent conditions exist:

1. **An effective recruiter has the ability to make employment opportunities known to prime candidates.** Even the most desirable job opportunities will go begging if

qualified candidates are not aware of them.

2. **An effective recruiter has the ability to interest highly qualified candidates in seeking employment once they are aware of the opportunities.** Jobs with noncompetitive compensation packages or with duties and responsibilities that hold little intrinsic interest to candidates are understandably more difficult to fill. In addition, organizations that have the reputation—deserved or not—of being an undesirable place to work also will have difficulty recruiting quality candidates.

3. **An effective recruiter has a hiring process in place that allows selection to occur in a timely manner and in a way that identifies those most likely to be successful on the job.** Being able to entice the "best and brightest" to apply for a job will be of little value if it takes months to process their applications. On the other hand, a speedy selection process is only useful if it also makes valid qualitative distinctions among candidates.

Based on these criteria, the federal government is not, for the most part, an effective recruiter of entry-level scientists and engineers. Except for the individual efforts of a few federal agencies at selected universities, the federal government is not seen as having an effective presence on college campuses. For example, when MSPB asked informed representatives from nine different schools of engineering if there were ways the federal government could improve its recruitment efforts, eight of the nine said there were and offered suggestions. The suggestions fell into two categories: (1) better and more active recruitment and (2) increased entry-level salaries. One respondent summed up the first point by noting, "Federal agencies must aggressively recruit students. Notice of vacancies and requesting submission of an application will not get the top students to apply." Another respondent said:

> Private industry is a formidable competitor for highly motivated engineering/computer science students, and particularly in the high tech fields, seems to offer more interesting career opportunities. Students have the impression that starting salaries are better in industry and that the differential continues over several years and adversely affects total potential career income.

On the issue of salary, although different methods for calculating salary comparisons between the federal government and private industry yield different results, all of the major comparisons that have been done show that the federal government pays less, often significantly less, at the entry level for scientists and engineers. For example, the Department of Labor's Professional, Administrative, Technical, and Clerical survey concluded that, as of March 1987, a federal engineer at a GS-5 salary level of $19,303 made 50 percent less than a private sector counterpart at $28,958, and at a GS-7 salary level of $23,956, an engineer in the federal government still made more than a third less than a private sector counterpart at $32,295.

Despite the salary differentials in some locations, the federal government still attracts at least some proportion of available candidates for its entry-level science and engineering positions. Assuming more than one qualified candidate is available for a given position, the competitive process for distinguishing among these candidates is an "unassembled" examination. Candidates do not assemble for a written test but rather are assigned a rating based on their education and experience as described in their applications. In the past, all applicants submitted their applications to OPM, which assigned each candidate a rating and then waited for a federal agency to request a list of names for a specific vacancy. Even if an agency had identified a candidate and submitted that person's application, it could still take months for the application to be rated and a determination made as to whether the candidate was among the "top three" compared to other candidates--including veterans entitled to extra credit for "veterans preference."

Currently, however, because the number of applicants for federal science and engineering positions has been so meager, the majority of scientists and engineers are reportedly hired into government through "direct hire" authorities. OPM may and increasingly has delegated direct hire authority to agencies when there is a shortage of candidates. Such an authority allows a federal agency to directly recruit, rate, rank, and hire qualified candidates. Because the agency controls the entire process, it can work rather quickly. Unfortunately, the current environment requires that the agency concentrate more on finding a qualified candidate to hire rather than trying to select the best-qualified from among a number of well-qualified applicants.

This transition to a more active role on the part of agencies also has created some confusion for the applicants. If an outside applicant should be interested in federal employment, perhaps because of the allure of an agency's mission or the unique facilities available in some agencies, he or she may find it difficult to discover how to apply for a job. In some cases the applicants can apply directly to the agency, but in other cases they must apply through OPM. Compounding the problem, not all agencies have accepted the increased responsibility for recruiting and disseminating information, which goes along with their increased examining and hiring authority.

Even when multiple outside candidates are available for a particular vacancy, the unassembled rating process historically has not done a very precise job of ranking them. Notwithstanding the impreciseness of the rating process, civil service law still requires selections to be made from among the three candidates assigned the highest ratings. Scores assigned to new college graduates, however, tend to cluster at the high end with little differentiation among them. In the past, applicants interested in different geographic areas would apply to different OPM regional offices to be rated. It was not unusual for the same applicant to receive different ratings from different offices even though each regional office applied the same criteria. Therefore, the ability of the federal government to meet even the last criteria of an effective recruiter—the ability to make valid qualitative distinctions among applicants—is suspect for engineers and scientists.

The Role of OPM

In a recent assessment of the first 10 years of the OPM, the MSPB Board (1989b) noted that under the Civil Service Reform Act, OPM was expected to:

- delegate personnel management authorities judiciously to other federal agencies, including authority to conduct

- competitive examinations, to enhance the operation of the federal civil service system within the context of the merit system principles;
- establish and maintain an aggressive oversight program to ensure that federal personnel management authorities are being used in accordance with the merit system principles and to gather data and analyses that will help improve the civil service system;
- conduct or facilitate the conduct of research and demonstration projects to ultimately develop more effective or efficient methods of human resource management; and
- execute, administer, and enforce civil service laws, rules, and regulations, for the president, as one aspect of the provision of leadership and guidance to the federal civil service system. This leadership is to be evidenced by active improvement efforts in a number of important personnel management areas, including the government's ability to recruit and retain highly qualified employees.

Although actual practice is more muddled, a reasonable division of labor in the recruitment of scientists and engineers is for OPM to play a major role by providing leadership, guidance, and oversight of the process. On the other hand, individual federal agencies are usually in the better position to carry primary responsibility for actual recruitment, examination, and hiring. Through both necessity and deliberate planning, OPM is starting to move in this direction (MSPB, 1989c). Ironically, decentralization of examining and hiring authority was largely the situation that existed in the mid to late 1960s until individual agency Boards of Examiners were consolidated into centralized Interagency Boards staffed by the then Civil Service Commission.

The philosophy behind this earlier centralization of examining authority was somewhat akin to that of the old typing pools, which was thought to be a more cost-efficient method of carrying out a repetitive function. It also was intended to provide greater quality control to the process and assure its integrity. Unfortunately, under centralization, quality proved to be an elusive variable to measure, let alone provide. It's also difficult to judge whether the integrity of the process was any greater under centralized examining because, except for some relatively isolated incidents, the integrity of the decentralized process was not found to be seriously compromised. On the other hand, timeliness of response to applicants (and, many would argue, the general responsiveness to legitimate agency needs) clearly suffered under centralization. What was different, however, was the greater number of applicants available in the late 1960s and early 1970s compared to today. The earlier excess supply of applicants relative to demand forgave some inefficiency, whereas today's tight labor market requires more efficient and effective recruiting, examining, and hiring—with little margin for error.

Although OPM seems committed to the goal of greater decentralization of examining authority, many federal agencies still need to shift gears and accept greater responsibility for active on-campus recruitment. The few agencies that already do so report generally favorable results. OPM should provide centralized assistance through general oversight and coordination, centralized job information, and research into more effective screening and selection techniques. Fortunately, there are indications that OPM is starting to accelerate its efforts in these areas.

Even the best recruitment efforts, however, cannot entirely overcome the obstacles presented by low pay and poor image. Congress shares responsibility and ultimately must be involved in any long-term solution to the issue of noncompetitive salaries and the negative image of federal employment. Although the government's current compensation system is generally seen as counterproductive and ineffectual, there is not yet agreement on the best solution to this problem.

The illogic of the pay situation was highlighted in a recent analysis by OPM and the Wyatt Company in a study of federal white-collar pay (OPM, 1989). Part of their analyses shows that an engineer hired into a federal position at the GS-5 level in January 1986 would have received a salary of $18,710, compared to a private sector counterpart who would have received the significantly higher starting salary of $27,670. However, because of the more rapid rate of advancement in the federal government, after four years both engineers could expect to be paid an average annual salary of $39,000. To achieve the goal of recruiting highly qualified engineers and scientists, how much better it would be for the government to have salaries that more closely match the private sector at the front end, even if that meant less rapid salary increases for the next few years. A recent budget proposal by OPM recognizes this fact by calling for a 5 percent increase in salary levels targeted specifically to GS-5 and -7 entry-level positions. In addition, over time OPM has authorized special salary rates for close to 200,000 hard-to-fill white-collar positions in specific occupations and geographic areas. Unfortunately, this patchwork approach does not obviate the need to reexamine the government's whole approach to compensation setting (see also MSPB, 1989d).

The fundamental changes needed in the federal compensation system will require congressional legislation, but OPM still has a significant role to play by proposing legislation. To their credit, OPM's proposed Civil Service Simplification Act of 1986 would have addressed some compensation-related problems, but it did not pass. OPM, as of this writing, is working on a new legislative proposal that will again attempt to address some of the issues requiring changes in the laws covering pay. A built-in limitation of the effectiveness of any OPM proposal may be OPM's stated belief that for any compensation legislation to be viable, it must be budget neutral. Unfortunately, no empirical evidence suggests that the most effective legislation would meet that criteria.

The federal personnel situation is not entirely grim, however. The relatively modest turnover rate among engineers and scientists suggests that the perception of the government as an undesirable employer is not fully shared by those in the best position to judge—that is, current employees. Indeed MSPB surveys have consistently found a very high level of job satisfaction among federal employees even though they also expressed dissatisfaction with certain aspects of the work environment, such as pay. For example, a representative sample of almost 16,000 federal employees were surveyed in the summer of 1989, and 70 percent agreed with the statement "In general, I am satisfied with my current job." Additionally, among those same employees, 88 percent agreed that they find their work meaningful. Efforts to improve the image of the federal government as an employer should build on the fundamental value of and interest in the work to be done within government. Image improvement, of course, must be a joint effort on the part of OPM, Congress, and the administration.

Conclusions

Efforts to manage the federal work force today must operate in an environment that is significantly different from 20 years ago. Although some of the related organizational and decision-making processes in place 20 years ago were effective at that time, there is evidence that they are effective no longer. Shifting demographics, the rapidly changing international climate, and the declining image of federal employment all argue for some fundamental shifts in the way federal personnel management is carried out. This may be especially true as the government struggles to recruit, motivate, and retain a large cadre of well-qualified engineers and scientists.

A recent MSPB report (1989c) found wide support among federal agency managers and personnel specialists for the concept of "simplification" of the federal personnel system insofar as that concept embodied the goals of increased decentralization and delegation of personnel authorities. "One size fits all" solutions to the problems of managing the huge federal work force no longer work, if they ever did.

The role of OPM in this changing environment is also being redefined. Rather than serve as the central hiring hall for government, OPM's role is better seen as providing guidelines and helping to provide the tools for individual federal agencies to wield in conjunction with an increase in their delegated personnel management authorities, including examining authorities. It is no longer a question of "doing more with less" but rather of "doing the best with what we have."

Although hampered by its own resource cutbacks, OPM has undertaken a number of recent and promising initiatives on a number of fronts. Part of the challenge will be in OPM's ability to follow through on these efforts. Even in areas where OPM's influence is less evident—such as the training and development of engineers and scientists and the degree to which their skills and abilities are well utilized—OPM has an impact by setting the policies, guidelines, and often the structure (e.g., the federal position classification system) governing activity in these areas.

Recommendations

MSPB has suggested that the future activities of OPM should reflect the following qualities:

- OPM should continue its renewed efforts to delegate personnel management authorities to the agencies but within the following parameters:

    - Delegations must not be abdications. OPM should closely monitor the ability of each federal agency to manage its responsibilities in a manner consistent with the underlying merit system principles.
    - Delegations should be accompanied, where appropriate, with the necessary support structures or guidance to assist in the use of these delegations.
    - When centralized examinations are still a useful option because of the number of applicants or the nature of the process, OPM has sought and should continue to seek methods for making the process as fast and efficient as possible. In this regard, OPM also should continue to

- encourage active involvement by other federal agencies in the development of the examinations.

- OPM must continue recent initiatives to develop its internal research capability so that it can provide timely legislative proposals, recommend Presidential initiatives, and develop improved personnel management tools that can be adapted to the varied needs of individual federal agencies.
- OPM needs to demonstrate leadership in causing or influencing constructive change to the federal civil service system in response to the changing demands and pressures. One measure of success might be the introduction within the next five years of a fair and equitable compensation structure consistent with the goal of attracting and retaining a highly qualified and motivated work force.
- Individual federal agencies, for their part, need to accept greater responsibility for recruiting and selecting new scientists and engineers. Part of that responsibility includes an ongoing college relations program. Furthermore, individual managers within many agencies need to play a more active role in the process. This is not an activity to be left solely to the personnel office—it's a shared responsibility.

Finally, solutions to the problems facing the federal government as it tries to recruit and retain well-qualified engineers and scientists must, of necessity, extend beyond the scope of OPM's role. For example, if a basic problem is ultimately that this nation's schools, colleges, and universities are producing an insufficient number of engineers and scientists, the long-range solution must aim at correcting that deficiency—something clearly beyond OPM's mandate, but not beyond the scope of federal involvement at some level (e.g., see Commission on Workforce Quality, 1989).

In the same vein, an argument can be made that federal managers need even more flexibility to address unique staffing problems, but that those flexibilities extend beyond what OPM can provide without changes to current civil service law. Congress, therefore, must be involved. The point is that we need more than a cosmetic reconfiguration of existing organizational and decision-making processes; some broader and more fundamental changes must be considered. Although some restructuring or further delegations of personnel authorities within the executive branch may well be necessary, we cannot afford to stop our search there. The stakes are simply too high.

Bibliography

Commission on Workforce Quality and Labor Market Efficiency. 1989. *Investing In People: A Strategy To Address America's Workforce Crisis.* Washington, D.C.: U.S. Department of Labor.

U.S. Merit Systems Protection Board (MSPB). 1988. *Attracting Quality Graduates to the Federal Government: A View of College Recruiting.* Washington, D.C.: MSPB.

_____. 1989a. *Who Is Leaving the Federal Government? An Analysis of Turnover.* Washington, D.C.: MSPB.

_____. 1989b. *U.S. Office of Personnel Management and the Merit System: A Retrospective Assessment.* Washington, D.C.: MSPB.

_____. 1989c. *Delegation and Decentralization: Personnel Management Simplification Efforts in Federal Government.* Washington, D.C.: MSPB.

_____. 1989d. *OPM's Classification and Qualification Systems: A Renewed Emphasis, A Changing Perspective.* Washington, D.C.: MSPB.

U.S. Office of Personnel Management (OPM). 1989. *Federal White-Collar Pay System: A Report on a Market-Sensitive Study.* Washington, D.C.: OPM.

DIFFERENCES IN RECRUITMENT, RETENTION, AND UTILIZATION PROCESSES: A COMPARISON OF TRADITIONALLY OPERATED FEDERAL LABORATORIES, M&O FACILITIES, AND DEMONSTRATION PROJECTS

Sheldon B. Clark
Senior Research Scientist, Labor and Policy Studies Program
Oak Ridge Associated Universities

Introduction

Concerns about the growing inability of the federal government to attract and retain the "best and brightest" scientists and engineers in the civil service have been persistent and well documented. Inadequate compensation is sometimes singled out as the most important factor limiting the government's ability to recruit and retain a highly qualified science and engineering (S&E) work force. On the other hand, low S&E salaries are considered by some to be merely a symptom of a more general problem—the inflexible policies and procedures of the civil service personnel system. Civil service laboratories,[1] which employ a significant proportion of the federal S&E work force, tend to view this external personnel system as a monolithic adversary that has little appreciation for the special needs of the research enterprise, especially its researchers and managers.

This paper examines, in comparison with personnel systems unlike the federal civil service system,[2] some of the elements believed to hinder the federal government's ability to attract and retain high-quality scientists and engineers. One of the alternative systems considered here is the management-and-operating-contractor (M&O) model, which the Department of Energy (DOE) uses for most of its laboratories. (M&O facilities were formerly referred to as government-owned, contractor-operated [GOCO] facilities.) Another group of alternative systems discussed in this paper includes two federal personnel demonstration projects. Also considered is a special-case federal agency, which has personnel policies and procedures that are markedly different from those of civil service agencies. For some problems, examples are drawn from traditional civil service labs that have developed means of coping with particular limitations of the civil service system.

---

[1] The term "civil service laboratories" is used in this paper to mean those government labs that are staffed by employees of the U.S. government who are covered by federal personnel law as contained in Title 5 of the U.S. Code of Federal Regulations.

[2] In this paper these personnel systems are referred to as "alternative systems."

Alternative Systems Considered

DOE M&O Contractor Facilities

DOE has a system of 67 M&O facilities operated by a variety of contractors—private-sector firms, universities, and university consortia. Since each of the operating contracts is negotiated separately with DOE, personnel policies and procedures vary significantly from one installation to another. The four M&Os that serve as the basis for comments in this paper are Argonne National Laboratory (ANL), Sandia National Laboratories (SNL), Oak Ridge National Laboratory (ORNL), and Oak Ridge Associated Universities (ORAU). ANL is managed by the University of Chicago; SNL by the Sandia Corporation; ORNL by Martin Marietta; and ORAU by a consortium of 55 colleges and universities.

Demonstration Projects

Demonstration projects are conducted or supervised by the Office of Personnel Management (OPM) to determine whether a specified change in personnel practices or procedures will result in improved federal personnel management. Such projects are typically designed to yield more flexible personnel systems that are more responsive to the needs of individual agencies. This paper examines two demonstration projects affecting white-collar workers in the demonstration laboratories: one involving two Department of the Navy labs, which began in July 1980 and is still under way; and one involving the National Institute of Standards and Technology (NIST), which began in January 1988 and was approved for five years.

Tennessee Valley Authority (TVA)

From its inception in 1933, TVA was given broad authority to establish its own personnel policies and procedures without regard to most civil service rules. One indication of the differences between TVA and civil service agencies is the volume of regulations governing its personnel system. TVA has fewer than 250 pages of policy guidance for personnel issues, compared to the more than 900 pages of regulations published by OPM to cover the same areas. The TVA personnel manual, which provides procedural guidance to personnel staff, contains about 800 pages, compared to the more than 6,000 pages that serve a similar purpose for OPM.

TVA's system provides for a great deal of management discretion and much employee involvement through employee unions. TVA's ability to make relatively major and timely changes in personnel policies and procedures can be valuable in meeting new or changing demands. By comparison, civil service agencies operate under a personnel system based more heavily on external controls and limited options for managers in the personnel process (U.S. Merit Systems Protection Board, 1989).

Selected Civil Service Laboratories

In addition to the above organizations, which have personnel systems that do not operate under normal civil service policies and procedures, a few positive examples in this paper are drawn from civil service labs that have devised methods of overcoming particular limitations imposed by the civil service system. These examples happen to be from the U.S. Army laboratory system (Clark et al., 1987), but they should be considered neither unique to that organization nor necessarily typical of it. In fact, the Army lab directors who reported on these methods of coping with civil service limitations stirred considerable interest among other Army lab directors.

Problems Identified in Civil Service Policies and Procedures

Identifying problems associated with the federal government's difficulty in attracting and retaining highly qualified scientists and engineers has long been the topic of many intra-agency, interagency, and external reviews. One way to gain insight into what the laboratories perceive to be their problems in this area is to examine the objectives of the demonstration projects undertaken to overcome these problems.

Navy Demonstration Project

The two Navy demonstration laboratories are the Naval Weapons Center (NWC) in China Lake, Calif., and the Naval Ocean Systems Center (NOSC) in San Diego. This demonstration project involved 3,076 white-collar employees at NOSC and 4,579 at NWC as of January 1988. About 50 percent of these employees were scientists and engineers. Two control laboratories also were chosen—the Naval Air Development Center in Warminster, Pa., and the Naval Surface Weapons Center in Dahlgren, Va., and White Oak, Md.

Prior to beginning the project, NWC identified its problems as (a) difficulties in recruiting adequate numbers of qualified personnel due to noncompetitive starting salaries and (b) troubles in retaining qualified senior personnel because of limited promotional opportunities above the GS-12 level. Many GS-12 scientists and engineers were leaving NWC for jobs in industry after 5-8 years because they saw little likelihood of being promoted to the GS-13 level. NOSC believed that its line managers (a) lacked flexibility in making work assignments because the General Schedule (GS) position classification process required too much paperwork and time and (b) were hindered in their ability to administer personnel resources effectively because the classification process was in the hands of personnel specialists rather than line managers.

The Navy demonstration instituted changes to the GS system in the areas of classification, performance appraisal, and pay. The project was designed to demonstrate that the effectiveness of civil service labs could be enhanced by allowing greater managerial control over personnel functions and by expanding opportunities available to employees through a more flexible personnel system (U.S. General Accounting Office [GAO], 1988b).

NIST Demonstration Project

The NIST demonstration involves both NIST labs—one in Gaithersburg, Md., and one in Boulder, Colo. This project covers all 3,050 NIST white-collar employees, more than 50 percent of whom are scientists and engineers. A comparison group consists of white-collar employees in selected Department of Commerce laboratories in Boulder. The project uses many of the same interventions that the Navy demonstration uses to meet similar objectives. One major difference is that NIST has set the goal of making the project budget-neutral throughout the five-year demonstration period, not just the first year, as required by law. NIST intends to accomplish this goal, despite the higher salaries expected under the new personnel system, by using fewer employees or employees with lower GS grades.

The objectives of the NIST demonstration are as follows:

1. To improve hiring procedures and to be more competitive for high-quality researchers through direct hiring and selective use of higher entry salaries and recruiting allowances;
2. To increase the motivation and retention of staff through higher pay potential, pay for performance, more responsive personnel systems, and selective use of retention allowances;
3. To strengthen the manager's role in personnel management by delegating personnel authority to him or her; and
4. To increase the efficiency of personnel systems by installing a simpler and more flexible classification system. The system is characterized by pay banding; automation; and a reduction of guidelines, steps, and paperwork in classification, hiring, and other personnel tasks. (OPM, 1989)

Recruitment of Scientists and Engineers

Interrelationship of Problems

The issues of recruitment, retention, and utilization may be conceptually different, but in practice they are inextricably linked. In the present context they share a common origin, the civil service personnel system, that influences all three through its policies and procedures. This centralized and external personnel authority slows down the hiring process, limits compensation options, and restricts the authority of managers to handle personnel matters. In addition to the effects of the policies and procedures themselves, such centralization of authority has been shown to be associated with poor morale, which in turn is associated with high turnover rates. Realizing that recruitment, retention, and utilization overlap in many respects, we shall now discuss certain elements of each and indicate how the alternative personnel systems are different from the traditional civil service system.

Role of University Interactions

In studying the disadvantages civil service laboratories have in recruiting scientists and engineers, one of the primary emphases has been on salary offers that are not competitive with those of private industry. NIST, for example, reports that 50 percent of its newly hired scientists and engineers had another job offer at a higher salary than NIST (OPM, 1988).

Clark et al. (1987), on the other hand, point out that salary is not necessarily the determining factor in recruiting success. They report that labs successful in recruiting high-quality scientists and engineers differed from their less successful counterparts in the perceived importance of developing and maintaining university ties. As one DOE lab director stated, "You have to recruit all the time—not just when you need to hire someone. University contacts are too important not to maintain." Labs with successful recruiting programs were emphatic about the significant positive effects of maintaining close ties with universities—through such activities as faculty and student research participation programs, consulting arrangements, lecture programs, participation in academic professional societies, and equipment-sharing programs. They felt that strong university relationships enhance the image of the lab and also its ability to recruit and retain highly qualified scientists and engineers.

Non-Salary Attractions

Unable to offer competitive salaries to new hires, at least one Army lab uses other incentives to overcome this disadvantage. To get a recruit to "sign on," the lab offers such perquisites as the following: support for participation in professional meetings, liberal sabbatical policies, opportunities for advancement, awards programs, and office refurbishing. It also offers a "Care" program designed to treat scientists and engineers with professional and personal dignity. This program includes such elements as flextime, alternative work schedules, work-at-home arrangements, and educational assistance. Although not many scientists and engineers take advantage of these programs, the knowledge that they exist seems to make a difference in how they feel about the lab (Clark et al., 1987). Special characteristics of the work environment in many civil service labs that help to overcome salary discrepancies include relatively stable missions and funding; national prominence; quality, quantity, and diversity of research services, equipment, and personnel; opportunity to focus full-time on research activities; rewarding research; and freedom from grant writing (Committee to Study Strategies, 1988).

Monetary Incentives

Unlike civil service labs, DOE M&O contractors are not limited by the rigidity of the civil service salary schedule. (It should be noted, however, that OPM has historically approved differential salary rates and given direct-hire authority to agencies for certain hard-to-hire positions. GAO also has endorsed this practice [GAO, 1988b]). Although their pay schedules have to be approved by DOE, the contractors develop multiple occupation-based pay schedules to reflect market rates. In the NIST demonstration project, in addition to higher starting salaries, recruitment and retention allowances are possible for all S&E positions. These allowances may not exceed $10,000 and are determined on the basis of relevant market factors such as special qualifications, turnover rates, and salary offer issues. One early outcome of the NIST demonstration, however, is that some salary inequities now occur between new hires and existing staff, caused by the flexibility in starting salaries (OPM, 1989).

Timeliness of Employment Offer

A major recruiting problem for civil service labs is the length of time the hiring process takes. Many labs report that it may take six months or more from the time an application is made until an offer is extended to a scientist or engineer. These delays also are common for other personnel actions (e.g., reassignment, promotion). None of the alternative personnel systems considered here has experienced undue delays in extending employment offers. One conclusion reached by OPM after the first year of the NIST demonstration was that there had already been a substantial reduction in the time necessary for making an offer of employment. Whereas it used to require three months to a year to hire a scientist or engineer under OPM procedures, it now can be accomplished within a few weeks (OPM, 1989).

Retention of Scientists and Engineers

Turnover

One of the most effective deterrents to excessive turnover is to hire the "right" individuals in the first place—a tenet that underscores the importance of the recruiting process. According to one survey of scientists and engineers, the factors most affecting job satisfaction are the employee's interest in the assigned projects, role in decision making, authority, potential for recognition, relative compensation, and compatibility with colleagues (Clark et al., 1987). In evaluating the Navy demonstration, OPM found that job satisfaction was affected less by pay and more by the work itself and the amount of control employees exercised over that work (GAO, 1988b).

The effects of high turnover are far-reaching, especially at the senior-researcher level and above. When senior staff resign or retire, the continuity and stability of research programs can be jeopardized and institutional memory can be significantly diminished. When top-notch senior researchers leave, recruiting success also may be affected. Some civil service labs count on their ability to employ noted scientists and engineers to attract promising young researchers (Clark et al., 1987). Another potential effect of high turnover is the loss of mentoring. When senior researchers and managers terminate, they cannot be mentors. When junior researchers and managers resign at a high rate, the senior researchers and managers may become unwilling to invest the time necessary for mentoring, since they do not realize a payoff for the loss in productivity associated with being a mentor.

OPM (1988) conducted a special study of the turnover rates at the Navy demonstration labs compared to the control labs. They found no differences in the turnover rates of scientists and engineers older than 40, but found lower turnover rates at the demonstration labs for younger scientists and engineers. Two generally accepted explanations for the decreasing turnover rate of civil service employees who are older than 40 are the lack of portability of federal pensions (i.e., they have too much invested in the Civil Service Retirement System to leave) and the relative amount of job security that federal employment offers.

Consistent with the desired outcome, OPM also found that there was a lower rate of turnover among the high-performing scientists and engineers at the Navy demonstration labs than at the control labs. Those in the demonstration labs who did leave were more likely to remain in the federal government than their control lab counterparts, probably because their higher salaries made private sector jobs relatively less attractive to them than to the scientists and engineers in the control labs.

Position Classification Systems

The position classification structures for the alternative personnel systems are the mechanisms by which line managers assume more responsibility for the personnel function. These classification systems tend to be simpler and require less paperwork than the civil service classification system. Perhaps more importantly, the new classification systems give labs more flexibility in managing salaries, including starting salaries.

The changes in the classification system in the Navy demonstration project primarily involved combining the 18 separate GS grade classifications into broad pay bands and simplifying the classification process. Instead of GS grades, there are five separate career paths (professional, technical, technical specialist, administrative, and clerical). Within each career path, employees are placed into one of several broad pay bands, which include at least two former GS grades (GAO, 1988b).

The NIST classification system has a similar design: there are four career paths (S&E professional, S&E technical, administrative, and support), each of which has a separate pay structure containing five pay bands. Each pay band replaces one or more GS grades, and salary ranges for adjacent pay bands within a career path overlap. To accommodate supervisory pay differentials, the pay bands are extended from 3 percent to 6 percent for supervisory personnel. NIST anticipates that pay banding will have several desirable effects: broader pay-for-performance salary ranges, fewer classification decisions, simpler processes for personnel classification, less paperwork, and more authority for line managers (OPM, 1989).

TVA uses a position classification system similar to that of civil service agencies, but it includes several pay schedules that are established through collective bargaining. The manner in which grades are assigned to particular positions also differs from the practice in the civil service, primarily because of the role that unions play in making that determination. The classification of management positions, however, is very similar to that followed by civil service agencies.

Compensation and Pay Structure

In studies of federal S&E employment, two problem areas that are consistently identified are entry-level salaries and senior-level salaries. In addition, pay freezes and the federal pay cap often are blamed for the widening salary differential between the government and private industry and the accelerating defection of the most experienced scientists and engineers to the private sector. The inflexible civil service pay schedule, with its inability to give performance its due weight, provides few incentives for hard work. With respect to policies and procedures governing pay structures and compensation, the alternative personnel systems considered here are rich with possibilities.

Role of Performance Appraisal Systems

Most of the alternative personnel systems have objectives-based performance appraisals very similar in design to those required throughout the civil service, but they are generally used quite differently. Many of the alternative systems have pay-for-performance compensation programs tied to the performance appraisal systems. TVA has separate and structurally different performance appraisal systems for managers and nonmanagers. Managers are given ratings that are tied to the pay-for-performance compensation plan, but the ratings of nonmanagers and executives are not.

Salary and Other Compensation

DOE M&O contractors develop salary schedules based on market analyses. All salary schedules and benefits programs have to be approved by DOE, and each contractor must provide a defensible basis for its own salary and benefits structure. Individual approval is required for each salary in excess of a certain amount (currently $70,000), but these salaries are not subject to the federal pay cap. Certain kinds of performance bonuses also are acceptable under the M&O contracts.

Because the pay bands incorporate at least two GS grades, the Navy demonstration labs have more discretion in determining the starting salary offers for new employees. Employees' salaries are then adjusted annually on the basis of performance and can include a salary increase within the same band, a one-time bonus or performance award, and/or a promotion to a higher band. In addition to these performance-based pay increases and bonuses, employees are also eligible for the same general pay adjustments (comparability) granted to employees under the GS system.

OPM found that, as of January 1986, employees at the Navy demonstration labs were paid salaries 6 percent higher than those in the control labs. This was attributed to higher starting salaries given to entry-level scientists and engineers and the larger-than-average salary increases given to employees both within a pay band and through promotions between the bands. Salary costs have increased at a rate of about 1 percent per year since the beginning of the project and are expected to continue to increase (GAO, 1988b).

The NIST pay-for-performance system bases salary adjustments on performance evaluations. Pay increases consist of comparability increases, performance increases, and bonuses and awards. One element of the pay-for-performance process requires the rank-ordering of peers by using the results of the performance appraisal, a procedure that managers feel may unduly increase employee anxiety (OPM, 1989).

What NIST considers to be one of its most serious recruiting and retention problems cannot be addressed by the demonstration project—the federal pay cap. It is viewed as an area of increasing concern under the new personnel system, which allows capable individuals to advance more rapidly. This rapid advancement could result in an increase in the number of NIST employees at the pay cap.

On the other hand, TVA has the authority to adjust total compensation to whatever it deems fit. TVA is only subject to the statutory <u>salary</u> ceiling, not to a ceiling for total compensation. Mechanisms by which total compensation is increased without exceeding the pay cap have in the past included the following: paying the full cost of medical and dental insurance premiums; paying the employee's share of social security;

and offering cash relocation incentives, supplemental retirement benefit payments, recruitment bonuses, and retention bonuses (MSPB, 1989).

One of the striking contrasts between TVA and civil service agencies is in the character of their relationships with unions. TVA has a history of using the collective bargaining process as the principal means by which compensation and personnel policies for its nonmanagerial employees are determined. Pay policies, salaries, job classifications, and the coverage and cost to employees of health insurance plans are among the issues largely decided through collective bargaining. The process for setting salaries of white-collar employees differs markedly from the civil service process because of the role of union negotiation. Although TVA initiated a pay-for-performance system for its white-collar employees, it abandoned it in 1988 (after 7 years) because of underfunding and perceived inequities in the distribution of performance awards. It currently has no mechanism for rewarding top-performing nonmanagers other than the negotiated salary increases or periodic step increases that are generally available to all employees. Managers are paid under a pay-for-performance system that has no comparability or cost-of-living component, but TVA can give bonuses to management employees who are in shortage occupations or who accept hard-to-fill positions.

Retirement

Civil service benefits for new government employees have recently become less attractive. Those hired after 1984 no longer have the automatic cost-of-living adjustments that were built into pre-1984 retirement packages. Retirement with full benefits is not available until age 57 instead of 55. The ability of demonstration projects to alter current federal benefits is highly restricted by law. As would be expected from the diversity of the contractors, DOE's M&O facilities have a wide variety of retirement programs, ranging from those typical of large private firms to those available to employees of colleges and universities. TVA has its own retirement system.

Other Personnel-Related Problems

Personnel Ceilings and Reductions in Force: Another constraint imposed by the civil service system is the limitation on the number of full-time-equivalent personnel a lab may employ. This ceiling, coupled with budgetary constraints, becomes a particular problem during periods of retrenchment, little growth, or low turnover, especially given the civil service restrictions on the lab's ability to remove the least productive personnel. Effective personnel management is hindered, since the ceilings tend to grow slower than budgets. Managers, who are best able to make decisions about how to allocate money and personnel to meet their programmatic commitments, are prevented from making the most productive decisions (IOM, 1988). Neither the DOE M&O facilities nor TVA are subject to such double constraints. DOE contractors in particular can better adjust to changing or diminishing funding by shifting researchers from one program to another or, if necessary, laying people off. Unlike civil service labs, these decisions can be made entirely on the basis of skills, abilities, and performance. Some traditionally operated civil service labs have been successful in dealing with personnel ceilings by significantly increasing their personnel pools through the use of university-based programs to bring adjunct personnel (e.g., graduate students, faculty, postdoctoral fellows) into the lab (Clark et al., 1987).

Aging Work Force: Concerns about the aging work force (especially at the senior-researcher and senior-manager levels) have been voiced by all of the organizations discussed in this paper. For example, approximately 40 percent of the NIST work force will be eligible for retirement during the five-year demonstration period (GAO, 1988a), and more than 60 percent of the senior managers and key researchers at one Army lab are already eligible to retire (Clark et al., 1987). This trend underscores the necessity of civil service labs' being able to attract qualified scientists and engineers to fill the depleting ranks and especially of their improving the retention of senior staff to assume leadership roles.

Conclusion

As concern grows about the role of the federal civil service personnel system in the increasing inability of government laboratories to attract and retain high-quality scientists and engineers, there has been a call for more demonstration projects to address the shortcomings of the civil service system. Opponents of demonstration projects claim that they create interagency competition for scientists and engineers. Even those who support the use of demonstration projects to identify viable alternatives to the civil service admit that it is extremely difficult to carry out a controlled study in a dynamic environment.

According to GAO (1988b), the Navy's demonstration project showed that a pay-for-performance system with simplified personnel procedures for classifying, appraising, and paying civil service employees is workable. It also showed that line managers could be given authority and responsibility for making personnel decisions. On the other hand, there was little evidence to support the conclusions that managerial flexibility to assign work had been enhanced by the project, that starting salaries higher than those permitted in the General Schedule were given, or that the salary increases and bonuses available to employees with good performance ratings made them more likely to stay at the demonstration labs than the employees who received poor ratings (and smaller salary increases and bonuses). It should be noted, however, that there were significant problems in the evaluation of this project: initial differences between the demonstration and control labs (different geographic regions, different organization and economic environments) and much missing data (some not available, some not standard, some not collected) (GAO, 1988b).

It is too early to reach conclusions about the NIST demonstration, but OPM (1989) reported several general impressions: managers feel that employee mobility could be reduced because of the differences between the new NIST personnel system and the rest of the civil service system; some evidence suggests that salary inequities can result from the flexibility in setting starting salaries; and supervisors feel that OPM has been too involved in the areas that were intended to increase the responsibilities of supervisors. On the other hand, there already has been a significant reduction in the time necessary for making an offer of employment, and most employees still feel optimistic about the eventual outcomes of the project.

As the federal government seeks ways to simplify its personnel system through greater deregulation and delegation of authority, the personnel system of TVA may be a useful example of a system that is already subject to fewer specific regulations and procedures. The considerable variability in the personnel systems used by DOE M&O contractors reflects their diverse private-sector origins. To consider this model for all federal labs, however, would require a major rethinking of the proper role and structure of the government laboratory system.

Personnel systems need to be customized to the organizations they serve. It is not reasonable to expect that a single model will fit all organizations or that a system, once developed, can remain static. The organizations themselves and the environments in which they exist are dynamic. Every organization needs a uniqueness in its personnel system, an opportunity to mold it to its own identity, and the freedom to change it when change is needed.

Bibliography

Clark, S. B., M. G. Finn, and L. B. Smalley. 1987. *Productivity Management Procedures in Department of the Army and Department of Energy Laboratories: Implications for Action and Compendium of Project Activities* (ORAU Report No. ORAU-279). Oak Ridge, Tenn.: Oak Ridge Associated Universities.

Committee to Study Strategies to Strengthen the Scientific Excellence of the National Institutes of Health Intramural Research Program, Institute of Medicine (IOM). 1988. *A Healthy NIH Intramural Program: Structural Change or Administrative Remedies?* Washington, D.C.: National Academy Press.

Kennedy, R. B. 1989. *Recruitment of White Female Engineers at the U.S. Army Missile Command, FY79-FY89* (MICOM Technical Report No. CPS-89-2). Redstone Arsenal, Ala.: U.S. Army Missile Command. NTIS No. AD-A211522.

Wilson, L. J. 1985. The Navy's experiment with pay, performance, and appraisal. *Defense Management Journal* 21(3):30-40.

U.S. General Accounting Office (GAO). 1988a. *Federal Workforce: Information on the National Bureau of Standards Personnel Demonstration Project* (GAO Publication No. GAO/GGD-88-59FS). Washington, D.C.: GAO.

_____. 1988b. *Federal Workforce: Observations in the Navy's Personnel Management Demonstration Project* (GAO Publication No. GAO/GGD-88-79). Washington, D.C.: GAO.

U.S. Merit Systems Protection Board (MSPB). 1989. *The Tennessee Valley Authority and the Merit Principles.* Washington, D.C.: MSPB.

U.S. Office of Personnel Management (OPM). *Implementation Report: National Institute of Standards and Technology, Personnel Management Demonstration Project* (OPM Publication No. PSO-204). Washington, D.C.: OPM.

_____. 1988. *Turnover in the Navy Demonstration Laboratories, 1980-1985* (OPM Publication No. PSO-101). Washington, D.C.: OPM.

THE POLITICAL APPOINTMENTS PROCESS AND THE RECRUITMENT OF SCIENTISTS AND ENGINEERS

James P. Pfiffner
Professor of Government and Politics
George Mason University

This paper examines the major factors that affect the recruitment of scientists and engineers in the political recruitment process and concludes that those factors are similar to the factors that affect PAS (political appointments requiring Senate confirmation) appointments in general. It further argues that the difficulties in attracting the best executives to public service are even greater in recruiting the best scientists and engineers. In addition, the nature of the science and engineering professions presents further impediments to recruiting and retaining the highest quality personnel. These negative factors, however, are often outweighed by opportunities present in the public service: the chance to work at the cutting edge of many areas of research, the challenge of tackling the toughest problems facing our society, and the opportunity to make a contribution to the public good or to serve an admired president.

The analysis and conclusions of this paper are based on systematic data from various studies and the considered judgments of experienced people. But it must be emphasized that defining "quality" and estimating the motives of potential government executives are inherently judgmental activities.

The Pressures of Transition

At the beginning of each new presidential administration, the President is faced with the daunting task of recruiting 3,000 to 4,000 political appointees. The Office of Presidential Personnel has the task of coordinating this effort, but it is directly responsible for the recruitment and selection of about 550 executives to lead the executive branch. Other political appointees include about 650 noncareer Senior Executives and about 1650 Schedule C appointments at the GS-15 level and below. A certain proportion of these political positions are appropriate for those with science and engineering backgrounds.

The pressures of the task seem overwhelming because it must be done under the additional burden of other transition pressures involving budget, policy, politics, etc. A flood of applications has inundated recent administrations, often amounting to 1,500 applications per day in the early part of the transition (National Academy of Public Administration, 1983). By June 1989 the Bush administration had received more than 45,000 applications for political appointments.[1] One of the main difficulties for the

---

[1] Interview with Chase Untermeyer, the White House, June 6, 1989.

President's personnel recruiters is to separate the wheat from the chaff, satisfying political obligations or appeasing those who are not appointed, and matching the right people with the right positions. The real challenge is actively to recruit the best and the brightest, rather than merely sifting through the resumes that come in "over the transom."

All of this is complicated by the inability of the President's personnel recruiter to do much preparation. Although presidential candidates Carter and Reagan had initiated some planning for political recruitment, because of political sensitivities, preparation can never be very thorough. Candidate George Bush refused to let his personnel recruiter, Chase Untermeyer, do any planning or even to recruit a staff until after the election.[2] One of the constant headaches of the President's personnel recruiter is to deflect political pressures for appointments so that those best qualified for the positions can be appointed. A tension that affects every presidential recruitment operation is between political pressures for patronage and the professional qualifications needed to perform the duties of the job. All Presidents legitimately demand loyalty, but the balance with competence is difficult to maintain.

Impediments to Recruiting the Best and Brightest

Although presidential appointments are prestigious, and many welcome an invitation to join an administration, Presidents do not always convince their first choices to accept presidential appointments. There will always be plenty of people eager to join an administration (as indicated by the 45,000 applications in 1989), but the real problem is finding those who are not looking for a job because they are successful and satisfied with their present position.

For the highest positions, cabinet secretaries and executive level II positions, there is usually not too much problem because of the prestige of the positions and the relatively close relationship to the president. But for the mid-level executive positions impediments to accepting a position and the quality of the experience in office have become increasingly important factors during the past several decades.

The relatively low level of pay is one of the major factors that keeps the President from recruiting the best and brightest for a period of government service. This reality is so widely recognized that it is not important to recite the results of salary surveys here. The main systematic analyses include the reports of the Quadrennial Commission and the Report of the National Commission on the Public Service.[3] The recent pay raise legislation passed in 1989 will help to ameliorate but not fully solve the problem.

Although pay levels may be the most highly visible and easy to document

---

[2] *Ibid.*

[3] The most recent "Quad Com" report was *High Quality Leadership--Our Government's Most Precious Asset,* report of the U.S. Commission on Executive, Legislative, and Judicial Salaries (December 1988). The Volcker Commission findings are in *Facing the Federal Compensation Crisis,* report of the Task Force on Pay and Compensation to the National Commission on the Public Service (Washington, 1989). See also the *Report of the President's Commission on Compensation of Career Federal Executives* (February 26, 1988).

impediment to presidential recruitment, other factors discourage the best and brightest from joining an administration. Among the most important of those factors are the series of laws and regulations that are meant to prevent appointees from taking advantage of their government positions to enrich themselves unethically. Regulations have been fashioned to require financial disclosure of personal finances when accepting a position, to remedy any potential conflict of interest (including blind trusts and recusals), and to limit employment and representation activities after leaving the government.

This is not the place for a close analysis of the specifics of the legal restrictions, but systematic data as well as anecdotal evidence show that these restrictions have a chilling effect on presidential recruitment. In a survey of all presidential appointees between 1964 and 1984, the National Academy of Public Administration (NAPA) found that while less than 5 percent of appointees in the Johnson, Nixon, and Ford administrations had problems with financial disclosure forms, 26 percent of Carter appointees and 34 percent of Reagan appointees had "significant difficulty" filling out financial disclosure forms. Some complained of sizable legal and accounting fees merely to fill out the required forms. There was a corresponding increase in the number of appointees who felt that the financial disclosure requirements have gone too far: from 40 percent in the Carter administration to 64 per cent in the Reagan administration (NAPA, 1985; Mackenzie, 1986a).[4] During the 1980s the restrictions became more burdensome and chilling, particularly the new postemployment restrictions that seemed to cause a number of senior federal executives at the National Aeronautics and Space Administration (NASA) and elsewhere to leave the government.[5]

Norman Augustine (1989), chairman and CEO of Martin Marietta, argues that complex ethics rules are a significant deterrent to attracting high quality federal executives:

> Exceptional career public servants are leaving government in alarming numbers, and qualified replacements are becoming harder and harder to recruit. The rash of resignations that preceded the effective date of the new "revolving door" ethics rules punctuates this concern.

Former Secretary of Defense Frank Carlucci (1989) has similar concerns:

> In my experience, the best people tend to be the most ethical. Yet, in the name of ethics, we are driving the best out of government. In other words, extreme and often absurd ethical standards are lowering the level of ethics.

---

[4] The NAPA 1985 survey was sent to 936 present and former presidential appointees. The response rate was 57 percent, and respondents were highly representative of the total target population of appointees.

[5] The chilling effect of postemployment restrictions was emphasized by several people interviewed for this paper: Stephen Andriole, former director of the Cybernetic Technical Office of the Defense Advanced Research Projects Agency; Lawrence Korb, former assistant secretary of defense; and Jeffrey Newmeyer, chief scientist of Lockheed Missile Systems. For examples of problems with the new ethics restrictions, see Linda S. Dix, "Recruitment, Retention, and Utilization of Scientists and Engineers in the Federal Government: Results of a Literature Review," earlier in this appendix.

> In every organization, there has to be an element of trust. A certain
> amount of regulation and even conflict of interest legislation is healthy, but
> a legislative effort to eliminate every conceivable conflict of interest
> creates a web of red tape and frustrations and demoralizes managers.

While recognizing the legitimate intent behind the ethics requirements and the very real abuses that they were intended to remedy, NAPA (1985) has recommended a reexamination of financial disclosure and conflict of interest legislation.[6]

Other problems face presidential recruiters. How do you convince a successful manager, scientist, or engineer to leave his or her job, step out of a career path for a short period of time (the average PAS term in position is 2.0 years), move a family to Washington, buy a house in an expensive housing market, and put up with the very real pressures of a political appointment?[7] The NAPA survey found that the proportion of presidential appointees who reported that they made a "significant financial sacrifice" to accept their appointment increased from 40 percent in the Johnson administration to 52 percent in the Carter administration to 64 percent in the Reagan administration. In addition, "quality-of-life" factors declined. Those who reported working more than 60 hours a week increased from 64 percent in the Johnson administration to 77 percent in the Reagan administration. Those who reported that their jobs caused "stress in personal life or family relations" increased from 51 percent in the Johnson administration to 73 percent in the Reagan administration (NAPA, 1985).

Although these data are discouraging, most appointees also reported that their periods of public service were among the most rewarding professional experiences of their lives. The point here is not to paint too bleak a picture but to isolate impediments to recruiting people for public service.

Another trend that affects the appointment process and the management of the government is the increasing length of time that transpires between when the President nominates a person and when that person takes office. These delays are attributable to internal executive branch clearances (including FBI investigation and financial clearances) and the Senate investigation and confirmation process. The average length of time has increased from 7 weeks during the Johnson administration to 14 weeks in the Reagan administration and probably longer in the Bush administration (NAPA, 1985). The reasons for this trend include new conflict of interest laws, more thorough White House clearance procedures, delays in Senate confirmation, and more thorough FBI full field investigations.

In addition to the delay in the average time that it takes to complete individual appointments, presidential administrations seem to take a longer time to complete their initial set of presidential appointments. Although comparable data have not been kept over the years, it was the consensus among published sources that in 1981 the Reagan administration had been slower than other recent administrations to fill its PAS positions (Pfiffner, 1988). In 1989 it was generally conceded that the Bush administration was

---

[6] See also Mackenzie (1986b) and National Commission on the Public Service (1989).

[7] In addition to the short average time of PAS appointees in office, former Assistant Secretary of Defense Lawrence Korb emphasized the psychological uncertainty of serving "at the pleasure of" the President and one's immediate superior.

slower than the Reagan administration: on August 10, 156 of 394 of the top executive branch positions had been filled, but there were no nominations for 160 of the positions (Pfiffner, 1990). By the end of 1989 the administration had not filled 46 of 116 PAS positions in independent agencies (40 percent) and 70 of 320 PAS positions in executive departments (22 percent) (Garcia, 1989).

The effect of these delays in recruiting presidential appointees depends on which positions are not filled. But where the incumbents of positions are, in effect, lame ducks for the first year of an administration, there will most likely be delays in the implementation of policy and management initiatives and possibly the recruitment of scientists and engineers at both the political and career executive levels.

Quality and the Number of Political Appointees

The creation of this panel was prompted in part by the concern that it is becoming more difficult to attract the best and brightest scientists and engineers to the federal service. The Report by the Carnegie Commission on Science, Technology, and Government (1988) stated, "It is generally agreed that the quality [of government technical personnel] has eroded." In 1989 Energy Secretary James Watkins said that the Energy Department did not have the officials with the skills necessary to run the country's nuclear weapons complex.[8]

This concern has been accompanied by a perception that there has been a decline in quality of some political appointees, which in turn has had a negative effect on the quality of political appointees in the government. Elliot Richardson (1987), former secretary of Defense; Health, Education, and Welfare; and Commerce, has noted "the increase in turnover and the decline in quality of second- and third-echelon political appointees" in the federal government. Richardson's concern is based on the observation that during the past 20 years there has been an increase in the number of political appointees in the government, a deeper penetration of political appointees into the career ranks, an increase in the turnover of appointees, and an increase in the emphasis on political loyalty in presidential administrations. These factors have had a negative effect on the recruitment and retention of scientists and engineers to the extent that the professional quality of appointees, institutional memory, and organizational stability have decreased.

The number of political appointees has increased during the past several decades. Although authoritative and comparable data are hard to find, there is no doubt about the trend. The number of PAS positions has increased from 152 in 1965 to 527 in 1985; noncareer Senior Executive Service (SES) positions increased from 582 in 1980 to 658 in 1986; Schedule C positions increased from 911 in 1976 to 1,665 in 1986. In 1986 there were 946 Schedule C's at the GS-13-15 levels, more than the total number of Schedule C's under President Ford (Ingraham, 1987). Although the absolute numbers of political appointees in relation to the total civilian work force may not seem high, the ratio of political to career positions at the mid-executive levels is increasing (e.g., the deputy

---

[8] "Energy Chief Says Top Aides Lack Skills to Run U.S. Bomb Complex," *New York Times,* June 28, 1989, p. 1. See also "Reversing Course at the Energy Department," *Washington Post,* January 24, 1990, p. 1.

assistant secretary level). The increasingly rapid turnover of these political appointees aggravates the situation, with PAS appointees' time in position averaging 2.8 years in 1965 and 2.0 years in 1984 (NAPA, 1985). From 1979 to 1986, noncareer SES executives stayed in office an average of 20 months (Ban and Ingraham, 1986).

Among the difficulties caused by the increasing number of political appointees is difficulty of recruiting high-quality people for positions that are lower in prestige than executive level I or II positions for relatively low pay. This is exacerbated by the centralization of White House control of political recruiting that reached a peak during the Reagan administration. In the 1950s and 1960s, even presidential appointees at the subcabinet level were often, in effect, chosen by cabinet secretaries in conjunction with the White House (Mann, 1965).

With centralization in the White House Personnel Office has come a greater emphasis on ideological or personal loyalty to the President as the primary criterion for appointment. According to Elliot Richardson (1987), the quality of political appointments has suffered from "the elimination from the pool of eligible prospects of those who cannot meet the ideological litmus test."

The argument is that cabinet secretaries are more likely to value competence and merit in selecting their subordinates who will run programs than is the White House, which is likely to be especially sensitive to the political claims of those who have supported the president's campaign. Richardson (1987) noted,

> A White House personnel assistant sees the position of deputy assistant secretary as a fourth-echelon slot. In his eyes that makes it an ideal reward for a fourth-echelon political type—a campaign advance man, or a regional political organizer.[9]

The Special Case of Scientists and Engineers

The impact of the above trends on the recruitment of PAS positions has the effect of narrowing the pool of candidates from which potential nominees are selected. The negative aspects of the job (low pay, financial disclosure, long hours, etc.) when combined with the political criteria often employed (ideological or personal loyalty) have a constraining effect on recruiting the best and the brightest for all presidential appointments except for the highest levels (e.g., cabinet positions). But good scientists and engineers are a special subset of potential appointees, and effectively recruiting them presents several additional problems.

Often scientists and engineers get into their professions because they prefer a rational, academic research atmosphere rather than the uncertain world of politics with its necessary compromises. It is less likely that they will become involved in partisan politics than, for instance, lawyers or business people. Thus it is less likely that scientists and engineers will possess the kinds of political credentials that are often demanded in order to get past an initial screening by president's personnel office.

As one presidential recruiter put it: "These people did not do a lot to help this

---

[9] For a full analysis of these issues, see National Commission on the Public Service (1989).

man get elected; they are just looking for an easy in." When asked for advice for scientists and engineers who might want to work in the public service at the PAS level, the recruiter replied: "If you are interested in serving, get involved in the political process early, not after the election." This mind-set on the part of presidential recruiters necessarily narrows severely the pool of people who will be considered for presidential positions. Scientists and engineers are not likely to become involved in presidential campaigns and those who do may not be those who are also experienced enough to fill successfully senior PAS positions. President Reagan's first personnel recruiter, Pendleton James, added that, even if offered a job in an administration, some scientists will turn it down for fear that their professional reputations might become "tainted" by political service.[10]

None of this is meant to imply that politics and political credentials are illegitimate in presidential recruiting, the point is that in looking for the best persons to run major programs for the government, the excessive use of political criteria may prematurely narrow the field and exclude those who might be best for the job but do not happen to have the right political experience. The argument is that an excessively political approach is particularly effective at eliminating scientists and engineers early in the recruitment process, for they are less likely to be involved in politics as a typical part of their professional lives.

The above analysis looked at the problem of recruiting scientists and engineers from the perspective of the political recruitment process. But the nature of the science and engineering professions themselves also impede recruiting the best and brightest for government service. The "tribal" values of scientists tend to cherish and give prestige to theoretical rather than applied or practical work. Thus academic or scholarly prestige comes in theoretical advances in the disciplines and publishing those ideas in scholarly journals. Those who do applied work are a bit lower on the pecking order in their disciplines, and those who do administrative work are even lower. Thus good scientists are less likely to get the administrative experience that qualifies them for public service positions running major programs.[11]

Finally, those who pursue scientific and engineering careers are often people who have a craftsman type of personality. That is, they focus on a single problem and enjoy the challenge of sticking to it until it is solved. These people are less likely to be good at or enjoy the job of a high-level executive that calls for the ability to move quickly from problem to problem in a very fluid environment. The political atmosphere of presidential positions intensifies these characteristics of high-level executive jobs (Maccoby, 1976). This is one form of the common problem of promoting very good professionals (accountants, doctors, lawyers, scientists, or engineers) from the work of their professions to management or executive positions. Those who are adept at one set of skills may not be adept at the other.

---

[10] Interview with Pendleton James, January 12, 1990.

[11] Interview with James Trefil, Robinson Professor of Physics, George Mason University, January 25, 1990.

The Role of Leadership and Vision

All of the above obstacles to recruiting scientists and engineers can be mitigated by visionary leadership. In recruiting for PAS positions, the role of the President is crucial. The President does not have time to be personally involved in recruiting for most PAS positions, but his attitude is decisive. He sets the tone for his recruiters, and by his final choices indicates whether he values professional qualities or prefers political loyalty over professional competence.

Another aspect of presidential leadership that affects the willingness of scientists and engineers to leave their professional careers to spend several years in public service is the value that is placed on the work they will be doing. Although it is impossible to measure easily, morale during the early years of NASA and during the Apollo program was high and made it easier to attract the best scientists and engineers to work on a program that was professionally challenging and clearly valued by the President, the government, and U.S. citizens.[12] The mission to Mars might become such a program. Unfortunately, to undertake such ambitious goals is very expensive, and in a time of constrained budgets is unlikely to happen.

The role of the President's science adviser is symbolically important insofar as it symbolizes the President's attitude toward scientists and science. The reestablishment of the position in the Executive Office of the President gave a positive boost to perceptions of the value that the President and the government place on science. The relationship of the science adviser to the President is something that is watched in the science and technology community and thus affects those scientists who are likely recruits for presidential positions (Stubbing, 1988). If the science adviser is perceived to have made politically driven compromises of his or her professional values, scientists may see this as evidence that if they come to work for the government, they may be pressured to compromise their own objectivity.[13]

Of course most scientists and engineers in the government are not at the PAS level, but the quality of scientists and engineers at lower, operational levels is influenced by the quality of those at the PAS and SES levels. Several scientists who were interviewed for this project emphasized that in order to retain good scientists in the career service, they must respect the technical competence of their superiors.[14]

Thus federal executives who want to recruit and retain good scientists and engineers will create the kind of atmosphere that will be attractive to them. They will set up professional recruitment and outreach efforts and will obtain the resources to do it well.[15] They will project a vision of the mission of the agency or program that will inspire and attract those who seek professional challenges. They will be sensitive to the professional values of scientists and engineers. They will ensure that the professional

---

[12] Interview with Richard Stubbing, public policy program, Duke University (former associate director, Office of Management and Budget).

[13] Interview with Jeffrey Newmeyer, chief scientist at Lockheed Missile Systems, February 10, 1990.

[14] Interviews with Jeffrey Newmeyer and Stephen Andriole.

[15] Interview with Stephen Blush, Office of the Secretary, U.S. Department of Energy.

products of scientists and engineers are given due consideration; that is, they will ensure that scientific research will have the chance to have an impact on policy, when that input is appropriate. Finally, they will be sure to buffer the professional work of scientists and engineers from the political whims of superiors and insulate them as much as possible from budget swings that are inherent in the political world of the federal government. The importance of "buffering the technical core" of organizations is especially appropriate in this context. This buffering role is one of the main responsibilities of chief executives and managers according to Thompson (1967).

Conclusion

One of the conclusions of this paper is that the ability to recruit and retain good scientists and engineers in the federal government is undercut by the combination of two factors. On the one hand is the difficulty of scientists and engineers gaining the type of political experience that provides them with the political credentials to be acceptable to a presidential recruitment operation. In addition, even if offers are made, scientists may be unwilling to serve in policy positions for fear that their professional values or objectivity might be compromised by political considerations.

On the other hand is the need for career scientists and engineers to have high levels of respect for the technical credentials of their political superiors. Thus federal recruitment of scientists and engineers at high levels is caught between the demand on the part of presidential recruiters that they have unquestioned political credentials and the demand on the part of career scientists and engineers that their political supervisors have impeccable scientific credentials. These two factors, in addition to the others mentioned above, reduce the ability of the federal government to recruit the best and brightest scientists and engineers.

This paper may seem to have painted an excessively negative picture of the prospects for recruiting top quality scientists and engineers for the federal government. The purpose of the project, however, is to examine problems in the process and potential avenues for improvement. Thus in accentuating the negative, the tone of this report should not overshadow the continuing very high quality of most political appointees and the scientists and engineers who have chosen public service.

It must also be emphasized that any arguments about the level of quality of federal employees is inherently judgmental. On the other hand, just because the factors involved cannot be quantified is not sufficient reason to make no judgement at all. The problems are real, and they should be addressed.

Bibliography

Augustine, N. R. 1989. Show our public servants some respect. *Washington Post.* August 13, p. B7.

Ban, C., and P. Ingraham. 1986. *Short-Timers: Political Appointee Mobility and Its Impact on Political-Career Relations in the Reagan Administration.* Paper presented at the National Convention of the American Society for Public Administration, Anaheim, Calif.

Carlucci, F. 1989. Public service: Are we sacrificing quality? Op-ed article written for the National Commission on the Public Service, November 1989 (unpublished).

Carnegie Commission on Science, Technology, and Government. 1988. *Science and Technology and the President.* New York: The Commission.

Garcia, R. 1989. *Presidential Nominations to Full-Time Positions in Executive Departments During the 101st Congress* and *Presidential Nominations to Full-Time Positions in Independent and Other Agencies, 101st Congress.* Washington, D.C.: Congressional Research Service.

Ingraham, P. 1987. Building bridges or burning them? *Public Administration Review* September/October 1987.

Maccoby, M. 1976. *The Gamesman.* New York: Simon and Schuster.

Mackenzie, G. Calvin. 1981. *The Politics of Presidential Appointments.* New York: The Free Press.

_____. 1986a. *The In-and-Outers: Presidential Appointees and Transient Government in Washington.* Baltimore: Johns Hopkins University Press.

_____. 1986b. If you want to play, you've got to pay: Ethics regulation and the presidential appointments system, 1964-84. In G. Calvin Mackenzie (ed.), *The In-and-Outers,* Baltimore: Johns Hopkins University Pres, 1986.

Mann, D. E. 1965. *The Assistant Secretaries.* Washington: Brookings.

National Academy of Public Administration (NAPA). 1983. *America's Unelected Government.* Cambridge, Mass.: Ballinger Publishing Co.

_____. 1984. *Recruiting Presidential Appointees.* Transcript of a group discussion of former White House Personnel Directors, December 13, 1984 (unpublished).

_____. 1985. *Leadership in Jeopardy: The Fraying of the Presidential Appointments System.* Washington, D.C.: NAPA.

National Commission on the Public Service. 1989. *Politics and Performance: Strengthening the Executive Leadership System.* Report of the Task Force on the Relations Between Political Appointees and Career Executives. Washington, D.C.: The Commission.

Pfiffner, J. P. 1987. Political appointees and career executives: The democracy-bureaucracy nexus. *Public Administration Review* January/February:57-65.

_____. 1988. *The Strategic Presidency: Hitting the Ground Running.* Pacific Grove, Calif.: Brooks/Cole.

_____. 1990. Establishing the Bush presidency. *Public Administration Review* January/February:67-69.

_____, and R. G. Hoxie, eds. 1989. The Presidency in Transition. New York: Center for the Study of the Presidency.

Richardson, E. L. 1987. Civil servants: Why not the best? *Wall Street Journal,* November 20.

Stubbing, R. 1988. Agenda Item for the Next President and Congress: Federal Science and Technology (R&D) Policy for the 1990s. Unpublished.

Thompson, J. D. 1967. *Organizations in Action: Social Science Bases of Administrative Theory.* New York: McGraw-Hill.

Trattner, J. H. 1988. *The Prune Book.* Washington: Center for Excellence in Government.

APPENDIX C
WORKSHOP ON RECRUITMENT, RETENTION, AND UTILIZATION OF FEDERAL SCIENTISTS AND ENGINEERS

- Agenda — 145
- Participants — 147
- Proceedings — 149

Agenda
Workshop on the Recruitment, Retention, and Utilization
of Federal Scientists and Engineers
National Academy of Sciences—Washington, D.C.
February 23, 1990

8:00 Continental breakfast

8:30 Opening Remarks and Findings of Previous Studies*
Alan K. Campbell, chairman, Committee on Scientists and Engineers in the Federal Government

9:30 Quantitative Inputs to Federal Technical Personnel Management*
Charles Falk, retired director, Science Resources Studies, National Science Foundation

10:30 Break

10:45 Organizational and Decision-Making Processes Affecting Recruitment, Retention, and Utilization
- The Role of OPM in Meeting Federal Work Force Needs with Regard to Scientists and Engineers*
John M. Palguta, deputy director, Office of Policy and Evaluation, U.S. Merit Systems Protection Board

11:30 Lunch, NAS Refectory

1:00 • Differences in Recruitment, Retention, and Utilization Processes: A Comparison of Traditionally Operated Federal Laboratories, GOCOs, and Demonstration Projects*
Sheldon B. Clark, senior research scientist, Labor and Policy Studies Program, Oak Ridge Associated Universities

1:45 • The Effects of the Political Appointment Process on Recruitment and Retention of Scientists and Engineers*
James P. Pfiffner, professor of government and politics, George Mason University

2:30 Break

3:15 General Discussion: Changes in organizational and decision-making processes that might improve the recruitment, retention, and utilization of scientists and engineers   *Alan K. Campbell*

5:00 Adjournment

*Discussion will follow each 15-minute presentation.

Participants
Workshop on the Recruitment, Retention, and Utilization
of Federal Scientists and Engineers
National Academy of Sciences—Washington, D.C.
February 23, 1990

Federal Agencies
U.S. Department of Agriculture:
Essex Finney, acting director, Beltsville Area Agricultural Research Service

Department of Commerce:
John Lyons, director designate, National Institute of Standards and Technology
Robert Mahler, deputy director, Environmental Research Laboratories, National Oceanic and Atmospheric Administration

Department of Defense:
Larry Lacy, head, Civilian Personnel Policy and Requirements
Susan Numrich, Office of Strategic Planning, Naval Research Laboratory
William B. Porter, technical director, Naval Weapons Center
Karl Steinbach, chief scientist, U.S. Army Belvoir Research and Development Center

Department of Energy:
Norman L. Howton, director, Organization and Personnel Division, Morgantown Energy Technology Center
Mary Parramore, assistant to the director, Argonne National Laboratory

Department of Health and Human Services:
Phillip Chen, associate director for intramural affairs, National Institutes of Health
James Eagen, director, Public Health Service
Mary Guinan, assistant director for science, Centers for Disease Control
Sharon Holston, Food and Drug Administration

Department of the Interior:
Stephen E. Ragone, acting assistant director for research, U.S. Geological Survey

Department of Transportation:
Brian Andrews, supervisory computer scientist, Federal Aviation Administration
Nancy Mowry, supervisory personnel management specialist

Environmental Protection Agency:
Clarence Hardy, deputy director, Office of Human Resources Management

National Aeronautics and Space Administration:
Dale Compton, acting director, Ames Research Center
Robert E. Sutherland, manager, Human Resources Division, Jet Propulsion Laboratory

Merit Systems Protection Board:
Paul van Rijn, research psychologist

National Science Foundation:
Margaret Grucza, director, Government Studies Group
Margaret Windus, head, Division of Personnel Management

Office of Personnel Management:
Jack Curnow, chief, Statistical Analysis and Service Division
Leonard Klein, acting associate director, Career Entry and Employee Development Group
Paul Thompson, project head, Research and Demonstration Division
Dona Wolf, director of policy

Carnegie Commission on Science, Technology, and Government
Jesse Ausubel
David Robinson

NAS/NRC/IOM
William D. Carey, chairman, Office of Scientific and Engineering Personnel (OSEP)
Claudia Dissel, associate executive director, OSEP
Alan Fechter, executive director, OSEP
Michael Finn, director of studies and surveys, OSEP
Steve Merrill, director, Office of Government Affairs
Lawrence E. McCray, executive director, Committee on Science, Engineering, and Public Policy

Others
Mark Abramson, executive director, Council for Excellence in Government
Barbara Bailar, executive director, American Statistical Association
Sandra Fiske, director, Federal Government Service Task Force
Ray Kline, president, National Academy for Public Administration
L. Bruce Laingen, executive director, National Commission on the Public Service

Proceedings
Workshop on the Recruitment, Retention, and Utilization
of Federal Scientists and Engineers
National Academy of Sciences—Washington, D.C.
February 23, 1990

Opening Remarks and Review of Previous Studies

Dr. CAMPBELL opened the session by explaining that the task of the Committee on Scientists and Engineers in the Federal Government—assigned to the Office of Scientific and Engineering Personnel by the Carnegie Commission that is examining major issues concerning scientists, engineers, and technology and the general capability of the United States in those areas—is to look at the issues of recruitment, retention, and utilization of scientists and engineers as they relate to the federal government with an emphasis on organizational and procedural mechanisms. The purpose of this workshop is for the Committee to gather as much information as it can in preparation of a report due to the Carnegie Commission in early summer. He noted that the commissioned papers reveal a lack of consensus in specific matters—for example, evidence that scientists and engineers are overpaid or that they are substantially underpaid in the federal government. The basic issue relates to inadequate disaggregation of the data. Among other matters of interest are the following:

- "inflexibility" of the civil service system and experimentation in the area of personnel management in the federal government, particularly contrasts between those labs directly operated by the federal government and those to which services are contracted;
- ethics, an area of counter forces: one dealing with issues that relate to people taking advantage of their federal positions and another advocating enough flexibility so that regulations and laws don't discourage prospective employees;
- differences in pay based on geographic location (Dr. CAMPBELL noted that, in the private sector, much of this is handled by up-front payments such as bonus sign-ons and special bonus opportunities rather than trying to deal with base pay issues);
- ownership of intellectual property;
- the quality of the working environment, which varies substantially from lab to lab; and
- the increase in the number of noncareer appointees in the federal government and their effects on the quality of people that are attracted to federal service and institutional memory.

**Quantitative Inputs
to Federal Technical Personnel Management**

Dr. FALK opened by asserting, "To say that effective management requires good information input is almost a truism. Nevertheless, that one facet of management frequently does not get the type of attention it should." His presentation was divided into three parts: (1) a description of the types of data needed and sources of relevant data, (2) an analysis as to the extent to which the data are being used, and (3) findings from the data. He divided the relevant data into two broad categories, descriptive and dynamic. Descriptive data provide information on the characteristics of the work force at a given point in time: demography (age, sex, and race); education (highest degree); work activity (occupation, type of work, its relevance to special national interests such as defense or environment, and salary); and quality of the work force. Dynamic data are important to assess what is happening to the work force, providing insights about why people leave, whether those who stay are satisfied with their jobs, and what is likely to happen in the future.

Do Needed Data Exist?

The Office of Personnel Management (OPM) regularly gets data from federal agencies about characteristics of their personnel; excepted agencies are the U.S. Postal Service, security agencies such as the National Security Council and the Central Intelligence Agency, and the uniformed services. Data from the Tennessee Valley Authority is not reported regularly to OPM but at certain intervals. OPM's Central Personnel Data File (CPDF) includes most of the descriptive elements and some dynamic ones, primarily those related to acquisitions and separations of personnel, as well as administrative data such as individual pay schedules. The data are compiled quarterly but published only every two years in *Occupation of Federal White and Blue Collar Workers,* which essentially presents descriptive data (mostly on sex, salary, occupation, and grade) but only in aggregated form by occupational codes.

Annual aggregated data are published by the National Science Foundation (NSF) by compiling the OPM data into occupational groups and subgroups—for example, the physical sciences in the sciences and mechanical engineering or electrical engineering in the engineering groups. NSF provides data in 13 different types of tables in its annual *Federal Scientists and Engineers.* In addition, NSF provides data on the whole national science and engineering labor force, including the federal sector, facilitating comparisons across sectors of employment. For sectors other than the federal government, the NSF data are obtained from the individual 5.5 million scientists and engineers themselves, on a sampling basis. NSF also obtains data from recent graduates, baccalaureates and master's recipients, about a year after they graduate; and the National Research Council maintains a data base on the entire U.S. doctorate population, based on responses to the annual Survey of Earned Doctorates.

The NSF numbers and the OPM data vary considerably because different definitions for "scientist" and "engineer" are used by the two organizations. OPM reports data on individuals who are classified in a science or engineering occupation. Based on individual responses to its surveys, NSF classifies as scientists and engineers those who meet two out of three criteria: (1) a degree in a science or engineering field, (2) a job in a science or engineering occupation, and (3) self-classification. As a result, NSF data include individuals who are not necessarily working in a science or engineering occupation at the time surveyed—for example, an engineer who is now in a nonengineering job but who considers himself or herself an engineer and holds an engineering degree. Discrepancies between OPM and NSF data are inevitable because they come from different sources: OPM data from employers and NSF data from individuals.

Two agencies in Washington, D.C., regularly provide projections about the entire scientific and engineering work force: the Bureau of Labor Statistics (BLS) and the NSF. A number of BLS publications deal with projections, one being the *Occupational Outlook Handbook*. NSF publishes projections of supply and demand both for doctoral scientists and engineers and for all scientists and engineers, showing what would happen under various scenarios.

OPM data are primarily used by the central management agencies of the government—OMB and OPM, for example—but the dynamic data are not published by OPM. Under those conditions, do the agencies ask for compilations to see how they compare to other agencies? According to OPM staff, this seldom occurs. Therefore, one wonders whether the agencies themselves will use the data that they provide to OPM to analyze their own performance.

Findings

- The Department of Defense (DoD) is the largest employer of federal scientists and engineers, about 50 percent of them, followed by the Department of Agriculture (USDA, 13 percent) and the Department of the Interior (7 percent).
- In essentially all major occupational subgroups, DoD is the largest employer with two exceptions: USDA is the largest employer of life scientists and the Veterans Administration employs the most psychologists.
- Only 25 percent of all federal scientists and engineers are actually engaged in R&D, with the rest employed in design, natural resource operation, management, and a host of other occupations.
- In the federal government, 58 percent of the doctorates in science are in R&D, in contrast to the national Ph.D. total of about one-third.
- Not all scientists and engineers working on a particular mission are employed in one agency. For example, although the Environmental Protection Agency (EPA) is only the seventh largest employer of scientists and engineers in the federal government, environmental issues are the second largest focus of work activities of federal scientists and engineers.
- An examination of scientists and engineers by their age group reveals that only 14 percent of federal scientists and engineers fall in the "over 55" group, as compared to 19 percent in the total U.S. work force.
- Information from a survey by the U.S. Merit Systems Protection Board (MSPB) indicates that members of the Senior Executive Service (SES) leave the government for four main reasons: ceilings on salary, changes in the retirement system, politicization of their organization, and inadequate use of their knowledge and skills.
- Because salary data are usually presented in terms of median or average salaries, comparisons assume that the distributions in each sector are identical with respect to age, occupation, and highest academic degree, but they are not.

Recommendations

- An examination should be made to determine when data available from OPM and other places are being utilized by the individuals agencies in the management of their science and engineering work forces.
- There ought to be an evaluation as to whether the dynamic data, those on separations and hires collected by OPM, should be more widely available in published form, at least to other federal agencies.
- Data on satisfaction or dissatisfaction in the job, as well as on the quality of the federal science and engineering work force—similar to that recently compiled by the DoD—should be generated on a regular periodic basis and made publicly available.
- Agencies should use projections about the future supply of scientists and engineers in the total U.S. work force to make projections of their own future demand for scientists and engineers.
- There should be a central body in the federal government that explicitly has the sole responsibility to evaluate the adequacy of the federal science and engineering work force.

Discussion

Dr. CAMPBELL said that this is a fascinating issue because aggregate turnover numbers are very low: in much of the private sector, turnover rates of 2 percent would be considered too low. He asked the agency representatives whether there would be ways to make the aggregate data more useful to them, or whether the current system of an agency building its own data base for its own management purposes (with the aggregated base being used essentially for broader policy questions) is more preferable. He noted that the Committee will address whether there should be changes in the nature of the federal data-collecting system and the character of what is being collected.

Reliability of the Data

Inconsistent Definitions: Dr. NORWOOD felt that the basic question really should not be "Why are the data not being used?" but rather "How good are the data?" Having responsibility for the measurement of occupational employment at all levels, BLS examined salary data for engineers—learning that those engineers who earn top salaries are managers of engineering work; thus, in the standard occupational classification structure, they are considered to be managers. Yet they are still engineers: they are trained as engineers and many of them are still doing engineering research, but they also are managing. Similarly, she noted that many SES people have to be classified as managers: they manage groups and cannot be classified as experts in a particular area if they are going to reach the higher salary classifications.

One also must take into account differences in the people and their skills. At BLS, for instance, there are statisticians and mathematical statisticians, each having different kinds of training. For example, although BLS employs three kinds of scientists, data on them is combined with data on scientists in other parts of the Department of

Labor (DOL); thus, the picture drawn from OPM data might reflect what is happening in DOL overall but totally miss what is happening in BLS.

Other problems arise when terms such as "turnover" are not clearly defined. For example, BLS may have a 16-17 percent turnover rate, but if BLS employees merely move to other parts of the DOL, the turnover rate for DOL is not affected. Mr. RAGONE commented on the 4 percent turnover rate cited in OPM data for hydrologists: of the 2,170 federally employed hydrologists, less than 200 work in the research program of the U.S. Geological Survey's Water Resources Division; thus, the aggregated data do not reflect the turnover rate in USGS. In addition, he noted that all employees in the Water Resources Division are considered to be hydrologists, even though their degrees may be in different fields, such as geochemistry.

The nature of the discussion pointed out that (1) dealing with the personnel system in the federal government is a very complex undertaking and (2) a main underlying problem is definitions and coverages—for instance, whether turnover just involves quits, includes separations, or recognizes transfers and whether the data deal with permanent staff, temporary staff, or seasonal employment. In the aggregate, one cannot deal with the multitude and myriad of problems that are unique to particular areas. That is why, according to Mr. CURNOW, the agencies themselves should conduct self-studies of turnover, separations, and quits. Using its aggregate data base, OPM looks at organizational supplements but not at program offices in any particular area. Furthermore, because the occupational classification that the government uses stays with an individual if he or she moves into a managerial or supervisory position, another definitional problem exists with respect to how managers are classified in the public sector as opposed to the federal sector.

Comparability of Data Sets: Mr. FECHTER said that information collected on individuals is good for tracking career trajectories. However, firm-based data, which is based on occupational classes, will not provide very reliable information about movement of individuals. Instead the issues of promotion and of moving into management, which are part of the dynamics of the system, need to be looked at very carefully.

Dr. VAN RIJN advocated the use of aggregated data available from the CPDF because various agencies have their own data bases, which may be incompatible and based on different definitions for key terminology. Using CPDF data, researchers can present the turnover rate for all occupations and show variations by length of service and from agency to agency. Although agency-specific data will always be more sophisticated and more detailed, based on the agency's purposes, aggregate data are necessary to determine the baseline. He pointed out that once definitional problems are resolved, agency data appear more similar to CPDF data. In fact, people in the agencies are using the aggregate data to stimulate their own internal research and definition of the problem of turnover.

Mr. RAGONE cited the danger of using national statistics, which do not reflect what is happening in significant but small parts of the work force. For instance, USGS has difficulty recruiting individuals at GS-12-15 levels for its national research program: it cannot compete with private industry at those levels. He emphasized that national statistics do not reflect the situation adequately; one must look at the agencies, their specific kinds of expertise, and what they are trying to accomplish.

Dr. MAHLER cautioned against comparing statistics on the federal work force with those dealing with the national work force because the government, in most cases, cannot hire foreign nationals. He also noted that the more widely available data do not reflect that an agency may employ more scientists and engineers as contractors who are paid on a different scale and do different work than the in-house scientists and engineers.

Usefulness of the Data

Dr. NORWOOD felt the bigger issue is identifying what statistics are really needed and the extent to which users of the data provide feedback to those who generate them. Mr. HOWTON responded that agencies don't use aggregated OPM data because those data have been massaged so as to be essentially useless at the field operations level. He agreed with others' comments that the federal data collection system does not take into account that private industry moves people into managerial titles out of science and engineering: they cease being engineers about the time they become branch managers, and all of a sudden their salaries are no longer reflected in the data base that OPM or BLS uses for its salary curves. However, Dr. AMBLER felt that the collected data are useful to a laboratory director in recruiting scientists and engineers by providing the reasons for leaving and the comparability of pay broken down by different ages and employment sectors.

At least three federal organizations—Naval Research Lab (NRL), DoD, and Centers for Disease Control (CDC)—have designed their own data collection systems to learn more about their own personnel. Dr. NUMRICH noted that NRL maintains two personnel data bases because it cannot make sufficient projections from the data that it sends to OPM. NRL keeps more detailed, exhaustive information to deal with its own problems, retaining items that have been dropped from the OPM data base. Data disaggregated by NRL have enabled the agency to compare its 1,800 scientists and engineers, more than 50 percent having Ph.D.s, with comparable agencies on a quartile basis, using maturity curves. Recruitment and retention data show that NRL's declination rate for firm offers increased exponentially during the last three years. Particularly disappointing is the inability to retain postdocs in the face of outside salary offers of as much as $55,000 (NRL can offer between $35,825 and $46,571 for postdocs entering at the GS-12 level). One solution is to use R&D contracts under which people perform research tasks at the laboratory, but that alternative has two negative results: (1) contractors working next to lower-paid government employees doing the same type of job and (2) government scientists spending their time managing contracts, which is inefficient use of their skills.

Mr. LACY said that DoD also has created its own central data base, which covers every civilian and military employee of the department and enables one to distinguish "quits" (departures from DoD) from other types of personnel actions (transfers from the Army to the Navy, geographic relocations, and changes in one's occupation). The actual quit rate for scientists and engineers is quite low, whereas "overall employee turbulence" is much higher, reflecting the large number of people changing jobs within DoD each year.

Dr. GUINAN said that because the CDC uses two personnel systems, aggregate data is really meaningless. At least half of CDC's research scientists are members of the commissioned corps of the Public Health Service and are eligible for bonus pay not available to veterinarians and physicians whom CDC hires. Because of the way the system works, the aggregated data do not reflect this phenomenon.

Dr. GUINAN posed another problem: unless the original purpose of OPM's data collecting was to help recruit and retain new employees, it is both useless and invalid to use the collected data for that purpose. Only the agencies themselves can define both what their needs are and how a system should be designed to respond to those needs—which are so agency-specific, especially in critical areas, that no aggregated data would be useful to a single agency.

Dr. GINZBERG asked if new and additional data would help agencies respond to their most urgent problems of trying to manage, attract, retain, and utilize effectively their scientific and engineering personnel. Dr. CAMPBELL doubted that such data would make any difference to internal management but could make a case for improvement in the broad employment system. Dr. NUMRICH responded that agencies would like market-based pay, pay banding instead of automatic promotion steps, and removal of the pay cap. When Dr. GINZBERG asked whether she would trade off some personnel slots to gain these changes while staying within a total financial budget, she responded that, as necessary, NRL's senior management would trade seniority rights and positions; however, the concept of total financial budget is meaningless for Navy labs, which are run under the Naval Industrial Fund. Labs are not funded as line items, but compete for research and development funds which include money for salaries. If their work is not cost-effective, the funder could choose to support the research elsewhere.

As a senior computer scientist, Mr. ANDREWS views himself as a "trench warfare scientist" who writes major contracts and is involved in computer development on highly sophisticated, highly reliable systems. He questioned the usefulness of data on new engineers and new scientists: his experience is that it takes about five years for new employees to learn the culture of the Federal Aviation Administration in order to be productive.

Dr. AMBLER cautioned against statements that the aggregated data are useless. The larger issue is the dynamics of the organization that make it what it is. He felt the main point is that the data are useless in hiring scientists and engineers at the agency level.

Mr. CURNOW noted the differences between micro- and macrostatistics. OPM data cover all scientists and engineers, but the problems cited by workshop participants deal with a small subset, those engaged in R&D in labs. Dr. GUINAN concurred that information on who is doing R&D and statistics on that particular group of scientists and engineers is more germane than knowing what all scientists and engineers are doing in a particular area of research.

Quality of the Work Force: Several workshop participants emphasized that the most useful data would be those that indicate the quality of the federal scientific and engineering work force. Dr. MAHLER was concerned about the quality of the future work force because (1) the best undergraduates are foreign nationals who cannot be hired and (2) in spite of changing demographics, agencies are not addressing the people coming up in the system, concentrating their efforts only on the averages. Dr. FALK concurred, noting that 50 percent of engineering Ph.D.s graduating in the United States are foreign, but most government agencies cannot hire them for security clearance purposes. Dr. ROBINSON stated that improving the quality of the federal science and engineering work force is probably the most important issue for improving the way the government deals with science and technology, and Mr. PALGUTA concurred but added that, in spite of this, we have found no acceptable way to measure quality. Dr. FALK responded that the educational institution attended provides some indicator of the quality at the entry-level, but determining quality at mid-level is difficult.

Based on studies conducted by the National Academy of Public Administration, Dr. KLINE said that most National Aeronautics and Space Administration (NASA) personnel officers believe they are not having great difficulties in hiring engineers of the quality they have had in years past: average entry-level engineers have GPAs around 3.2, just as they did during the height of the Apollo program. Federal agencies have seldom attracted people with GPAs in the 3.6-4.0 range, although people use numbers like those to show declining quality. Neither Dr. STEINBACH nor Dr. NORWOOD considered GPAs to be a very good measure of quality without reference to the major area of studies and the school.

Negative Impacts: Dr. COMPTON said that data not only are not useful at the field laboratory level, but they are used against agencies. For instance, low turnover rates are used to prove that the federal government does not have an attrition problem: whenever an agency asks for something special, it must turn in turnover numbers to prove that it has a problem. He felt that although turnover numbers are low, a serious problem exists, particularly after 5-7 years of employment. Of 50 new scientists and engineers hired by Ames Research Center a year ago, Dr. COMPTON projected that 30-40 percent of them will leave within the first five years.

Mr. HARDY said the EPA has problems with the data because they presume more stability and less diversity than what the agency is experiencing. He noted that in implementing EPA's Superfund program, the aggregated data were used to keep EPA from getting the salary flexibilities and other requisites for recruiting and retaining needed people. In some cases, the data need to be disaggregated by agency, by individual agency within a larger group, and by individual programs in the agency.

Timeliness of the Data

Dr. NORWOOD noted that obtaining personnel data from the federal government is the most difficult problem of BLS, which gets good response from industry to surveys whose data are incorporated into its standard occupational classification.

Coordination of Data-Collection Efforts

Dr. GINZBERG, who agreed with the view that no office in the federal government has overview responsibilities for scientists and engineers, voiced concern with the weaknesses and quality of the data systems. He asked the agencies if a lack of data ever affected the planning of their operations and whether any particular kind of data was needed "to improve their management of scientists and engineers."

Conclusions

Mr. CAREY said that some of these points of "information" have secondary and tertiary effects throughout the decision system. The data need to be examined much further, not to question their quantitative accuracy but to see whether they reflect positively or negatively on government's ability to utilize and manage its very critical human resource. If government retains only 25 percent of its scientists and engineers in actual R&D, how does that compare with other sectors that are heavy users—for example, manufacturing or some of the Federally Funded Research and Development Centers (FFRDCs)? He felt that if a number like that is isolated in terms of the way government behaves, it could suggest things that are either true or false relative to the productivity and utilization of scientists and engineers; such data just cannot be left hanging. Before trying to make a case for higher compensation for scientists and engineers, isolating that population of specialists away from the general population of career people in other government occupations, we must better understand the data points.

Mr. PALGUTA mentioned the difficulty of getting Congress to look at even the aggregated data on federal civil service issues, let alone disaggregated data. He felt the most appropriate use of disaggregated data (e.g., data unique to an agency or agency subunit) is at the agency level. He suggested that the best solution is to allow greater discretion for each individual agency to tailor its personnel system to any unique needs identified in the data. This may require convincing Congress of the need for major changes in the civil service system to allow that discretion.

Reminding participants of the Committee's charge, Dr. CAMPBELL asked if there is a sufficient set of problems and difficulties with scientists and engineers to recommend the establishment, some place in the government, of a collection of data that is more disaggregated and thereby more usable for management. He wondered whether there is something so unique about scientists and engineers that there should be recommended a special set of institutions to deal with both data collection and policy recommendation in that area. Dr. NORWOOD made two points: (1) at least 100 other areas would request that same thing, and (2) before one can argue that the federal government has to do something, one must deal with the broader problem of a potential shortage of scientists and engineers in all sectors of the work force (although it is true that the private sector is much more flexible than the federal government). Dr. MESSNER agreed but noted that the federal government has a problem beyond the general condition.

Meeting Federal Work Force Needs With Regard to Scientists and Engineers: The Role of the U.S. Office of Personnel Management

Mr. PALGUTA explained that the MSPB is interested in recruiting and retaining not just scientists and engineers but the federal work force as a whole. As part of the civil service Reform Act enacted in 1978, the MSPB was established to hear and adjudicate appeals and to conduct periodic studies of the health of the federal civil service system. Scientists and engineers are an extremely vital and necessary resource for government to carry out its assigned role of service to the nation, and it is in the national interest to recruit and retain scientists and engineers who are among the most capable. Yet there is growing evidence that federal agencies are not very successful in this regard.

Policy-makers have two concerns in this area: (1) the quality of the individuals coming into government service, especially compared with those who are leaving, and (2) whether interventions might reduce any undesirable turnover. As to turnover, MSPB has found that nationally only about 5 percent of engineers and scientists leave the federal government each year, and this is split about evenly between retirements and resignations. Because many federal employees retire as soon as they are eligible, one goal might be to induce some of them to stay a few more years before retirement. Among the 2-3 percent of engineers and scientists who resign each year, Mr. PALGUTA noted, some of them undoubtedly are not well matched to their jobs and, therefore, agencies would not want them to stay. Other resignees are among the "stars" who leave for salaries of $150,000 and higher. Although these are the extremes, it is clear that difficulties in meeting current federal work force needs with regard to scientists and engineers will not be overcome solely or even primarily by reducing turnover.

On the national level, therefore, Mr. PALGUTA felt emphasis should be placed on recruitment interventions. The government simply is not effectively filling its vacant engineering and science positions. Recruitment is a multifaceted function, having three interrelated aspects, each of which is necessary for good recruitment but none of which alone is sufficient: (1) an agency's job opportunities have to be known; (2) the jobs, as well as the agency itself, have to be attractive to potential applicants; and (3) the hiring process must operate in a timely manner and also allow employers to make qualitative distinctions among the candidates for employment. The question is "What should the government do to improve its recruitment process?"

To answer that question, one needs to understand the changes that have occurred in the environment within which the government recruits. Twenty years ago, the hiring process for federal scientists and engineers was largely centralized in the U.S. civil service Commission. This policy was partly justified by a large influx of applications from individuals who found the image of government as an employer fairly good: we had recently put a man on the moon, the EPA had just been established to improve and protect our environment, world hunger might be conquered through federal agricultural research, and so on. The federal government was viewed as an exciting, interesting place to work and had the reputation of seeking to hire the best and brightest. Federal pay, while still not a match for many private-sector jobs, was closer than it is today. The weak spot 20 years ago was the government's centralized screening process: it could take six months or longer for a person to even have an application acknowledged and to get a numerical rating, and then even longer to be referred to an agency having a vacancy. Further compounding the recruitment process was the "rule of three": after screening the applicants available, the Civil Service Commission referred the three best applications to the agency, but the agency often rejected all three, believing that better applicants were available.

The current situation and conditions are much different. Recruitment today rarely involves screening massive numbers of applicants but rather tries to find a "live" applicant willing to accept a federal position. Today approximately 75 percent of engineering and science recruiting is done on a decentralized basis, in large part through authority delegated to individual federal agencies to directly hire any qualified applicant. OPM maintains a list of eligible candidates. Thus the question has changed from how to best screen a large number of applicants to whether the federal government can attract a sufficient number of well-qualified applicants in the first place. We have gone from a centralized process to a decentralized one.

We have seen an evolution and a shifting of roles between Congress, OPM, and the agencies, but the changes in government's organizational or procedural mechanisms that should accompany such a shift have not all been made. For instance, because of a traditionally rigid compensation system, salary remains a major issue: OPM's data show that an engineer hired at a GS-5 level in 1986 would be offered $18,700 versus a private industry offer of $27,000. More revealing is that four years later, in January 1990, those two individuals—the one who entered government as a GS-5 and the one who chose private industry employment for the additional $8,000 or $9,000 annual starting salary—end up earning about the same, about $39,000 a year. Government salaries rise more rapidly in the early years, but industry had learned that it could "front-load" salaries to attract employees. The government currently does not have this flexibility.

Once someone has entered the work force, however, inertia sets in: as long as an employee is being treated decently and is making an acceptable wage, there is a certain tendency not to shift to other employers. This may account partly for the low turnover rate in engineering and science occupations, as compared with other occupations that are affected by different dynamics. In addition, although the government could take care of any turnover problems by hiring people that nobody else wants, worse problems would obviously arise. The goal should be to recruit a good applicant pool at the outset. The individuals hired may be in government for a long time.

With regard to OPM's role in the process, MSPB has looked at delegation and decentralization as part of its review of efforts to simplify personnel management. MSPB supports OPM's efforts to delegate more authority to the agencies to recruit, select, and hire. The agencies, in turn, must take the initiative for developing their own college relations programs to recruit well-qualified employees and accept greater responsibility for the process. To assist in this regard, OPM and Congress must address the issue of salary through legislative change. OPM is aware that it should provide leadership to address not only the pay issue but also the process of recruitment, and it is attempting to do so. OPM should provide the tools for the agencies to use to recruit and retain well-qualified engineers and scientists and, through oversight, assure that they are properly used. OPM need intervene only where there is a problem, and then usually only on an agency-specific basis as opposed to a government-wide level. Finally, although it is not OPM's charter to be a champion of the federal employee per se, OPM is expected to be the champion of effective and efficient human resource management. In the long run, good human resource management involves treating employees and applicants for employment fairly and earning a reputation as a good employer.

Discussion

Need for More Personnel

Workshop participants stressed the need to look at the work activity and maturity curve to make the case for more personnel. Mr. HARDY noted that nothing in the current system will help EPA fix its Superfund problem—total comparability, facilities, equipment, etc.—short of some statutory or legislative remedy to help recruit and retain people. Although the recruitment, retention, and pay problems are significant, EPA generally does not experience these problems. However, because the Superfund program is a new activity that uses scientists and engineers in nontraditional ways, turnover is as high as 25 percent in some cases; people leave for higher pay, doubling the average $37,000 a year salary paid by the government.

Competition with Other Employment Sectors

Mr. ANDREWS said that because scientists and engineers have very marketable skills, the government must be very careful in how they manage them: there is a lot of parallel contractor activity, and contractors are willing to pay much more money for these marketable skills. Mr. HARDY said that in a new and emerging industry, EPA finds itself competing with its own contractors. This led EPA to undertake a self-study, concluding that the agency was creating its own problem and that less work would be done by contract.

Ms. MOWRY noted that the Department of Transportation (DOT) cannot compete not only with private industry but also with federal agencies such as National Institutes of Health (NIH) and NASA, which have more visible programs. Thus, DOT is not able to attract the higher level, quality applicant. As a result, the agency has little attrition at the mid-level, but instead is stuck sometimes with lower quality employees who really cannot compete in private industry because they lack the necessary talents and background. Compounding the situation is that the department has little training money to advance mediocre applicants. Thus some hope that the proposed defense cutbacks and current hiring freeze will result in gravitation and cross-line transfers from DoD to DOT. Finally, Ms. MOWRY cited the effects of the Gramm-Rudman five-year plans: DOT is analyzing how to operate with less money and still improve programs in all hard-to-fill occupations.

When Dr. LYONS expressed concern about the loss of National Institute of Standards and Technology (NIST) employees to academe, Mr. CAREY asked why that movement causes more concern than movement to industry: is there not a value in strengthening academic flow, too? Mr. LYONS replied that the flow used to go the other way; the National Bureau of Standards (NBS, predecessor to NIST) would lure people from academe. The real problem is not that the agency's top scientists and engineers are moving to academe but that the agency is losing them to second- and third-rank schools.

Mr. RAGONE asserted that (1) although the agencies have good theories about how to better recruit, retain, and pay scientists and engineers, the decision on implementing these theories is a political one determined by Congress, and (2) the three big research sectors of this country—the federal, private, and university sectors—are not really engaged in competition but actually reinforce each other.

Other Problems

Ms. MOWRY said that OPM has made it a lot easier for agencies to recruit but cited some factors detracting from effective recruitment:

(1) Most recruiters are untrained, having recruiting as a collateral duty.
(2) Most recruiters are much older than the college applicants whom they face at career fairs or on college campuses.
(3) Most agencies cannot compete at career fairs with private industry because the monies are tight. Agency recruiters do not have the glitzy displays or the number of recruiters actually needed to do a one- or two-day career fair.
(4) There is also much confusion among the different agencies as to what the direct-hire authorities are: because they differ agency to agency, applicants become confused.

She also said that most college graduates are looking for program stability; salary is not their primary consideration. In fact, many college counselors advise young people to work for the federal government to get the experience of beginning a project and seeing it through for several years. However, the federal government may not continue to offer such stability. Because of cuts to many programs, a lot of employees are being shifted or moved geographically.

Mr. KLEIN noted that disillusionment sets in among entry-level scientists and engineers when they find they won't be doing real engineering work but rather preparing to be contract managers because so much federal work is contracted out. This has led to congressional examination of how government work is conducted, to questions on the role of government R&D, and to discussions of what should be done in-house versus what should be done by contractors. Several workshop participants said that scientists and engineers in the government want to do things, not just manage the work of others, although that experience often serves as a means for them to acquire even more marketable skills. As mentioned earlier, this disillusionment is heightened when contractors sitting next to civil service people earn almost twice as much. This as a problem of some importance in terms of the health of federal science and engineering and the R&D establishment: How will federal agencies maintain the intellectual, managerial, and technical strength needed for government to do what will be required of it?

Decentralization

Dr. NORWOOD observed that although OPM attempted decentralization, the Office of Management and Budget (OMB) advocated centralization. She wondered whether there is any conflict between the decentralization required, since both OPM and other agencies to whom these tasks are decentralized have had their staffs reduced markedly because of OMB directives.

Mr. PALGUTA responded that problems do arise because agencies are given more work but their staffs are reduced. He noted, however, that agencies are directed to cut overhead by a given percentage but are free to determine the job classifications that such cuts will affect. Because of decentralization and tighter budgets, individual managers, not personnel staffs, find themselves tasked with greater responsibility for recruitment, which is probably as it should be (although many agencies and agency managers do not recognize that they are being tasked with a greater responsibility). Some activities must be centralized because agencies need basic tools such as a flexible, realistic compensation system.

OPM has tried to assist agencies in two areas:

(1) Because many students do not know where they might apply and how to find a federal job, in September OPM set up the college hotline: by calling a 900 number and answering a series of questions about one's specialties, degrees, and college(s) attended, a person can learn how to apply for a job and is sent the appropriate federal forms for applying. A prerecorded voice explains the process and the basics of the system. If an individual wants to find out about specific agencies, he or she may call a given number to talk to an actual recruiter.

(2) OPM has replaced the FS-171 with an automated form processed within 24 hours at its Macon, Ga., facility. The rest is left up to the individual agencies. For example, if an agency wants to recruit an engineer, it uses a specific code to hook into this automated system; after specifying the series, grade, and specialty wanted, within 13 minutes the agency will receive either a particular application or a referral of all the candidates who qualify for that job.

Mr. KLEIN enthusiastically noted that many agencies find this system useful, after expressing disbelief that the federal government had created it. Besides its facility and speed, this system benefits agencies because the referrals allow direct hire of anyone on the list. A disaggregated system could never be imposed on the total federal government, for the resulting paperwork would be mountainous. He felt that uniform definitions are not the solution: some agencies would find that those definitions do not work for them. Furthermore, if the general movement during the past 10-15 years of granting greater authority to the departments and agencies should continue, one must be careful not to impose from the center even data requirements that can influence how management operates. Determining how much flexibility and decentralization are needed in government is very difficult because of the overwhelming pressure of the centralizing site, whether it is the central agencies, the data collectors, Congress, or the General Accounting Office. All of those things tend to force centralization, and maintaining a decentralized operation in that context is very difficult. In spite of Mr. KLEIN's enthusiasm, most workshop participants said they were unaware of this automated system.

Hiring Authority

Dr. CAMPBELL reinforced the idea that, if there is one major cultural difference between the federal government and the private sector, it is the degree to which the chief personnel officer is the line officer. In the private sector, the personnel people provide assistance but also get involved in every personnel decision because the success of their unit depends on those people who are recruited and given training. It is important not only that line managers and senior executives go out and recruit but that established relationships with universities continue between recruiting trips. Dr. NORWOOD thought many agencies have done that. Dr. CAMPBELL added that agencies should be given the authority for hiring on the spot and thus avoid the situation whereby desired individuals have taken employment elsewhere. Many participants were grateful that agencies are allowed to hire college graduates off the campus.

As a result of decentralization, 70 percent of all new federal employees are hired through delegation, as opposed to the 14 percent under a more centralized system in 1981; 95 percent of scientists and engineers are employed through direct-hire authority—that is, the agencies find potential employees and hire them. OPM has taken the stance that if individuals are qualified and agencies are satisfied with those qualifications, the agencies should go ahead and hire them.

Dr. NORWOOD asked, "How hard is it to get OPM to declare a particular occupation in shortage?" Mr. KLEIN responded that it is becoming easier because there are more shortages. Dr. CAMPBELL was alarmed that the delegation of hiring authority results from a shortage of candidates rather than from a change in philosophy in the central personnel agency. But Mr. PALGUTA explained that the greater delegation of hiring authority during the transition from the civil service Commission to OPM was a planned action, although it was followed by a rescission of those authorities along with much negative feedback from the agencies that had enjoyed them. Redelegation and re-decentralization are supply and demand problems as well as a resource problem, since OPM cannot handle the hiring of government employees by itself.

Essentially, all engineers, "hard" scientists, medical specialists, mathematicians, and computer scientists are direct hire. Dr. STEINBACH said that he had been informed that direct hiring authority extends only to engineers and not to physicists or statisticians, but Mr. KLEIN noted that that was false information.

Flexibility

Dr. GINZBERG asked whether anybody has been clever enough to structure the job classification system to have less trouble hiring at the entry level. Dr. CHEN responded that NIH uses a special authority of the Public Health Service Act, its enabling legislation, to bring in young scientists primarily in the biomedical area without being restricted by the civil service classification system: a tenure-type system similar to that of a university enables NIH to keep these individuals for up to seven years in a temporary appointment. Because salaries are negotiated and set administratively, supervisors feel they have more power at the entry level. At the end of seven years, either these individuals receive tenure, usually as a GS-13, or they leave; about 10 percent achieve tenure. Mr. HOWTON added that agencies have some hiring flexibility at the entry level—based on GPA, one can be hired above step one. However, when a GS-7, step 10, can only be offered only $27,000 by the government but can earn $40,000 in private industry, problems arise.

Concurring with others about the importance of initial recruiting, Dr. AMBLER emphasized that Congress, OPM, and the departmental personnel offices should have no role in that process after granting agencies the flexibility, but Mr. PALGUTA concluded that a higher level decision-making, that of Congress and OMB, currently preempts OPM and the agencies from achieving greater flexibility.

Both Dr. GINZBERG and Dr. CAMPBELL thought the agencies' most important need is flexibility to respond to the market in real dollars and other benefits. What it would take for an agency to tell Congress that, instead of providing a personnel budget, 100 percent in terms of jobs, it wanted a 5-10 percent conversion possibility of its personnel budget to establish super-grades at the bottom and at the middle levels? The different agencies have different problems, and with a little flexibility on the dollar side and benefit side, they could better handle many of the problems they face. However, Dr. NORWOOD said that the term "agency" should be clearly defined.

The Federal Employees Retirement System

Many participants felt that the federal retirement system also stymies recruitment and retention. Dr. GUINAN advocated a federal retirement system compatible with that in most universities; it might lure a scientist from academe to contribute five years of very productive time in federal service.

Dr. NUMRICH wondered about the effect the Federal Employees Retirement System (FERS) will have on attrition in about 10 years, when mid-career people will be on FERS, highly mobile, and facing college tuitions of their children. Mr. PALGUTA responded that the conventional wisdom is that FERS will have a negative impact because the very concept behind FERS was portability. However, he pointed out that in its periodic government-wide samplings of 20,000 federal employees, the MSPB consistently finds that federal employees like their jobs, by and large, although they may be dissatisfied about particular conditions of employment such as pay. Once individuals enter government, agencies have a strong ability to keep them if they are given at least a living wage, meaningful work, and good management and if agencies use their skills.

Dr. GUINAN felt that most agencies would advocate more flexibility in the retirement system as a mechanism for enhancing their recruitment and retention capabilities, facilitating movement from academe to government and back. Dr. CAMPBELL asked how much difference it would make if the government were able to make contributions to TIAA-CREF when it attracted academics enrolled in the program. Dr. GUINAN responded that it would make a big difference in a small percentage of cases—for a director of a center, for example. Such an individual would be willing to go for five years, and the agency would have five years of leadership in a very important position. Dr. WINDUS indicated that NSF does this now but cautioned that, besides TIAA-CREF, some visiting scientists to NSF belong to retirement systems—such as state systems—that prohibit contributions by NSF during the individual's tenure at NSF. Dr. ROBINSON asserted that this can be mandated legislatively; some states do it. Dr. WINDUS noted the problem posed by the restriction on the amount that can be paid to visiting scholars, congressionally limited at $95,000.

Future Projections

Dr. GINZBERG asked whether people from DoD saw any change in the labor market in terms of "the changing outlook for the defense budget." Individuals may not want to get involved in the defense area, which is expected to be downgraded among federal priorities and lead also to less money for the private sector in the defense-aerospace area. He wondered whether the federal government has made any hypothetical adaptations to this changed labor market and asked how quickly in the short run the tightness on the scientific and engineering front can change. He noted that when the NASA and defense budgets went down simultaneously in the early 1970s, both that market and the federal government's position toward it changed rapidly.

Dr. STEINBACH responded that DoD has not noticed any changes because it has a hiring freeze. Dr. NORWOOD added that the proposed cutback in defense is really a cutback from levels that have not been achieved, that is, future levels. Therefore, DoD will not really be affected for some years. Supporting that idea, Mr. LACY said that data on successions reveal that 1989 was a banner year for hiring new engineers: DoD added about 7,000 new engineers as civil service employees, compared with about 4,300 in 1988. However, he added that DoD is looking at what effect the hiring freeze will have in the long run: although DoD expects only a limited problem with the retention of scientists and engineers because they turn over so slowly, soon everybody will be doing their own typing because of a shortage of secretaries.

Dr. CAMPBELL disagreed, expecting very substantial changes in terms of employment for engineers and physicists both in the broader defense industry as well as in DoD. Mr. PORTER said that because the broader defense industry has begun to react to the proposed cutbacks, the Naval Weapons Center is able to use the advantage of its demonstration program to offer higher salaries than other federal agencies and to still offer jobs, with acceptance rates jumping to 43 percent since 1987.

Differences in Recruitment, Retention, and Utilization Processes: A Comparison of Traditionally Operated Federal Laboratories, M&O Facilities, and Demonstration Projects

Dr. CLARK discussed some imaginative and different approaches to the management of the federal government's R&D activities, looking at labs directly operated by the government, contracted labs, and some of the civil service demonstration projects undertaken to provide increased flexibility to federal agencies. Most of the Department of Energy (DOE) laboratory systems are contractor operated. The Department of Commerce's NIST and the Navy labs examined are demonstration projects. The Tennessee Valley Authority is special in that it is a federal lab but not subject to the same policies and procedures as most civil service labs.

Talking about DOE laboratories as a group is difficult because they are more like the private sector, the types of contractors that run these labs are quite varied, and the personnel policies and procedures that they use also vary significantly. Even though DOE has approval authority of the personnel systems employed in these labs, they still are negotiated with DOE's nine operations offices, each of which has responsibilities for several DOE labs.

Recruitment and retention are interrelated, and separating cause from effect is not easy. The organizational factors that may cause a scientist or engineer to leave a federal lab after X number of years are the same ones that may keep a well-informed candidate from joining the lab initially. Dr. CLARK listed the kinds of problems experienced in federal R&D labs and discussed some of the techniques that labs use to resolve them:

Problems	Solutions
Compensation	One compensation issue of concern to most lab directors is the federal pay cap and its effect on the ability to retain senior administrators and outstanding researchers. Alternatives include nonsalary compensation, pay banding, recruitment bonuses, relocation bonuses, and occupation-specific pay scales.

Time required to extend an offer of employment	Direct-hire authority, simplified hiring procedures, and increased personnel authority for line managers.
Difficulty of promotion after reaching the GS-12 level	Pay banding, increased personnel authority for line managers, and occupation-specific salary schedules.
Restricted role of line managers in personnel decisions	Flexibility in increasing salary without promoting, increased personnel authority for line managers, and occupation-specific salary schedules.
Excessive paper work	Direct-hire authority, computer-assisted classifications, and more generic classifications.
Questionable tie between performance and pay	Performance appraisals, multiple components of pay increase that are not mutually exclusive, and bonuses and awards.
Personnel ceilings and reductions-in-force (RIF)	Use of adjunct personnel such as postdocs, flexibility in considering things other than seniority, and simplified classification systems that enable the labs to retrain RIFed staff.
The aging work force	Well-thought-out institutional planning is necessary to ensure long-term health of the lab, but not much is being done
Job satisfaction, morale	See above.

Lab directors and managers, in general, seem to feel that the civil service system is external to them. It operates outside the lab that it is serving so its accountability is less than would be desired. In DOE, for instance, each lab has its own personnel system. Also, the civil service system is designed to be an efficient, effective system for the "average" federal employee in the "average" federal agency.

Discussion

Demonstration Projects

Mr. THOMPSON cited the measurable benefits of the Navy demonstration projects as identified by OPM:

(1) An increase in quality of people who have been recruited, even in less advantageous geographical settings, as indicated by increases in GPAs;
(2) Easier recruitment because of the ability to offer starting salaries reasonably close to the industry average;
(3) Pay progression more similar to that employed in the private sector (start higher and advance slower);

(4) Pay for performance: high-quality people are often attracted by a system that will reward them differently from people performing less well;
(5) Satisfaction with the revised job classification system, which is as accurate and certainly more expeditious than the old system;
(6) Improved attitudes of managers, who feel significantly more empowered to run the personnel system through the various flexibilities built into it; and
(7) Increased job satisfaction.

China Lake: According to Mr. PORTER, the Navy's demonstration program at China Lake has been considered a real success since its establishment in 1980. It began as a five-year experiment, was extended for a second five years, and now has been extended indefinitely by congressional legislation backed by OPM. Although lacking authority to grant recruitment bonuses, China Lake does have direct-hire authority and the authority to adjust beginning salaries beyond the broad pay band to be competitive in the marketplace. Assignment of position classification is the responsibility of line managers, with audits by the personnel department after the fact. The personnel office, instead of being in an adversary relationship, is supportive, helping China Lake to provide better training of staff. China Lake also employs a dual-career ladder, whereby top technical people are promoted based on their technical skills and can earn as much as or more than the managers.

Mr. PORTER said that the annual additional cost for implementing these changes during the project's first six years was only 1 percent more than the expenditures of similar labs that operate under the traditional civil service system; that cost difference appears to have stabilized. Although the Navy believes a 6 percent change over a 10-year period is not all that significant, OMB staff, looking at the possibility of extending the project government-wide or laboratory-wide, have a different opinion. Dr. KLINE advised that concerns about budget neutrality should be balanced by recognition of the lab's improved performance, which the Packard Commission report and other studies have pointed out.

NIST: Mr. LYONS explained that in 1982 the White House Science Council asked David Packard to convene a subcommittee that visited a number of national labs and made four recommendations, one of which dealt with personnel problems and focused on the China Lake experiment. Presidential interest in those findings led the science adviser to convene a Committee on Federal Laboratories, chaired by Jim Ling, to look into the Packard report. That committee responded to its charge by drafting a bill that proposed even more flexibility in regard to personnel issues than the China Lake experiment allowed. NBS had one goal in mind—to maintain and increase the quality of its staff. However, under review by OMB, OPM, and the agencies, the proposed bill engendered stiff opposition, but Dr. Packard personally delivered the draft to Don Fuqua, then chairman of the full House Science and Technology Committee.

Congress eventually passed that legislation as a part of the reauthorization bill for the NBS, detailing line for line what its demonstration project could do. One provision is direct-hire authority for the whole agency, except for blue-collar workers: even a division chief can make a hire, offering what he or she thinks the market demands up to the 75th percentile of the top salary stated in the DOE salary surveys. In addition,

NIST can make an on-the-spot offer and hire in a matter of days, offer $10,000 recruitment and retention bonuses, and pay whatever starting salary seems valid.

Another important aspect of the demonstration project is having line managers do the classification and the qualification check, with personnel officers authorized to audit the programs. As a result, entry-level problems experienced by NBS seem to have been resolved, as have those associated with recruiting. Retention problems have arisen, however, as division chiefs and senior scientists accept professorships at mid-level universities for more than $100,000 (but aggregate statistics do not show that loss, which only concerns the top 5 percent of employees). Some participants believed that some turnover is necessary to prevent a laboratory from becoming static.

Dr. ROBINSON expressed concern about the mechanism by which the operations of a federal demonstration project achieve full-scale implementation. He described, from his own experience, the difficulty in moving from research into production, particularly when there is an institutional barrier between the research lab and the production facility; the major role of the manager is to overcome these barriers before they arise. Similarly, he believed, before beginning a demonstration project, there should be a mechanism for determining what one hopes it will achieve and criteria on which to base decisions about implementing the demonstration on a permanent basis, as well as a mechanism for providing continuing oversight.

Both Dr. AMBLER and Dr. CAMPBELL asserted that just getting authority to establish a demonstration project was a major feat and that taking steps during the planning stage to ensure its life beyond the experimental period would be too time-consuming and involved. Nonetheless, Dr. CAMPBELL, concurring with Dr. Robinson's analysis of the barriers to implementation, agreed that a major question is how to overcome those barriers to make the leap from the current personnel management system in the federal government to a more effective one: How do you select mechanisms for deciding to go beyond the experiment and implement its policies and procedures on a permanent basis? Discussion among participants provided no answer to this question.

Dr. GINZBERG felt that if Congress will not give the executive departments more leeway in spending their allocated funds, implementation of demonstration projects will be difficult; he advocated substantial decentralization of the personnel budgets of the agencies. Dr. AMBLER added that one must recognize from the beginning that designing a demonstration project is a lot of work for senior managers, who must plan and clear it with the relevant department and OPM and get the technical people enthusiastic about it.

Dr. AMBLER asked how OPM and the congressional committees would react if the President's science adviser said, "I have read about these demonstration projects. They are the best thing since sliced bread." Dr. CAMPBELL felt that OPM would support demonstration projects, but Dr. NUMRICH believed OMB would oppose increasing the number of projects involving scientists and engineers; furthermore, OMB has criticized the existing demonstration projects as having not proved success through the use of acceptable metrics such as increased productivity. Dr. FINNEY said OMB's support would depend on whether the project is revenue neutral. However, Dr. NORWOOD said that even more important is the political reality of concern to

OMB: when the President says we are going to put the government on a diet but the result is not fewer people, it becomes a political issue.

Dr. MESSNER offered two other relevant points: (1) OMB has become less aggressive about setting arbitrary numbers as controls, focusing mainly on a guarantee that the demonstration project not exceed its funding level set by OMB; and (2) it takes a long time for Congress to move.

Dr. KLINE said that when he attended Cabinet meetings during the 1980s, support for demonstration projects that would enhance the recruitment and retention of scientists and engineers was not forthcoming because the data showed an attrition rate of only 5 percent for scientists and engineers, half of the government-wide rate in general. He felt that instead the focus should be on how a demonstration project can enhance the performance of government laboratories. However, Dr. AMBLER mentioned the lack of a productivity measure for an R&D institution.

M&O Facilities

For the management-and-operating-contractor (M&O) facilities, the DOE operations offices negotiate personnel policies and salaries with the contractors at each lab. Although salaries vary from one lab to another, the contractor itself must conduct a market survey to justify the proposed salary schedules. On the other hand, because DOE has final approval authority, staff in the operations offices are aware of the relationships between the salary schedules of their contracted facilities and the GS schedules.

Mr. HOWTON said that DOE does operate two GOGO (government-owned, government-operated) research laboratories, one in Morgantown, W.Va., and one in Pittsburgh, Pa., as well as the on-site M&O contractors. In a broad sense, the contractors' salaries are significantly (10-15 percent) above the federal salaries, although the GOGOs and M&Os are almost mirror organizations. There are differences, however, in the deferred compensation costs associated with each type of facility; such costs for the M&Os show up in contract costs to DOE, not in base salary. M&Os also have stock ownership plans and other benefits not offered by the government.

Dr. SUTHERLAND described the strong working relationship between the Jet Propulsion Laboratory (JPL) and Cal Tech, whose faculty serve as principal scientists or investigators on JPL projects and whose students are involved in the lab's research projects. All of JPL's policies and procedures are Cal Tech policies, not federal ones. JPL advises NASA of planned changes, and NASA can object within a certain period of time, but the relationship with NASA is superb. In fact, many JPL staff are detailees to NASA headquarters on a non-conflict-of-interest basis, and some Cal Tech faculty are on loan to NASA through JPL.

Other Possible Solutions

Dr. COMPTON said that the NASA Ames Laboratory had two options to the civil service system: to fix it or to get out. The use of demonstration projects is an example of fixing the problem. Becoming an FFRDC or an M&O is a way of moving out of the civil service system; JPL is a fulfillment of that option. He described the difficulty in acquiring university sponsorship of Ames activities. Respected universities were not interested in picking up a federal research center as part of their institution for two reasons: Ames was too big an operation, and universities want more control over the lab's activities, particularly because of adverse publicity that might occur if something went wrong in the lab's operations. Dr. COMPTON observed that to establish a strong relationship, a university and a federal agency must "grow up together": they are difficult marriages to make once two mature institutions are involved.

Mr. CAREY, mentioning his membership on the University of Chicago's Board of Governors for Argonne National Laboratory, agreed that the university places a high value on its relationship with the laboratory. They have established a positive, mutual relationship, although the inevitable tensions between the parent government department, DOE for example, and the laboratory are sometimes difficult for the trustees of the university to accept. In other words, constraints exist, even in the flow of appropriation funding to the laboratories.

Mr. HARDY observed that some federal organizations such as the Atomic Energy Commission (AEC) offer a number of the flexibilities associated with the demonstration experiments. However, the AEC opted for contractor-operated labs because of the frustrations associated with hiring and the desire to use their work force effectively.

Dr. CAMPBELL asked whether managing a contractor requires special skills, whether it is more difficult or easier to manage a contractor than it is a federal work force. Mr. HOWTON replied that comparisons are inappropriate because each involves an entirely different set of laws and procurement regulations; management problems that do arise tend to be legal and liability issues associated with nuclear energy: people are scared of what the costs will be for them. However, Mr. HARDY noted that in the Clinch River Breeder Reactor project, which involved both contractor and federal employees, dealing with the federal part of the system was more frustrating and more difficult, having more "traps" and rules.

Responding to Compensation Concerns

Entry Level: Dr. VAN RIJN was concerned about morale problems that may arise when scientists working in different divisions receive different entry-level pay because they have different managers. Dr. LYONS did not consider that a serious problem: the NIST demonstration project resembles an industrial personnel system.

Dr. STEINBACH pointed out that the entry pay in the government is low. For example, hiring a physicist in the area of electromagnetics is difficult not only because there are so few available but also because their initial pay is less than that of a secretary in the Washington area. He also observed that the median salaries indicate insufficient flexibility in the government: just about everybody gets the same pay.

Mr. FECHTER noted that a recent review of DoD's science and engineering work force reinforces the impressions that the salary disparity is quite large at the entry level but narrows dramatically after four to five years of employment. Promotion is a mechanism for managing one's work force, although it may not be the right mechanism. The DoD study also examined movements of individuals within the federal government, between positions and across grades.

Dr. NUMRICH presented data based on the national Hay Survey of R&D

organizations contracted by DOE. On a maturity curve basis, NRL lags about 40 percent at the 90th percentile for entry-level engineers (special rates are included in the NRL figures). At the higher experience levels, the differences are about 20 percent for nonsupervisory positions. However, when the comparison is based on a comparable private-sector organization, salaries for all types of degree recipients (B.S., M.S., Ph.D.) working in either supervisory or nonsupervisory roles lag by a figure closer to 25 percent, representing dollar lags of as much as $25,000 for lead researchers. Fully aggregated data show only a 2-5 percent lag. She emphasized that analyses of data relating to federal recruitment and retention should include examinations of private-sector organizations doing similar work.

Mid-Career and Senior Levels: Agencies—particularly demonstration projects—have devised special provisions to address issues dealing with supervisors and senior scientists. At NIST these included higher salary offers, a program of NBS fellows, and supervisor differentials of 3 percent for group leaders and 6 percent for division chiefs (NIST has no employees in the super grades GS-16 to -18, about two dozen on the ST salary schedule, and slightly more than 100 in the SES).

Dr. MAHLER noted that although both NIST and the National Oceanic and Atmospheric Administration (NOAA) have facilities in Boulder, Colo., the initial concern—that the higher salaries offered by NIST would encourage NOAA employees to transfer to NIST—has not been realized. He felt that NOAA was able to retain its staff because salary is not the only issue: nonsalary items such as the work performed are important, too.

CDC has no trouble recruiting young scientists, both because of the bonus pay option and because of its research orientation: the excitement of research institutions in the federal government is a lure for young scientists, who are willing to put up with a lot of things to work in an exciting environment. However, Dr. GUINAN noted CDC's difficulty in recruiting at the middle and upper levels because the excitement of the environment is overshadowed by prospective employees' concerns about money and sending their kids to college. A middle-level scientist with two children in college cannot survive on a federal salary.

In spite of the difficulty of recruiting at the mid-level, Dr. GUINAN felt there is not enough turnover once career scientists reach the upper levels: the lack of new blood coming into the upper strata could lead CDC away from the cutting edge. She concurred that there is a particular shortage of scientists in any emerging field: CDC needs molecular biologists to conduct research on retroviruses but cannot compete with the higher salaries paid in the private sector.

Mr. RAGONE found it difficult to justify noncompetitive salaries at a time when the research work force is aging dramatically. At GS-5-9, the U.S. Geological Survey is being "eaten alive" by the consulting firms that offer hydrologists much higher salaries. He also noted the lack of discretionary funds that would enable federal employees to attend professional meetings.

Pay for Performance: The criteria for evaluating performance is based on comparing an individual with his or her peers in the scientific area—how many papers they write and how much basic research they do. In general, scientists seem satisfied with these criteria. Mr. PORTER said that China Lake has been able to establish a link between pay and performance that works better than the old system; although there is not universal satisfaction with the new system, external studies indicate that, in general, it is accepted and people are happier with the system now than they were before.

According to Dr. AMBLER, pay for performance was implemented at NIST before the demonstration project; it is a lot of work but is considered to be much better than the alternative. In fact, NIST hesitates to give retention bonuses because the whole system is based on pay for performance, and it is better to give employees permanent adjustment to base salary. Dr. AMBLER also clarified that its authorizing statute says nothing about revenue neutrality, but the NIST administration wanted it. (After the authorizing act was passed, NIST was told to be budget neutral and not to exceed the civil service pay cap. However, because half of NIST's income comes from other federal agencies, Dr. LYONS wondered whether anybody knows what "budget neutral" is.) He concurred with Dr. CAMPBELL that, in order for a pay-for-performance system to work, there must be clearly established objectives to be achieved in a particular time period.

Responding to a question of Dr. Numrich, Mr. THOMPSON said that OPM considers the Performance Management Recognition System (PMRS), established in 1984 by Congress, to be a system based on pay for performance. However, he noted two important distinctions between pay for performance in the Navy and NIST demonstration experiments and the PMRS: (1) the potential for large rewards under the demo systems has been much greater because of greater funding, and (2) the demonstration project systems have won greater employee acceptance because of the way they were implemented, beginning with communication of objectives and follow-through dialogue between employee and supervisor.

Dr. CAMPBELL questioned whether promotions in the federal government are a result of performance or simply a way of catching up and making the government competitive. Dr. NORWOOD responded that federal scientists almost automatically progress from GS-5 to GS-11; after reaching GS-11, it becomes harder to get a promotion.

Dr. CAMPBELL said that a variety of gain-sharing programs exist in private industry but are primarily restricted to mid-level management as opposed to being total-employee programs. Dr. MAHLER cited the inequities in the federal government's bonus systems: A scientist could receive a bonus under the PMRS, while the bonus system for nonmanagers is the General Workforce Performance Appraisal System (GWPAS). The PMRS has a finite pool of money that can be used for bonuses, whereas GWPAS has limitations only on the size of each individual award. Thus an outstanding manager might receive an $800 bonus while an outstanding performer under GWPAS could receive $2,000. Dr. CAMPBELL contrasted this policy with that in the private sector: companies want everybody to maximize their bonus because if that is true, the corporation is doing great.

Dr. GINZBERG said that this awkward, inflexible, complicated system of personnel management in the federal government is closely connected with less-than-optimal performance. That fact should be the basis of any case for greater agency discretion. In response, Dr. NUMRICH declared that NRL has historically performed excellent research and continues to do so: "We are in a situation of diminishing returns and maintain our influx of talent only because of heroic efforts in recruitment and retention and the presence of excellent scientific leadership." The real issue is that in 10 years the federal government can expect catastrophic failure because senior leadership will be eligible for retirement, and new employees (those under FERS), although they may be well-trained and have sound scientific reputations, will leave because of being in high demand and facing the financial problem of meeting college tuition payments: the federal government will be like a university without senior professors.

Dr. NORWOOD asked whether demonstration projects have been tried in an atmosphere where at least the middle-level employees are unionized. Dr. CLARK responded that Tennessee Valley Authority used a pay-for-performance system for its nonmanagerial, white-collar workers for seven years but abandoned it because of perceived inequities, both individually and across organizational units.

The Political Appointments Process and the Recruitment of Scientists and Engineers

Dr. CAMPBELL said that certain facts and observations prompted the Committee to consider the relative significance of noncareer appointments to the recruitment, retention, and utilization of scientists and engineers. Of concern were the increase in the number of political appointments; the number of vacancies in those positions; their influences on the culture, performance, and productivity of the federal organizations that make extensive use of scientists and engineers; and the slowness of the appointment process.

Dr. PFIFFNER began by describing the pressures of a Presidential transition: at a time when policy, power, and position are "up in the air," one must handle personnel recruitment, likened by some to "trying to take a sip from a fire hydrant." Of about 550 PAS positions (Presidential appointments with the advice and consent of the Senate) in the executive branch, the subset of scientists, engineers, and people that supervise them equals about 250 (according to National Research Council calculations). These numbers exclude noncareer SES and Schedule C appointments. Recruiting the best and brightest people for these positions is not difficult at the Cabinet level because of the prestige and power associated with Executive Level I appointments. However, recruitment of the subcabinet—that is, Executive Levels II through V—and noncareer SES is difficult for a number of reasons: noncompetitive pay, ethics requirements, financial disclosure, post-employment restrictions, the short tenure in office, and the daily risk of being dismissed (because one serves at the pleasure of the President).

Determining how the increased numbers of political appointees affect the career force may be difficult, but the size of the increase is significant: PAS positions increased from 152 in 1965 to 527 in 1985; the number of noncareer SES rose from 582 in 1980 to 658 in 1986; and Schedule Cs increased from 911 in 1976 to 1,665 in 1986. These increases reflect a deeper penetration of political appointees into the career bureaucracy. In addition, control of political appointments has been centralized in the White House. Although PAS's are all presidential appointments, in the 1950s and 1960s, most sub-Cabinet appointments were determined by Cabinet Secretaries. But beginning in the Nixon administration, Presidents have felt that they gave away too much of their appointment power, leading the Reagan administration to centralize all political appointments, including noncareer SES and Schedule C, in the White House. The potential implication is that agency heads and cabinet secretaries might have different criteria in mind than the White House staff. Certainly an agency head will look for somebody who has expertise and competence in management because that person will make the agency work or not work. The White House, on the other hand, may very well have a different perspective and be especially sensitive to political pressures for rewarding the party faithful and appointing those with certain ideological values. Dr. PFIFFNER agreed with a Volcker Commission task force chaired by Elliott Richardson: the problem is systemic such that higher numbers in combination with deeper penetration and centralization do have some relationship to the diminishing quality of political appointees.

Also important to scientists is the leadership and vision of the President. In addition, the President's science adviser plays an important symbolic role: if it appears that person has to compromise his or her professional ideals to do something political, fewer scientists will be willing to enter public service, even for a few years. Scientists and engineers said that it is important that they be able to respect the technical competence of their boss and feel comfortable with his or her ability to evaluate their work. Finally, scientists and engineers expect political appointees to duly consider their work and to buffer these technical people from the whims of the political wind.

Discussion

Dr. CAMPBELL asked for comments on the degree to which it makes any difference whether assistant secretary or deputy assistant secretary appointments, which have some supervisory responsibility in relation to the R&D side of government, (1) are filled or left vacant and (2) affect the quality and tenure of people appointed to those jobs.

Problems Associated with Unfilled Positions

Dr. CHEN pointed out that the NIH director was not a presidential appointee until passage of the National Cancer Act in 1972. Since that time the job has become quite political, to the point that for the last six months, NIH has not had a director, resulting in a certain loss of momentum, morale, and overall sense of purpose. A search committee suggested individuals to serve as NIH director, but there were sufficient political ramifications that none of those candidates were interested in the job. The secretary of the Department of Health and Human Services has convened a second high-level committee to determine how to make the job more attractive. Once issues such as salary and authority are worked out with the Secretary, it is hoped that the job can be made sufficiently attractive to initiate a second search. Dr. CHEN felt that such situations would be less prevalent if the position were not a political appointment. Dr. ROBINSON believed that having an assistant secretary for health who can override decisions of NIH staff, including the director, is a problem—as is the fact that the director is many levels removed from the actual running of a $6 billion agency.

Quality of Presidential Appointees

Many participants said that having a boss who has a reputation in his or her respective field is important, even more important than salary levels, all the way down the line, even in hiring decisions.

Dr. NUMRICH felt that having both political appointees and vacant positions at the top leads to less stable funding. When department heads lack institutional memory and knowledge of what ought to be going on, particularly in the administration of funding, fewer risks are taken. She said that R&D labs perform risk-oriented work that is possibly high gain, but such work is not now regarded as primary.

Another issue brought to the Committee's attention is the inadequate management preparation of career executives and career managers. More than once, a newly appointed SES member admitted to attending his or her first management training session after being appointed. Dr. PFIFFNER said that the uniformed services develop their executive talent by sending them to special schools, but less is done on the civilian side. Dr. CAMPBELL agreed that moving people from technical specializations into managerial positions has always created problems; he prefers to take a specialist and give him or her managerial training rather than assume that a manager can manage anything.

Tenure of Presidential Appointees

Dr. MESSNER stressed that the engineering and scientific community in the government cannot exist separate from the political process; it would not be a realistic goal to build a wall around the scientific engineering community, treating it differently from other government employee groups. Without political participation, however, there is no way to prevent the erosion of the attributes of the scientific and engineering existence in the federal workplace. If an agency does not have an advocate at the table when budgets are reviewed, an agency not only will not get training money, but also probably will not get facility money, parking places, or health care for its occupational safety program.

MS. MOWRY said that the current system makes a big impact. During the first year political appointees must develop loyalties with the career employees. A PAS member must develop a better image of the federal employee and be open-minded and willing to cooperate with the career staff. Since the average stay of a political appointee is 18-24 months, there is constant change at the top, with subsequent change in loyalty as well as much reorganization.

Dr. AMBLER said that when Presidential appointees are not allowed to do the job they are supposed to do, they start to micromanage. They are appointed because, presumably, they are of the same opinion as the President on political affairs; however, scientists and engineers become nervous by the implication that ideology would overwhelm scientific objectivity. Advocacy, in the budgetary sense, will go to agencies whose programs fit what the President is trying to do.

Fixed Term of Office

Workshop participants offered several insights and suggestions:

(1) According to Dr. KLINE, a fixed term is not a bad feature but does not guarantee that the appointee will hold the position for the entire term.
(2) Dr. ROBINSON advocated a fixed term for the directors of NSF and NIH so that when the time comes for appointment, consideration can be given to reappoint-

ment of the person in a technical position who has done a good job. Some thought that fixed terms established so as not to expire around the time of a presidential election would be beneficial. While not disputing this point, other participants considered having the confidence of the Administration more important to agency staff: if an appointee has a six-year term but not that confidence, he or she has little besides an office.

(3) There are inconsistencies within the system: the commissioner of Labor Statistics has a four-year term, but the director of the Bureau of the Census does not; therefore, the latter position is considered a political appointment.

Designated Positions

Dr. CAMPBELL asked where political appointees should be in the system. The civil service Reform Act, which eliminated the designation of positions as either political or career and specified that no more than 10 percent of the SES appointments could be noncareer, attempted to open up higher level positions to career people, thereby making it possible for them to be appointed to assistant secretary positions and the like. He wondered whether the government should return to a system of designated positions, rather than leaving the classifications open. According to Dr. PFIFFNER, after lengthy examination, the head of personnel at the Department of Health and Human Services has concluded that we might as well use the former system, because as soon as a political appointee is placed in a job that was formerly a career position, the job becomes politicized; the next administration thinks that is its slot. Dr. CAMPBELL said that, if that occurs, career people can never aspire to become assistant or deputy assistant secretaries: taking a political appointment would eliminate their rights back into the civil service system.

Mr. CAREY said it is important to give career people the opportunity to accept political appointments with some fallback protection. Dr. NORWOOD said that during her long tenure in a PAS position, even though it has a fixed term of office, she has seen a continuing erosion: many positions that could be filled by either a careerist or a presidential appointee have been designated PAS unless a career position has been clearly protected. The 10 percent limit on the number of PAS positions has been maximized.

Dr. MESSNER observed, based on personal experience with the White House personnel office under five different administrations, that the political appointment process as it regards scientists and engineers is nonexistent. He wondered, if one really cannot resolve this issue by designating jobs as political or career, if a solution might be to advocate identifying positions that should have professional criteria, limiting the President's appointment power.

Dr. ABRAMSON added that staff in the White House personnel office complained that they did not have enough names of scientists and engineers for PAS positions. He suggested that national groups supply the personnel office with names of qualified people in the scientific community. In addition, the personnel office staff find that the individuals whom they do contact think the pay offered is not worthwhile and the ethical requirements are bothersome.

Based on his own experience, Dr. CAMPBELL said that the White House personnel office does not try to identify and recruit people except for the Secretary positions. Dr. MESSNER agreed and added that the source of the name that is sent to them is screened by the personnel process; one must have certain political prerequisites to have his or her suggested nominee even considered. Mr. HOWTON agreed that a long-term civil servant with the right political connections will not get through the personnel office because the Hatch Act prohibits such contacts. He said that political appointees can be good or bad, but if an agency has no political appointees, it will instead have a congressional oversight committee—a situation that creates its own set of complications.

General Discussion

Dr. MESSNER opened this session by saying that in a buyer's market, one can afford to be much more sloppy in dealing with human resource issues, but in a shortage situation, one can get in trouble quickly. The engineering community is concerned about the potential lack of human resources in the near future partly because of the changing demography:

- There are fewer young people.
- During the next 15 years, 85 percent of the entering work force will be women and minorities, but historically the engineering profession has been unsuccessful in attracting women and even less successful in attracting minorities.
- Enrollment in engineering schools is down, even for women, who for a short time were enrolling in engineering schools in greater numbers; 50 percent of the students now in U.S. engineering schools are foreign and could be a resource if they choose not to return to their own countries.
- Statistics show that the United States will have a shortage of about 400,000 engineers as we enter the 21st century.

Dr. MESSNER questioned the effectiveness of the U.S. education system, stating that some scientific and engineering specialties are more successful in preparing students for the work force. As an employer, he is concerned about investments in the engineering person power and felt the federal government must engage in forward thinking about the human resource pool and how it will attract that pool to its programs.

Dr. NORWOOD asked whether the supply of scientists and engineers is actually a bigger problem for the federal government than for the private sector. In response, Dr. FALK said that his industry contacts say they can get the people they want, as long as the pay is high enough. Mr. RAGONE said that federal agencies provide a training ground for industry, hindering the agencies' abilities to fulfill their missions, but the loss of small groups of highly trained scientists and engineers is not reflected in aggregated statistics. Mr. ANDREWS said that he had had the same experience: the Federal Aviation Administration hires engineers who, after a training period of three to four years, take positions in industry at salaries $10,000 higher. Dr. STEINBACH noted similar problems in the fields of electromagnetics and computer software and predicted that the current national shortage will get worse. Dr. NORWOOD concurred that many agencies face similar problems: scientists and engineers come in, get valuable experience, and then go on.

Dr. MESSNER said the federal government must plan with greater because its infrastructure causes the government to move so slowly. Industry can move more quickly because firms can operate without adjusting to the labor market, either through pricing or, more importantly, through strategies to recruit from underparticipating groups. For instance, industry can attract more women by responding to special problems that women have in the work place.

Constraints

Mr. FECHTER asked participants to define the real constraints. He noted that mechanisms are being used to get around pay caps, and promotion is a mechanism to get around pay inequities. However, what other constraints exist and what are the mechanisms for getting around them? Dr. CAMPBELL pointed out that today OPM may delegate most personnel authorities other than pay caps and some other limitations.

Dr. CHEN said that NIH, because of the Public Health Service Act and some of its special authorities, does not have the same constraints as many agencies about hiring foreigners. As a result, about one-third of its doctorates are foreign. In ensuing discussion, participants suggested that language in appropriation acts might be changed so that other agencies could hire foreign nationals.

Two other points raised by Mr. ANDREWS are that technology now has a more international focus, and the rate of technology changes so quickly that engineers must spend much time to even keep pace with it.

**Past Initiatives To Recruit
Scientists and Engineers**

Dr. NUMRICH suggested looking at various initiatives, including DoD's attempt to extend the Naval Ocean Systems Center/Naval Weapons Center demonstration project to the rest of the department's laboratories, and evaluating why they have failed. To move forward we must understand how and why those failures happened so they will not recur.

Dr. CAMPBELL said that some initiatives fail because of opposition based on the proposition that they should be made government-wide rather department-specific. He surmised that legislation now before Congress to grant special salary pay rights to specific departments and agencies may, in fact, be attractive but lead to further fragmentation of the total federal employment system. Dr. CHEN cited an example to support that belief: NIH developed a legislative proposal for higher salaries for its scientific faculty (equating its scientists with comparable ranks in medical school faculty) based on an annual salary survey conducted by the Association of American Medical Schools. Another aspect of the proposal was to link the retirement system to the TIAA-CREF, allowing faculty from medical schools to come into the government for a brief period, remain in the same retirement system, and then maybe move out of government. The proposal was not successful because of objections by OMB and by other sectors that wanted to have similar special legislation.

Dr. MAHLER mentioned NOAA's Environmental Research Laboratories' use of a large part of its global change money to finance six joint institutes done cooperatively with universities and co-located in its laboratories. ERL does not pay the principal investigators' salaries but does pay postdocs' and graduate students' salaries, thus promoting the study of science and engineering by providing monetary support. There are not many environmental scientists, and the supply has been going down. Thus NOAA is trying to encourage potential environmental scientists by putting more money into the universities, where the training is available and these cooperative institutes work. NOAA hopes not only to encourage undergraduate students but also to broaden the spectrum of new entrants.

This discussion led Dr. GINZBERG to ask: To what extent does the government really get in its own way in terms of attraction, retention, and utilization of people by underinvesting in the continuing education of its scientific people? Participants described the effective programs of DOE, NRL, and CDC but noted that training money is being cut back for 1991, and providing such training does not ensure that those in agency-sponsored education programs will not use that training to acquire higher paying jobs in industry or academe.

Future Initiatives

Dr. MAHLER believes there is a new mode of operations whereby the government runs programs across agencies, not through agencies. An intergovernmental committee on earth sciences, for instance, is advocating the global change program now: each agency involved has agreed on its contribution to the program, and the committee has created realistic budgets and is selling the program to Congress. Such programs are more salable, but they take some control from the agency heads and put it in the program areas. These interagency committees have broad scientific and management support of attempts to find solutions across the board, a far more effective mechanism than single-agency programs.

Dr. FALK said that although such committees could be effective, the real solution is establishing one central organization responsible not only for the welfare of science but also for the effectiveness of the federal science and engineering work force; such an organization could be the one to fight the political battle.